Ethics at the Heart of Higher Education

Ethics at the Heart of Higher Education

EDITED BY

C. R. Crespo AND Rita Kirk

PICKWICK *Publications* · Eugene, Oregon

ETHICS AT THE HEART OF HIGHER EDUCATION

Copyright © 2020 Wipf and Stock Publishers. All rights reserved. Except for brief quotations in critical publications or reviews, no part of this book may be reproduced in any manner without prior written permission from the publisher. Write: Permissions, Wipf and Stock Publishers, 199 W. 8th Ave., Suite 3, Eugene, OR 97401.

Pickwick Publications
An Imprint of Wipf and Stock Publishers
199 W. 8th Ave., Suite 3
Eugene, OR 97401

www.wipfandstock.com

PAPERBACK ISBN: 978-1-5326-9048-8
HARDCOVER ISBN: 978-1-5326-9049-5
EBOOK ISBN: 978-1-5326-9050-1

Cataloguing-in-Publication data:

Names: Crespo, C. R., editor. | Kirk, Rita, editor.

Title: Ethics at the heart of higher education / edited by C. R. Crespo and Rita Kirk.

Description: Eugene, OR : Pickwick Publications, 2020 | Includes bibliographical references.

Identifiers: ISBN 978-1-5326-9048-8 (paperback) | ISBN 978-1-5326-9049-5 (hardcover) | ISBN 978-1-5326-9050-1 (ebook)

Subjects: LCSH: Education (Christian theology). | Education—Religious aspects. | Education, Higher—Aims and objectives—United States. | Ethics—Study and teaching (Higher)—United States. | Education, Higher—Moral and ethical aspects—United States.

Classification: LB2324 .E84 2020 (print) | LB2324 .E84 (ebook)

Manufactured in the U.S.A.   08/24/20

This book is dedicated to Cary M. Maguire for his constant dedication and support of ethics education across the United States. We at SMU owe a special debt to him for his support, encouragement, and resolve. Not only did he establish the Maguire Center for Ethics & Public Responsibility at SMU but he also endowed chairs at numerous universities as well as the Library of Congress. Mr. Maguire is a visionary. He asks tough questions. Yet he also demonstrates through his own life actions that questioning ethical decisions takes a dedication to enacting values. Countless students have benefitted from his endowment of our summer Public Service Fellowships that support students financially so that they can spend the summers researching ethics-related issues or pursuing volunteer opportunities with nonprofit organizations. Professors have been supported through course development grants, yearly Public Scholar lecture, and teaching fellowships. The community has been engaged as a result of public forums on issues of the day, the Ethics & Compliance program, the yearly Conference of the Professions and our annual J. Erik Jonsson Ethics Award for community service. Ethics is about more than words on a page but a living habit of mind and action. Thank you for investing your energy in us.

Contents

Contributors

Mary "Molly" Camp (MD, University of Texas Health Science Center at Houston) is an associate professor in the department of psychiatry at UT Southwestern Medical Center. She specializes in geriatric mental health and cognitive and memory disorders. Dr. Camp is the director of the Neurocognitive and Geriatric Psychiatry Program in the UTSW Psychiatry Outpatient Clinic and the associate program director of the combined Psychiatry and Neurology Residency Program. She completed residency training in psychiatry at Baylor College of Medicine and UT Southwestern.

Alexander Cole (MD, University of Chicago) is the chief resident in the department of psychiatry at UT Southwestern Medical Center. After graduating from residency in 2019, he will be joining the faculty at UT Southwestern as an inpatient psychiatrist for University Hospitals. He graduated magna cum laude from Baylor University, earning a bachelor of science with a major in biochemistry and minor in great texts of the Western tradition. He attended medical school at the University of Chicago Pritzker School of Medicine. At UT Southwestern, he is a member of the educator track and was awarded the department's Outstanding Resident Contribution to Medical Student Education award in 2017.

C. R. Crespo (MEd, Southern Methodist University) is the associate director of the Maguire Center for Ethics and Public Responsibility and an adjunct professor in the department of corporate communications and public affairs at Southern Methodist University. Her editing experience includes *Annals of Dyslexia: An Interdisciplinary Journal of The International Dyslexia Association* as well as other university publications. She completed the Management Development Program at the Harvard Graduate School of Education

Institute for Higher Education. She oversees the operation of SMU's Maguire Center for Ethics and Public Responsibility and focuses her work on higher education policy and administration. Her previous experience includes extensive work in communications at domestic and international nongovernmental organizations, and public affairs and policy research for Fortune 500 companies and national professional associations.

Charles E. Curran (STD, Academia Alfonsiana and Pontifical Gregorian University) is the Elizabeth Scurlock University Professor of Human Values at Southern Methodist University. He has served as president of three national professional societies—the American Theological Society, the Catholic Theological Society of America, and the Society of Christian Ethics. He was the first recipient of the John Courtney Murray Award for Distinguished Achievement in Theology given by the Catholic Theological Society of America. In 2003, the College Theology Society gave him its Presidential Award for a lifetime of scholarly achievements in moral theology. The Society of Christian Ethics gave him its Lifetime Achievement Award in 2017. In 2010, he was elected to membership in the American Academy of Arts and Sciences. Dr. Curran has authored or edited more than fifty books in the area of moral theology and taught for more than twenty years at the Catholic University of America and has also taught at Cornell University, the University of Southern California, and Auburn University.

Robert J. Howell (PhD, Brown University) is a Dedman Family Distinguished Professor and is the chair of the department of philosophy at Southern Methodist University. He is the author of *Consciousness and the Limits of Objectivity* (Oxford University Press, 2013) as well as numerous articles on the problem of consciousness, self-knowledge, and the nature of moral character. With Torin Alter he coauthored *A Dialogue on Consciousness* (Oxford University Press, 2009), *The God Dialogues* (Oxford University Press, 2011), and coedited *Consciousness and the Mind Body Problem: A Reader* (Oxford University Press, 2011). Dr. Howell's current research focuses on consciousness, self-knowledge, and the ethics of emerging technologies.

Rita Kirk (PhD, University of Missouri) is the William F. May Endowed Director of the Maguire Center for Ethics and Public Responsibility as well as an Altshuler Distinguished Professor in Corporate Communication & Public Affairs at Southern Methodist University. Her research focuses on the development and ethical targeting of public arguments, campaign communication, and a phenomenon that cannot be ignored in current discourse: hate speech. Dr. Kirk's books include *Political Empiricism: Communications Strategies in State and Regional Elections*, which won the "Best Book in Applied Communication" from the National Communication Association; *Hate Speech*, a book analyzing implications for hate discourse in public communication, with coeditor David Slayden, which was awarded the Outstanding Book on the subject of Human Rights in North America and the James Madison Prize for work on free speech; *Solo Acts: The Death of Discourse in a Wired World*; and her most recent book, *Political Communication in Real Time: Theoretical and Applied Research Approaches*, edited with Dan Schill and Amy Jasperson. Kirk has more than thirty book chapters and articles in scholarly publications and is a frequent commentator in the media.

D. Stephen Long (PhD, Duke University) is the Cary M. Maguire University Professor of Ethics at Southern Methodist University. Dr. Long is an ordained United Methodist Minister in the Indiana Conference. He has served churches in Honduras, North Carolina, and Milwaukee, Wisconsin. Dr. Long works in the intersection between theology and ethics and has published more than fifty essays and fourteen books on theology and ethics, including *Divine Economy: Theology and the Market*; *The Goodness of God: Theology, Church, and Social Order*; *John Wesley's Moral Theology: The Quest for God and Goodness*; *Calculated Futures: Theology, Ethics, and Economics*; *Christian Ethics: A Very Short Introduction*; *Saving Karl Barth: Hans Urs von Balthasar's Preoccupation*; and *The Perfectly Simple Triune God: Aquinas and His Legacy*. Dr. Long was baptized by the Anabaptists, educated by the evangelicals, pastorally formed by the Methodists, and given his first teaching position by the Jesuits, which makes him ecumenically inclined or theologically confused.

Robin Lovin (PhD, Harvard) is the former William H. Scheide Senior Fellow at the Center of Theological Inquiry at Princeton and is the Cary M. Maguire University Professor of Ethics *emeritus* at Southern Methodist University. He joined the SMU faculty in 1994 and served as dean of Perkins School of Theology from 1994 to 2002. Prior to this, he was dean of the Theological School at Drew University in Madison, New Jersey, and a member of the faculty at the Divinity School of the University of Chicago.

Dr. Lovin's most recent books are *Christian Realism and the New Realities* and *An Introduction to Christian Ethics*. He has also written extensively on religion and law and comparative religious ethics. In 2013, he held the Maguire Chair in Ethics and American History at the Library of Congress. He is a Visiting Scholar at Loyola University Chicago, an Honorary Trustee of the Center of Theological Inquiry in Princeton, New Jersey, and a member of the advisory board for the McDonald Centre for Theology, Ethics, and Public Life at Oxford University.

Richard O. Mason (PhD, University of California Berkley) is the Carr P. Collins Distinguished Professor Emeritus at the Edwin L. Cox School of Business at Southern Methodist University. Dr. Mason currently serves on the Mercy Regional Medical Center Ethics Committee in Durango, Colorado, is a member of the Professional Associates advisory group at Fort Lewis College, and was recently on the board of the Women's Resource Center. He served as director of the Maguire Center for Ethics and Public Responsibility from 1998 to 2005. The author of numerous academic articles and books, in 2001 he received the AIS Fellow LEO Award for lifelong contribution to the information systems field from the Association of Information Systems. In 1992 he was made a Foreign Fellow of the Russian Academy of Natural Sciences in the Infomatics and Cybernetics section.

William F. May (PhD, Yale) is a retired professor and has since served as a visiting professor in the department of political science at Yale, a chair holder in ethics and American studies at the Library of Congress (established by Cary M. Maguire), and, most recently, a fellow at the Institute for Practical Ethics and Public Life at the University of Virginia. Earlier, he chaired the department of religious studies at Smith College and founded and chaired the department of religious studies at Indiana University. Thereafter he held the Joseph P. Kennedy Chair at the Kennedy Institute of Ethics at Georgetown University, and the Cary M. Maguire Chair in Ethics at Southern Methodist University, where he also founded and directed the Maguire Center for Ethics and Public Responsibility. Professionally, Dr. May has cochaired the research group on death and dying at the Hastings Center and served as president of the American Academy of Religion and the Society of Christian Ethics. In public life, he served on the Clinton Task Force on Health Care Reform and as a member of the President's Council on Bioethics.

Thomas Wm. Mayo (JD, Syracuse University) is an Altshuler Distinguished Teaching Professor of Law at Southern Methodist University Dedman School of Law and adjunct professor of Internal Medicine at UT Southwestern Medical Center, where he teaches medical ethics, and is Of Counsel to Haynes and Boone, LLP. After practicing law in New York and Washington, DC, and serving as a law clerk to the US Court of Appeals for the District of Columbia Circuit, he joined the SMU law faculty in 1984. He has taught seventeen courses, most recently Health Care Law, Bioethics and Law, Nonprofit Organizations, Public Health Law & Ethics, Legislation, Torts, and (for the past twenty-three years) a joint offering with UT Southwestern Medical School: Law, Literature and Medicine. He was a "Co-Principal Investigator" (with Prof. William F. May) in the creation of SMU's Maguire Center for Ethics and Public Responsibility and served as its third director from 2005 to 2010.

John Sadler (MD, Indiana University) is a professor of psychiatry and clinical sciences and the Daniel W. Foster, MD Professor of Medical Ethics at the University of Texas Southwestern Medical Center. Dr. Sadler directs the division of ethics in the department of psychiatry and is the institution-wide Director of the Program in Ethics in Science & Medicine at UT Southwestern. Dr. Sadler's career has spanned research, education, administration, and clinical practice. His main research area has been in the philosophy and ethics realm—from clinical ethics, to research ethics, to the philosophy of psychiatry. He is editor-in-chief of the Johns Hopkins University Press journal *Philosophy, Psychiatry, & Psychology* and the Oxford University Press book series International Perspectives on Philosophy and Psychiatry.

Gratitudes

WE ARE GRATEFUL TO this book's many contributing authors—renowned academics, researchers, and practitioners—each of them committed to the study and practice of ethics. Their diversity of perspective and wisdom allowed for a robust conversation on the teaching of ethics across university disciplines and makes the case for a systematic and academic effort to develop a multidisciplinary approach to the development of ethical cultures.

The role of four groups of people at SMU is also notable. Our professional advisory board, cochaired by our founder Cary Maguire and the spirited Bobby B. Lyle, is an ever-present source of wisdom. Their ideas, involvement with the larger Dallas community, and vision for what ethics education might produce have been instrumental in our programming and development. Our academic advisory board challenges us to avoid the trite and dig deeply into the thoughtful and inquisitive that characterize a university. And, of course, our board of trustees led by President R. Gerald Turner who gave ethics education full weight in our strategic plan.

Finally, we are thankful for the students that fill the university and our classrooms with their curiosity and spirit and allow us to share in this very special phase of life.

To our colleague Adria Richmond, and to our families, John Phillips, Robert Whillock, and Rene and Caroline Crespo. We couldn't have done this without you.

Introduction

WE USED TO BELIEVE that our ethics are learned at our mother's knee, that the formation of our ethics is completed at an early age. But that is not true. Our ethics are developed throughout our lives, first as children from our family, then by modeling others we hold in regard, and further influenced by interactions with our peers, communities, media, books, and environment. In previous generations, education supplemented religious teaching by implementing and practicing the manners of civil society. Students were taught to read, reason and debate. They practiced memorizing lofty words of wisdom through declaration and poetry. Yet that is not the education today. Despite the hand-wringing of critics, students today have more knowledge available to them than can be absorbed; mastery of a subject area creates siloes where most every course is tailored to comprehending subject matter that may be outdated before they graduate. But learning is more than subject-matter expertise.

This book begins with the questions that plague academics who are unsure of the proper role of ethics courses in the curriculum. What should an ethics course seek to do? What are its outcomes and measures of success? Our fast-paced environment requires instantaneous reactions to complex questions. Our instant messaging age champions quick response over reflection or thought—even the president governs by Twitter. Yet the ethical dilemmas are no less complex than the subject matter; cyber security, prison reform, labor rights, abortion, artificial intelligence, or gun laws are common table topics over lunch. Struggling through that complexity is central to understanding its implications for our culture. As scholar D. Stephen Long so eloquently writes in his chapter, "It is insufficient to inform students that they already have an ethical formation. It must be subject to examination."

This book brings together some of the leading ethicists in the country together to consider the rightful place of ethics in the university today. Twenty years ago, William F. May, a distinguished ethics scholar, set the foundation for an ethics program at SMU when he stated, "A university does not fully discharge its duties to its students if it hands out knowledge—and the power that knowledge yields—without posing questions about its responsible uses." Philosophy, religious studies and theology professors still engage students on topics related to contemporary moral issues but there is another movement on campuses, one that we should support: the teaching of applied ethics by professors of practice. When a self-driving car hits a pedestrian because it misinterpreted a sign, or when another corporation defrauds its investors, we will wish that we had spent more time thinking not only of what it is possible to do with our knowledge but also what is right, just, and honorable. Educators have a duty to empower students to cultivate their character, ethically assess situations and prepare them for an ever-hostile world. However, just as accomplished professionals look to physicians, lawyers, and engineers when they need the help of a professional, so too can individuals look to ethicists for solving complex moral issues.[1]

The question of the proper role of ethics courses in the university curriculum takes on particular debates when considered in light of the secular focus of most universities. Robert Howell considers this debate in light of our own experiences in developing an undergraduate curriculum that requires ethical education for all students. So what does it mean when we say we teach ethics? As he addresses the issue of the Secular University's Dilemma ("either Morality and Ethics encode God's will [and thus have a religious backing] or they are merely a matter of cultural custom"), Howell claims that the debate does not lessen the importance of the concepts.[2] In fact, in a highly secular world of diverse belief frames, learning how to reason with one another across religious and cultural contexts is more important than ever. Contextualized in the framework of Howell's concept of "Google Ethics," he explains the criticality of doing more than what is thought to be right and just. Students must also know *why they do what they do*.

This book also provides a much-needed overview of the field of Christian ethics, including the Social Gospel movement, Christian realism,

1. See Charles Curran, chapter 3.
2. See Robert Howell, chapter 2.

Catholic social teaching, the proper role of the state in social and economic life, subsidiarity, religious liberty, human rights, the Christian right, and liberation theology. This grounding demonstrates the depth and complexity of Christian ethics and concludes that the rightful place for such thinking and debate also resides at the university.

The university faces unique institutional challenges when it claims a commitment to ethics education. Its core population is often comprised of the traditional college-aged student who is leaving home perhaps for the first time, faced with an expanded range of possible experiences, seems unaware of the consequences for risky behavior, and is certainly not thinking about the impact of actions on the image of the university. To be fair, students are not the only ones who make poor choices, perhaps not even the most impactful ones. Still, our country is blessed with some excellent university ethics programs, numerous ethics-based community groups, and shelves of books to enlighten our journey. Yet as David Brooks, author of *The Road to Character*, notes, "We've accidently left this moral tradition behind. Over the last several decades, we've lost this language, this way of organizing life. We're not bad. But we are morally inarticulate."[3] It's time we got that back. Our future depends on it.

That's why this book is important.

3. Brooks, *Road to Character*, 15.

1

Can Ethics Be Taught? Connecting the Classroom to Everyday Life

D. Stephen Long

CAN WE, SHOULD WE, teach ethics in the modern university? Teaching ethics differs from teaching other disciplines. Few students arrive at the university aware of Organic Chemistry and the importance of Grignard reactions. They most likely have not studied the causes, major dates, or key persons in the French Revolution. The means for teaching and evaluating students in these subjects can be relatively straightforward. Either one has success in the laboratory forming carbon-carbon bonds or one does not. One can give the dates for Robespierre's life and describe his role in the revolution or one cannot. But what about ethics? Our assumptions about teaching ethics cannot be the same as they are for teaching Organic Chemistry or French History. On the one hand, we assume students already have some sense of ethics before they arrive, which is why we hold them accountable for their behavior from their first day on campus. No one can avoid being disciplined for a violation of an honor code by protesting, "But I have not yet had my ethics course!" We would not hold a student accountable for her ignorance of Grignard reactions or French history prior to receiving instruction in the field, but we do hold students accountable for their actions with or without a course in ethics. On the other hand, we also assume that students should reflect on ethics across the curriculum, and that assumes that ethics needs to and can be taught. How do we make sense of both these assumptions? (1) Students arrive capable of being held accountable for ethical behavior. (2) Students arrive in need of an education in ethics.

A cursory reading of these assumptions might find them to be contradictory. If students can be held accountable for ethical behavior without an ethics course, then why teach ethics? If students need an education in ethics, then why hold them accountable for ethical failure? This essay explores these two assumptions, noting why they are not contradictory, and why the teaching of ethics should depend and build on the ordinary formation with which students arrive on campus. Teaching ethics in the university will be most successful when it connects with students' previous histories of doing good and avoiding evil in their everyday life, connects that to the university's moral history, and points toward the ordinary events that will constitute their future endeavors. It is in these histories that teaching ethics makes best sense.

If the two assumptions of my opening paragraph are granted—first, we assume students arrive at the university with some understanding of ethical behavior so that we can hold them accountable for their actions even if they never had a course in ethics; second, we assume students should be taught ethics in their curriculum, including courses in ethics across the curriculum—then two possible objections arise based on the possible contradiction present in the assumptions. We could argue that students do not arrive at the university with a sufficient understanding of proper ethical behavior such that we should hold them accountable for their actions. This argument, however, would make the life of the university nearly impossible. Even if we cannot give convincing theoretical reasons why we hold the first assumption, living together in a complex space like the university requires that practically we assume students arrive with at least a tacit awareness of doing good and avoiding evil. We do not need to assume they all share the same ethical convictions, or that every student has the same level of ethical awareness, but the practice of everyday, university life assumes students (along with everyone else associated with the university) have some tacit ethical awareness.

Universities are composed of adults who have already been formed into ways of seeing the world and acting within it from a diversity of social forms of life. They are also composed of persons who should reflect on what virtuous human action is, for as Socrates said, "the unexamined life is a life not worth living." If the two assumptions above are conceded, then the task of teaching ethics must address these two questions: (1) from whence does ethics come? and (2) to where should ethics go? The first question assists us with the first assumption that students and others arrive at the university with a tacit awareness of proper ethical behavior. The second question assists us with the second assumption that students (and others) benefit from examining and reflecting upon that tacit awareness to bring it to a fuller one that can assist them in living well. They can do so by confronting the question of what is a good human life? But as most people already know, and as we shall see, answers to this question are so contested that the question readily gets neglected or abandoned in the modern university for fear that the answers will produce too much conflict.

From whence does ethics come?

Ethics never begins in a vacuum. Ethics cannot be taught like a science experiment that seeks to remove the contingencies of everyday existence and create ideal conditions. Human action is too complex for such a possibility. Plato famously argued that to have a just city we would need drastic actions. We find ourselves already in the middle of preferences and injustices that prohibit the necessary harmony for justice to prevail. Plato proposed that to acquire justice we would need to start anew by exiling or killing everyone over the age of ten. Whether Plato was being ironic or conveying how difficult it is to bring about justice in a city has been debated and never fully answered, but he found the contingencies of human existence thwarting ethical pursuits. Unfortunately, some political leaders have attempted his experiment, trying to destroy everything that stands in the way of ideal conditions. Teaching ethics in the university can fall into the trap of assuming the university is an ideal condition in which students can now slough off everything that prevents them from adopting a putative ideal ethical theory. This assumption rejects the first assumption above that students arrive at the university with some measure of ethical formation, a formation that can be built upon but does not need to be destroyed. From whence does this ethical formation come?

It arises from diverse sources—family, friendships, attention to nature, participation in culture through a diversity of means such as novels, television, education, oral stories, worship, and everyday practices like athletics, music, theatre. These means are mediated through neighborhoods, local schools, urban, suburban or rural living, ethnic and racial identities, citizenship in nation-states, participation in civil society or in corporations and the market. Ethical formation takes place in religious institutions, churches, synagogues, mosques. Students who enter an ethics class already have a complex formation derived from these and other sources. Of course, student's formations from these sources differ widely. Perhaps this complexity is why ethicists are tempted to reduce students to either autonomous, rational or self-interested individuals. It is easier and gives them something in common, but it is also similar to Plato's odd counsel in that it takes the history of the student as something to overcome rather than build upon. It treats an ethics course as if it is a retraining camp in which everything the student has been taught to this point must be destroyed for the sake of making him or her anew.

Let's briefly consider how we receive ethical formation from these diverse sources beginning with the family. For most of us, ethical formation begins with the care received from immediate or extended family located within neighborhoods. We learn practices before we learn any theory. I doubt few parents set their children down at a certain age, went over possible ethical theories by which they could live, and encouraged them to choose one and live consistently with it. John Mill, J. S. Mill's father, approximated such an education with his son. J. S. Mill published an autobiography in which he tells of his father's rigid educational instruction. He was taught Greek at the age of three, Latin at eight and had a complete course in political economy by thirteen. In 1822 at the age of sixteen he started a Utilitarian society, and when he turned twenty he had a nervous breakdown.[1] Perhaps his strict education had no bearing upon his breakdown, but few of us are given a rigid ethical and political education as he was. Our ethical formation was less planned, less systematic and we are the better off for it.

How are we formed by our familial and neighborly relations? It usually occurs informally. Within them we learn to cooperate, to care for others, to eat appropriately so that others might be able to do so as well. We learn to take our turn, and ask for and give forgiveness. We learn by example, both positive and negative. Let me offer an example. My grandfather never returned from World War II. He did not die in the war; in fact, he was never deployed overseas. He betrayed my grandmother, took up with another woman and had children with her without my grandmother's knowledge. It devastated her emotionally and financially. She had to raise five children by herself, my father being the oldest. They were so poor that he would be "farmed out" in summer to a local family who gave him shelter, food, and a stipend to work their farm. He remembers that time fondly, but he also taught his children and

1. Mill, *Autobiography*, 94, 97, 112, 118.

grandchildren that there were consequences to sexual and marital relations. We were not supposed to be like our grandfather, whom we never knew. Each family has narratives like mine that set forth positive and negative ethical exemplars that make possible the ethical projects that we find ourselves in the middle of, and that is why acknowledging students arrive at the university with an ethical formation matters—they are already in the middle of ethical projects of which they may or may not be aware.

Families and neighborhoods bring with them histories that make possible the exercise of virtues or vices; those virtues and vices will differ depending upon those histories. In his retrieval of an Aristotelian virtue ethics, Alasdair MacIntyre wrote, "What the good life is for a fifth-century Athenian general will not be the same as what it was for a medieval nun or a seventeenth-century farmer. But it is not just that different individuals live in different social circumstances; it is also that we all approach our own circumstances as bearers of a particular social identity. I am someone's son or daughter, someone else's cousin or uncle; I am a citizen of this or that city, a member of this guild or profession; I belong to this clan, that tribe this nation. Hence what is good for me has to be good for one who inhabits these roles. As such, I inherit from the past of my family, my city, my tribe, my nation, a variety of debts, inheritances, rightful expectations and obligations. These constitute the given of my life, my moral starting point. This is in part what give my life its own moral particularity."[2] MacIntyre distances his virtue approach from individualism. An individualist approach to ethics falsely assumes each student emerges without moral particularity so that their histories do not matter. If we take their histories as moral starting points, then teaching ethics will connect more with their lives and become more complex. For instance, a white student from the US inherits ethical obligations arising from the long history of the slavocracy, Jim Crow, segregation and mass incarceration that will differ from a black student in the US. Someone with a Christian, Jewish, Islamic or secular history will also differ in their moral starting points.

Beginning with particular histories raises the question, But do we not have anything in common, anything we share by nature? The question is important. There is no reason that a focus on histories should reject the assumption that some of our ethical formation also comes from what we hold in common such as "nature." Humans have a "nature," which is why the term "human nature" makes sense. The term "nature," like the term "culture" that

2. MacIntyre, *After Virtue*, 220.

we will examine momentarily, is a complex and difficult term, especially when it is appropriated for teaching ethics. The ancient Stoics founded ethics upon a "natural law." The universe has a natural purpose amenable to the right use of reason. There are a variety of teachings about the natural law, but on the whole the natural law assumes this basic form: moral norms are present in nature and can be accessed by reason. Within that basic form, natural law teaching has great variation. Some interpret the natural law as a set of rules. Jean Porter contests this interpretation. Drawing upon Thomas Aquinas she suggests that the natural law is better "described as a capacity or power for moral discernment rather than as essentially or primarily a set of rules for right conduct."[3] As a capacity for moral discernment rather than a rigid set of rules, the natural law can be common—everyone has a sense that they should pursue the good and avoid evil—and at the same time what is common gains concreteness through our histories and actions. Vincent Lloyd's work on *Black Natural Law* exemplifies this natural law approach. He cites Frederick Douglass's emphasis on our common humanity made in the image of God as a basis for ethics. Douglass, like many others, professed that all humans share a similar human nature. Yet Douglass was born a slave and treated by his oppressors as if he had no nature in common with them. This disconnect between a common human nature and a history that denies it reveals that it is insufficient simply to appeal to nature; too many people miss what the natural law is. It, too, is only a starting point. For this reason, Lloyd argues that the history of Black suffering provides Blacks with an access to what this common humanity should be that is unavailable to others without a similar history.[4] Everyone can and should learn from the history of those denied their common humanity to discover what it is. Our natures are historical so learning about what we have in common also requires discernment arising from our histories.

Students arriving at the university have already engaged with "nature" and learned from it. Take as an example something as trivial but morally significant as stopping at red lights. It is a form of natural knowledge in that laws intrinsic to being human are present in such a simple practice. One such law is that two automobiles cannot inhabit the same space at the same time and any attempt to force them to do so will have bad consequences. Yet how should we define the moral significance of the "natural law" that we learn from this practice? Is it self-preservation that

3. Porter, *Nature as Reason*, 4.
4. Lloyd, *Black Natural Law*, 4.

causes us to honor this natural wisdom, or a desire to cooperate with others, or an instinct to do no harm? The practice itself is not self-interpreting, and when I use this example in teaching ethics I find students who will staunchly defend all the possibilities noted above. Although all might agree that stopping at red lights is ethically important, how they conceive of its ethical importance will have entailments for how they think about politics, economics, family life and much more. Are our relations within each of these based on virtue, grace, dignity, utility or caring? The answers we give affect how we inhabit forms of ordinary life.

Related to "nature" is culture. Stopping at red lights conveys natural knowledge, but red lights are also cultural artifacts. We can easily imagine societies where the natural law that two bodies cannot inhabit the same space at the same time is present, but someone might learn it from something other than red lights. Perhaps it is a society without automobiles, or a society where every red light has been replaced with roundabouts. Nature is mediated to us through culture. "Culture" is as confusing a term as is nature. The two are usually set in contradiction to each other. Culture is human activity that transforms nature in some way. Nature is the "stuff" upon which culture works. Yet clearly delineating where nature ends and culture begins, as with the previous red light example, is not easily done. It is natural to eat, sleep, reproduce, reason, study, act and so on, and yet each of these natural activities only occurs within specific cultural contexts.

No student arrives on campus or in an ethics course without having already participated in some of these ethical sources. I hope the above brief discussion will convince the reader that students have ethical formations that should provide the university with confidence that they can abide by some basic norms. They share a nature, but that nature has been mediated through diverse cultural means. The diversity of their ethical formation, however, will be both a strength and a weakness in the classroom. It gives us enough in common to discuss and debate ethical matters, and differentiates us so that those discussions and debates have the potential to be lively, if not conflictual. Think of any ethical issue: abortion, sexuality, war, pacifism, torture, eating, economics, reproduction, euthanasia, technological enhancements, alcohol or drug use. Most students already have some intuitive sense of these issues based on the intersection of their histories, interaction with nature, and diverse cultural mediations. That mediation may have come through television or novels, through formal education or oral stories told around the dinner table. It may have come through worship or conversing with friends. That cultural mediation may have been profound or superficial. Students may have had a serious training in the virtues or they may be emotivists who think moral judgments are primarily subjective preferences. They arrive with a moral starting point from their histories that should be honored and built upon at the same time that it will be subjected to scrutiny, not in order to free them from it, but to assist them to inhabit it. A tacit assumption in teaching ethics is that students still have work to do; there is something that they should know or practice that they might not yet know or practice. It is insufficient simply to inform students that they already have an ethical formation. It must be subject to examination. This implies normative judgments, and here is where teaching ethics gets tricky. Whose and which normative judgments should prevail?

To where should ethics go?

Teaching students to be aware of their ethical formations is one thing. Teaching them to examine and build upon it is another; the latter assumes that not all ethical formations are the same; some are better than others. How is it possible to make normative judgments about deeply held ethical convictions? Take for instance the morality of obliteration bombing in World War II. Many of our relatives were involved in it, and it is the case that without it some of us might not be here. Directly targeting civilian populations may have brought that war to a quicker end and saved relatives who were soldiers preparing for invasion. To subject this event to moral scrutiny raises all kinds of questions, especially after the fact. And yet—this scrutiny is what a course in ethics must do, not so that we judge our forebears, but so that we might know how to own our histories and act morally given the times in which we live. According to both the Stoic natural law and Roman Catholic teaching, directly intending to kill the innocent, even if it reduces the amount of suffering in the world, is an evil that should be avoided. Questioning one's country's role in the bombing of London, the fire bombing of Dresden, dropping the atomic bomb on Hiroshima and Nagasaki can be unsettling, as can reminding students that there were voices at the time who spoke out against these practices.[5] Once a teacher points out that Roman Catholic and natural law teaching oppose them, some students will respond by noting that they are neither Roman Catholics nor natural lawyers so that they feel no moral compunction about those teachings. On what grounds

5. Ford, "Morality of Obliteration Bombing," 261–309.

then do they justify or reject directly targeting innocents? This example often demonstrates that most students are utilitarians or emotivists, who argue that no universal, objective moral norms exist.

A common experience in teaching ethics is dealing with students who are primarily emotivists. Emotivism is a theory of meaning in which moral statements are expressions of preference. To say directly killing the innocent is intrinsically evil is to assert that the one making the statement does not like directly killing the innocent; one expresses his or her emotional dislike. If another person disagrees and likes it, then no rational adjudication between them is possible. Of course, emotion is an important aspect of moral education. We rightly question the probity of someone who observes moral horrors such as genocide or lynching with emotional detachment. But the wrongness of moral horrors must be something more than individual preference. Upon a little reflection students can usually be dissuaded from an emotivist theory of moral meaning. They unanimously agree, in my experience, that genocide is morally objectionable. When asked why, some students give an emotivist answer: "I don't like it," or "It just feels wrong to me." When you follow up by asking if they truly think that such a moral horror is wrong because of their feelings, many (although not all) acknowledge that there must be something more to its wrongness than the way they feel about it.

Where is its wrongness located? An important way to begin to answer this question is to ask students if they think there is a purpose to human existence and what that purpose is? The question assumes that there is an answer to the question, What is a well-lived life? or What does it mean to be human? but identifying a common answer provokes disagreement. One compelling reason for teaching ethics is to gain clarity on the broad disagreements that quickly arise when we seek to answer these important and basic questions. Some awareness of the discipline assists us in that clarity.

Ethics is both a practical and theoretical discipline; in fact, it is unique in that it combines practical and theoretical reason. Practical reason culminates in an action. Theoretical reason culminates in thought or contemplation. Let me provide a famous example from W. D. Ross (1871–1977) to illustrate the difference. Imagine you promised to meet a friend for lunch. You are on your way to keep the appointment when you come upon someone drowning, and being an expert swimmer you can save the drowning person. Immediately you jump into action by kicking off your shoes, diving into the water and saving the person. The result is that you were unable to keep your promise to your friend, but you saved another human being. You exercised your practical reason—you observed someone in trouble, knew that you had the ability to assist and concluded that you were obliged to act. You tacitly exercised theoretical reason as well. The action suggested that the immediate need to save someone overrode the obligation to keep a promise to meet someone for lunch. However, your consideration of the matter did not result in thought or contemplation alone. You did not sit down and ask yourself if this episode fell under Ross's theory of *prima facie* duties—duties that should be kept other things being considered. Ross uses this example to help us think or contemplate about such an episode. His theory of *prima facie* duties states that we should keep our promises unless there is a compelling reason not to do so. In so far as we contemplate what we might do, we are engaged in theoretical reason. It may not lead to an action. For instance, in a classroom on ethics, teachers and students consider and discuss *prima facie* duties without the discussion concluding with an action. If they were holding class outside next to the lake on campus and saw a drowning person, one would not expect a theoretical discussion but an action to save the endangered person.

Ethics then assumes practical reason and students arrive having already been formed to some degree by practices of everyday life that have already required actions from them, actions that ended in moral failure or success. They most likely have also contemplated what was the proper course of action and thus engaged in theoretical reason. Both assume that the subject of ethics is human action either directed to the good (or right) and/or away from evil. "To do good and avoid evil," wrote the thirteenth-century theologian Thomas Aquinas, is the first principle of the practical reason. This first principle should resonate with Southern *Methodist* University because the first two rules of the original Methodist societies, rules that remain in theory binding on all Methodists to this day, are first "do no harm, avoiding evil of every kind," and second "do good." (There is a third rule to attend upon the ordinances of God.) These first two rules restate the first principle of practical reason. It is, however, only a beginning point that assumes, on the whole, people in the course of their life try to do good and avoid evil. There may be persons who are sociopaths who seek evil and avoid good, but ordinary life would not be possible if they were the norm. Whether out of self-preservation or concern for others, most people do not drive willy-nilly through red lights. Why is this true? Is it because we seek to be (1) virtuous citizens, (2) faithful creatures before God, (3) moral agents who treat others as we desire to be treated, (4) individuals who maximize utility, or (5) agents who have been cared for by others and seek to extend that caring to others? Each of these options offers a theoretical response to the practical question of ethics. They describe how we go about being ethical and they prescribe how we should act. They also bring out five important moments in the history of ethics. One reason for the need to teach ethics is to know how those who came before us thought about ethics.

(1) Aristotle's Virtuous Citizen

Perhaps we refuse to run through red lights because we have been trained in virtues that make us good citizens in our cities and neighborhoods. This would be the reason given by one of the earliest philosophers who taught ethics, the Greek philosopher Aristotle (384–322 BC). Although much has changed in the twenty-four hundred years since he lectured and wrote on ethics, his work is still widely used to help us understand what ethics is. Aristotle identified five "virtues of thought" that assist us in knowing what is true: craft (*techne*), scientific knowledge (*episteme*), practical wisdom (*phronesis*), wisdom (*sophia*), and understanding (*nous*). *Craft* is concerned with production similar to what builders, engineers and manufacturers make. The end product is external to the one who makes it so this kind of knowledge does not necessary produce virtue. For instance, one could be a morally compromised person and an excellent surgeon or car mechanic. It would be better if a surgeon were virtuous, but it is not necessary for her or his specific craft. *Scientific knowledge* is "demonstrative." It discovers universals either through deduction or induction. Deduction begins with premises that are universally true and argues from them to conclusions that will also be universally true. Inductive reasoning begins with particular observations or probable premises and argues to conclusions that will be sound albeit not necessarily true. *Understanding* begins with principles that are undeniable; they are intrinsically known. Understanding provides the first principles for scientific knowledge. *Wisdom* is the ability to use understanding and scientific knowledge to arrive at conclusions that are "the same in every case." Aristotle distinguished this from practical wisdom; its conclusions are actions that are not the same in every case. For instance, you should stop at red lights, but if you are driving your injured child to the hospital in the middle of the night, the light is red, and you clearly see there are no cars coming, practical wisdom would tell you to run the red light.

11

For Aristotle, ethics is not a "speculative" discipline that provides necessary knowledge like mathematics, but a practical discipline whose knowledge can be other. That is to say, ethics cannot create a method, or a computer program, where we input an ethical dilemma and if everything works properly it concludes with a necessary result that would fit anyone in any context with any kind of education, formation or knowledge. Ethics is not a deductive science that is "demonstrative" and known universally. It is about "particulars," contingent features of everyday life. How we see, define and act on those particulars will always be a matter of judgment made possible by our character. For this reason, practical wisdom is not productive in the same way that a craft is. It affects who the agent is more profoundly than a craft. Practical wisdom is the cultivation of virtue over time within a community that allows a moral agent to see well what is going on in a situation and, in turn, act virtuously. Ethics is as much about vision as it is about action because what we are unable to see excludes proper action. It is also about friendship and happiness or *eudaimonia*. The latter term translates as happiness or flourishing. For Aristotle, all action has a purpose, end or telos; it aims at a particular end—happiness. It alone contributes to human flourishing. Wealth, honor, status, health, or pleasure are not ends in themselves because even if we have them we want them for something other than themselves. They are means to some end, an end he identifies as *eudaimonia*.

Aristotle's ethics depends on the formation of character that requires "habituation." It is the education resulting from practices that forms young boys into virtuous men. For Aristotle, ethical formation primarily occurred within the Athenian city by free males who had the leisure to pursue their flourishing. Ethics was not available to anyone, and for that reason contingency resided at the basis of ethics. Did a person have the right birth at the right time in the right place that would let him pursue those goods that made for human flourishing? Aristotle's discrimination against women and slaves is no longer acceptable. His understanding of the ethics of virtue has, however, been translated into contemporary practices that remove these discriminations. Aristotle took as the paradigm for his ethics "the great souled man" who did not depend on anyone else while he himself had many who depended upon him. Few contemporary virtue theorists adopt the "great souled man" as a moral exemplar. Aristotle also argued that friendship was necessary for ethics; many contemporary virtue theorists adopt friendship as an essential aspect for virtuous living. Ethics is not accomplished by an isolated individual, but by a person with friends who assist him or her in the cultivation of virtue.

(2) Thomas Aquinas's Faithful Disciple

Perhaps we do not run red lights because we seek to be faithful creatures before God, and doing harm to other creatures would at the same time be an offense to God in whose image they are made? However, despite our best efforts we find ourselves not doing the good we think we should do. We look for assistance, for something outside of us given by grace that causes us to do good works in the world. Thomas Aquinas (1225–74) was a Christian theologian and a member of the religious order known as the Order of Preachers who may have given this kind of answer. He accepted much of Aristotle's teaching on ethics, but transformed it with theology. Like Aristotle, friendship was of central ethical importance, but Aquinas taught that the true end of the ethical life is found in friendship with God. For Aristotle, friends were primarily friends with others of a similar stature so the differences between God and humans ruled out the possibility that they could be friends. For Aquinas, friendship with God was not something that could be achieved on one's own; it comes as a gift. Aristotle taught that virtues were acquired; they were habits that we achieve through proper habituation. Like many before him, he stated that the most important virtues were the "cardinal" virtues, from the Latin *cardus*, meaning "hinge"; they are the "hinge" that allows one to live well. Aquinas taught that friendship with God required something more than the acquired virtues; it required "infused" virtues that came from the Holy Spirit. They are "faith, hope and love," and direct us to both God and our neighbor because to love God and neighbor fulfills the two tablets of the Ten Commandments given by God to Moses. To love God we must participate in God's own love, and that participation makes possible infused virtues.

(3) Immanuel Kant's Autonomous Reasoner

Although both Aristotle and Thomas Aquinas's ethical teachings are still present in practice and theory today, they are not often the dominant ethical theories used in the modern university. They are considered too parochial. Modern ethical thinking originated with two seminal thinkers, Immanuel Kant (1724–1804) and J. S. Mill (1806–73). Perhaps we do not run red lights because if we lived by such a rule—I will willy-nilly run red lights—we could not will that everyone act by the same rule. Driving would be impossible.

For Kant, the only truly good thing in the world is a good will. Ethics was not about contingency, habituation, happiness, or friendship; it was about the rational, autonomous individual willing an action that could be done by anyone in any circumstances at any time. This gave rise to what is referred to as the "universalizability" thesis. Unlike Aristotle and Aquinas, ethics did not depend upon a community like the Athenian city or the Christian Church, it was available to anyone who was willing to do his or her duty. Accomplishing one's duty consists of obeying commands or imperatives. Kant taught that there were two kinds of imperatives—hypothetical or categorical. Both are forms of practical reasoning. In the hypothetical imperative, an action is performed not for its own sake but for the sake of something else, for instance that it makes one happy or righteous in the eyes of God, one's family, city or nation. In the categorical imperative, an action is performed for its own sake. Kant gave several versions of the categorical imperative. One version is to always treat others as ends and not as means. Our action, if it is to be moral, must always honor the dignity of another individual. Another version stated, "act only on that maxim which you can at the same time will that it be a universal law." A maxim is a rule one adopts to live by. It should be adopted freely by the ethical agent and not because anyone else, parents, teachers, rulers or priests, told you to adopt it. Ethics is about autonomous actions that arise out of one's own individual thought and will, and not the thought or will of another.

Simply adopting a maxim does not make it moral. We could always imagine an immoral maxim one might live by such as "always steal when you can get away with it." What makes an action moral, what fulfills the categorical imperative, is that the maxim you live by can be made a universal law. The categorical imperative asks that if you are on the receiving end of a maxim, could you will it? In other words, if someone steals your goods because they can do so with impunity, would you be willing to adopt that maxim as a universal law? Reasonable people would refuse to make such a maxim into a universal law so it fails the categorical imperative. Kant's ethics, then, are an extension of the adage to treat others the way you would want to be treated. His ethics began a tradition of ethical thinking known as "deontology" from the Greek word *deontos*, which means "binding." Ethics is doing your duty because it is your duty whether you benefit from it or not.

(4) J. S. Mill's Utility Maximizer

Perhaps we refuse to run red lights because it increases the utility to our lives, that is to say it increases pleasure or diminishes pain. John Stuart Mill was a trained economist like his father John Mill who taught utilitarian ethics. He was part of a radical group of thinkers in the nineteenth century who challenged how we think about ethics. Like Kant, ethics is about action, but Mill built on his predecessor Jeremy Bentham's work that took pleasure or utility as central for ethics. He, too, started a tradition that has developed and grown into a variety of theories, but what the tradition has in common was best expressed in three articles Mill published in 1861 that were collected into a small book in 1863 known as *Utilitarianism*. Mill wrote, "Actions are right in proportion as they tend to promote happiness; wrong as they tend to produce the reverse of happiness."[6] This statement sounds similar to Aristotle or Aquinas's *eudaimonia*; ethics seeks its end in happiness, but what is meant here by happiness has shifted. Happiness is the "intended pleasure and the absence of pain." There is no sanction for it except the desire each has for his or her own happiness. Ethics is about increasing utility and/or diminishing disutility. For Kant, utilitarianism commands a hypothetical imperative in that it tells us to follow a rule not because of the rule itself but because of its consequences, either in making us or the greatest number happy.

(5) A Feminist Ethics of Caring

Much modern ethical thinking pits deontology against utilitarianism and defends some version of one or the other. But not all ethicists are happy with this situation. Feminists, in particular, find it wanting. Perhaps the reason we do not run red lights is because we have been nurtured by caring others who pass on to us a desire also to care. Neither a universal categorical imperative, nor a desire to increase utility, explains our ethical actions. Ethics is more local, more grounded in relationships of trust. Some feminists argue that the deontological/utilitarian binary is little more than a debate within dominant forms of masculinity. Virginia Held suggests that these two forms of ethical theory assume a male agent fit for liberal political or economic theory; deontology assumes the person as rational autonomous agent and utilitarianism as a self-interested individual. They are based on

6. Mill, *Utilitarianism*, 7.

capacities putatively intrinsic to maleness, but ones that overlook capacities that women possess, one of which is "the capacity to give birth to new human beings."[7] Based on this and other capacities, Held develops an "ethics of caring" that draws upon "the universal experience of care." Every person, she claims, has been cared for or cares for others at some point in his or her life. This universal experience makes more sense of our ethical practice, and can lead to a better ethical theory. Like Aristotle and Aquinas, it has a place for something more than autonomous reason. It emphasizes neglected aspects of being human—desire, passion, emotion. Unlike them, it is not found in only some communities, religious or otherwise, so it can satisfy the universalizability premise. It is modern without privileging the autonomous rational or self-interested individual.

The five ethical theories above do not exhaust the diverse ways philosophers and theologians think about ethics, but they suffice for demonstrating some of that diversity. They help us see why no single answer can be given to a perceived need to teach ethics. If in response to discovering that someone teaches ethics, a person responds that we need more of it, it would be appropriate to ask them, what do you think we need more of—acquired virtue, infused virtue, binding imperatives, maximizing utility, care? Some of these answers might overlap, but they also have different conceptions of what the purpose of ethics is, and they assume different social contexts in which it makes sense. All five assume that they are telling us how the common person (if there is such an entity) thinks about morality, and how the common person should think about it. Yet there is an interesting correlation that should not be missed in these diverse theories. Each of them privileges some underlying social context that renders them intelligible. Aristotle's ethics assumes a small, manageable city and a moral agency fitting its citizens. Aquinas's ethics assumes a church and a moral agency fitting disciples; Kant's a nation-state securing the dignity of autonomous rational individuals through rights; Mill's a market where self-interested individuals trade and barter; and Held's an extended family where persons relate to each other as caregivers and receivers. What this demonstrates is something that the contemporary Aristotelian moral philosopher Alasdair MacIntyre has argued—every ethics implies a sociology. Ethics cannot be abstracted from the social and political contexts that both make it possible and which it then in turn serves. Ethics done well will require us to consider the social orders which we think human actions should serve, orders such

7. Held, *Ethics of Care*, 60.

as nations, the state, the market, a city, a neighborhood of friends, family, a church or other religious institutions like a mosque or synagogue. Any teaching of ethics that does not attend to the correlation between social orders and ethics does students a disservice by inviting them to conceive of their lives in terms of such orders without giving them the tools to acknowledge that they are doing so.

Now we find teaching ethics, especially in a diverse context, to be veering into precarious territory; ethics has become inseparable from politics. When we ask students what is a well-lived life, they may give a diversity of answers, but with those answers also comes a tacit affirmation of the goodness of social orders and their arrangements. Students might suggest that the good life is one that pursues and achieves, wealth, honor, pleasure, or health. Thus, anything that discourages or impedes this pursuit is evil and anything that enhances it is good. From Aristotle to Aquinas, however, the pursuit of wealth, honor, pleasure or health was insufficient as an answer to what it means to be human because it could not lead to human flourishing. If students gave such an answer, they stood in need of correction. Perhaps Aristotle and Aquinas could make such a claim because they lived in societies in which there was a common conception of what human flourishing is. We do not, and for that reason making judgments on students' answers to the question "what is a well-lived life?" is often perceived as inappropriate. How are we to proceed?

One way to do so is to let each student define his or her own answer to the question "What is a well-lived life?" without subjecting it to examination. Then the purpose of an ethics course is to encourage them to find the right means to achieve their end no matter what that end might be. This procedure is to my mind deeply flawed. Although it might appear to honor each student's particular history and refuse to impose moral norms on them, it actually does the reverse. The assumption that ethics is about an autonomous decision to choose your own way of life and pursue it consistently is one ethical option among others. To assume that a course should proceed along these lines is to narrow down ethical possibilities, not expand them. It also neglects the inevitable link between ethics and politics. The answer to the question of a well-lived life will assume some underlying social formation that is worthy of our lives.

Normative ethical judgments should not be imposed on students, but how one teaches them without imposition—implicit or explicit—is exceedingly difficult. I once had an ethics teacher who was well known for beginning his course by stating, "In this class you do not have minds to make up for yourself about ethics. Your purpose is to think like me." Most students were immediately appalled and raised their resistance to whatever he said next. His purpose was to challenge the default position of emotivism that he found among students, as if whatever they felt or thought about ethics was somehow in itself sufficient to the task. He did not say that students were to arrive at the same normative judgments that he did, although I think he hoped they would. He stated that they should follow a way of thought that he had inherited from others in order to think better about ethics. Part of that way of thought was to recognize that living one's life for wealth, pleasure, honor, or health was insufficient for human flourishing, and to trust those forms of social life whose end was wealth, pleasure, honor or health alone were insufficient for one's loyalty. Another part was to dissuade students that ethics was a pursuit of individual preference. These two parts are, however, negative. They tell us what should not to be done, not what should be done. Can we do more than this?

What is a well-lived life? What is human flourishing? What is the purpose for human existence? If ethics is to become more than a description of the diverse ethical sources student already have, and engage the normative task present in the second assumption, then it cannot avoid these questions. No single answer to the purpose for ethics suffices in the university, but below are ten well-known possible answers.

1. The purpose of ethics is to maximize utility.

2. The purpose of ethics is to honor and respect the dignity of every individual.

3. The purpose of ethics is to cultivate virtue in order to be a loyal citizen.

4. The purpose of ethics is happiness, learned within a context of friends.

5. The purpose of ethics is to obey Torah.

6. The purpose of ethics is to submit to Allah.

7. The purpose of ethics is to love the Blessed Trinity, enjoy God forever and in so doing love one's neighbors and enemies.

8. Ethics has no purpose. It only expresses subjective values or preferences of approbation or disapproval.

9. Ethics is a practical skill to match means to ends whatever end one chooses for one's self.

10. Ethics is nothing but a disguised form of power by which the privileged take advantage of those without privilege.

Let me offer a brief commentary on each of these possible answers. The first two are the dominant forms ethics takes in the modern university. They assume an isolated individual as the basic subject of ethical action, and provide a formal, putatively universal account of ethics. They tend to be reductive. The first answer makes individuals into utility maximizers, but no discrimination is made about the content of utility. The second also assumes the basic subject for ethics is the individual, but rather than a utility maximizer, the individual is now a rights bearing entity whose rights should be respected by all other rights bearing entities. It too is formal in that it does not attempt to give content to those rights. The first option is an ethics for the marketplace; the second for modern democratic nation-states. Both options do not take a person's history as her or his moral starting point, but abstract from it by reducing persons to individuals.

The third and fourth answers take a more manageable political entity or small association of friends as the subject of ethics. We would need to know the content of the political entity in which the person is a citizen or friend to know what virtues matter. Large modern nation-states have a difficult time offering this kind of content because they are too big to facilitate the encounters necessary for the cultivation of virtue. Smaller units such as cities, villages, parishes or neighborhoods would provide the proper size, but they would need to have venues for political engagement with each other to determine what a good citizen is in specific contexts. Broad based community organizing is one place where virtuous citizenship is cultivated.[8] Association of friends is an even more manageable size for the cultivation of virtue. It assumes that one's ethical possibilities will in part depend upon the character of one's friends and the common objects of love that they share. For instance, friendships determined by a shared passion for drug use will inevitably be vicious. Friendships determined by a shared passion to assist the poor, or to bring aesthetic joy to others bear great potential for virtue.

The fifth through the seventh answers obviously place the ethical life within religious institutions. There are well defined disciplines of Christian, Jewish and Islamic ethics. To police them out of any ethical conversation is to make the secular the default position. While a secular

---

8. Stout, *Blessed Are the Organized.*

ethic has its advantages, it should not simply be assumed as the norm without some attempt to explain why it is preferable to religious ethics. One such attempt, one that has been discredited in practice and theory, is that a secular ethics is not as violent as religious ethics.[9] Religions have, undoubtedly and unfortunately, contributed to violence. As the twentieth century amply demonstrated, secular polities did so as well. So what is the advantage to a secular ethic over a religious one? Anyone who argues for it will need to explain what the secular is and why it is preferable to religion. One common answer is known as the "subtraction thesis." The secular is what remains once superstition is removed and only reason remains. Here the secular is a narrative of inevitable progress in which "secular reason" is primarily understood as negative. It is what you have once the world is disenchanted from all religious influence. Both the first and second answers could be forms of a secular ethic; God or religion is not necessary for them. Nor are they a priori opposed to God, which leads to a second definition of "secular," one put forward by Charles Taylor. The secular is not what remains once religious influence is removed, but religion becomes a private preference individuals choose. It is one option among others.[10] This secular ethics is another form of emotivism or expressivism. A third account of the "secular" arises from Christian theology, especially from St. Augustine (354–430). The secular is the time between Christ's first and second advents in which religious and non-religious people must learn to live together in harmony. They will share common objects of love such as peace, health, basic services like food, shelter and protection, but they will also differ in objects of worship.

To this point, I have not made a case for a religious ethic, whether it be Jewish, Christian or Islamic, but only attempted to question if a secular ethic should be given the default position as it often is in the modern university. Like religious ethics, it too should have to give an account of itself—tell us what it is, what purpose it serves, and why it will let us flourish as human beings more so than other kinds of ethics. What account might a religious ethics give for itself? At a minimal level, anyone who seeks to be conversant with the ethics of the vast majority of the earth's inhabitants should at least be aware of the ethical teachings among the world's religions. Because each religion has contested teachings on ethics, it would behoove us to encourage the religious persons with whom we inhabit this world to be the best

9. Cavanaugh, *Myth of Religious Violence.*
10. Taylor, *Secular Age.*

representatives of that religion's teachings. For instance, I think it is preferable to encourage the world's religions at least to take seriously their just war traditions over holy crusades. For that matter, a secular war ethics would benefit from the practical wisdom of the just war tradition.

Beyond this minimal reason for teaching religious ethics is the important ethical question of whether or not God exists, and what it matters in everyday life. For if there is a God, and a God like the transcendent deity at least in part shared among the Abrahamic faiths, then God is not one more object in the world. God's existence will change everything, especially concerning the ethical life. What difference God would make to ethics as that knowledge is mediated through religions should be part of any quest for moral purpose. To police it out a priori is to force secular conversions upon the ethical conversation. A third important reason to make space for religious ethics is an important point made by Alasdair MacIntyre about the basic subject of ethics. To this point I have agreed with most ethical theories that the basic form ethics takes is *action*. As noted above, practical wisdom culminates in it. MacIntyre, however, has made the point that *action per se* is not the basic form of ethics but *intelligible action*. To act is not an isolated event, but one that arises from an ability to see and construe the world in specific ways. Ethics is as much about vision and narrative as it is about action. Narratives provide a vision by which we can see a situation that allows us to act within it. Part of the ethical task will be to get students to clarify the narratives that provide them with a vision to act in the world, and then ask if those narratives are worthy of their life? Religions offer narrative construals that render actions intelligible, but the same of course is true of secular visions.

The eighth through the tenth answers slightly differ in content, but are similar in kind. The eighth depends on the "emotivist" theory of meaning for ethics. Although it was once popular among scholars, and still has a resonance with popular culture, I find it misguided for the reasons already noted. Faced with horrible moral failure few people find it adequate to say "*x* is wrong because I don't like it." The ninth answer is one based on managerial expertise, a peculiarly modern form of instrumental reasoning that claims to be able to match means with ends without making judgments about the worthiness of those ends. Ends should matter; it avoids the reason for teaching ethics altogether. The tenth answer is less deceptive than the instrumental reasoning present in putative managerial expertise. It denies that we have purpose at all and thus claims to be "beyond good and evil." This is the fascinating position of Friedrich Nietzsche (1844–1900) who claimed that morality was a "soporific appliance."

Nietzsche wrote, "I hope to be forgiven for discovering that all moral philosophy hitherto has been tedious and has belonged to the soporific appliances—and that 'virtue,' in my opinion, has been MORE injured by the TEDIOUSNESS of its advocates than by anything else; at the same time, however, I would not wish to overlook their general usefulness. It is desirable that as few people as possible should reflect upon morals, and consequently it is very desirable that morals should not some day become interesting!"[11] Moral philosophy as a "soporific appliance" induces sleep in order to numb patients so that an operation can be performed on them without their knowledge. Moral philosophy masks what is really going on. There is no good or evil, no up or down, no purpose to life. We are on a little blue ball spinning aimlessly through the universe and the most we can do is what Nietzsche called the "artistic taming of the horrible." Take the horrors of life and using aesthetic means make it as beautiful as it can be. Moral philosophy, like religion, soothes immature minds who cannot look upon our horrifying reality and affirm it for what it is. Answers eight and nine inevitably lead to ten when we look with the utmost seriousness at what they are suggesting because, in the end, they conceive of ethics as nothing but a will to power.

These ten answers are not the only answers to the question of moral purpose; others can be found. The difficulty in teaching normative ethics is the step that comes after presenting these possible answers. As I noted earlier, if we tell students to "choose" a moral purpose and live consistently with it, we are not giving them independence but imposing something like answer nine upon them. Such an answer will tacitly assume that the role of the bureaucrat-manager is the normative role for ethical practice and theory. We cannot divorce the teaching of ethics from proposing some form of good life within a social context.

Conclusion

So what should be done in teaching ethics? The first task is to take seriously the ethical formations students already bring with them into the class room, and help them gain the practical and theoretical wisdom to be able to name them. The second task is to have them subject it to scrutiny

11. Nietzsche, *Beyond Good and Evil*, 578.

through an examination of human flourishing by attending to the question, What is a well-lived life? But if the answer to this question is not simply to be emotivist, it must be something more than subjective preference. Here is where not only the student's history, but the history and tradition of the university should come into play. Students and teachers are not the only ones who have histories, so do universities. They exist in specific locations and have traditions of practical reasoning present through their ceremonies, architecture, monuments, mission statements, etc. They help us answer the question, What does this university stand for? Where does it want to take you ethically? Is it primarily to gain wealth, status, health, virtue, faith, abandon faith? What does it think a well-lived life is? If it has no answer to this question, then perhaps ethics courses will be unintelligible. Those answers are usually present and can be found, for better and worse, in those mission statements, monuments, and architectural structures. For instance, the motto at Southern Methodist University is *Veritas liberabit vos* ("The truth will make you free"). This motto is found throughout its history and marks significant moments and monuments of SMU's life and architecture. It comes from Christian Scripture, John 8:32, and bears traces of SMU's Methodist heritage.

This heritage is worth considering as an answer to the question, What is a well-lived life? The mission statement in the university's strategic plan makes this explicit: "Among its faculty, students, and staff, the university will cultivate principled thought, develop intellectual skills, and promote an environment emphasizing individual dignity and worth. SMU affirms its historical commitment to academic freedom and open inquiry, to moral and ethical values, and to its United Methodist heritage." Some debate and discussion about what that heritage is, and how it helps us answer the question of moral purpose should be noncontroversial. It can be done without assuming everyone must join the United Methodist church, sign some confessional document, or even have faith in God.

The university is a complex space where no single authority should define it. It has relations with many other "spaces"—the market, government, the military, church, other religious and civic institutions, but it also has its own identity. While it must have relations with each of these other "spaces," it must also keep an arm's length distance from them so that it can engage in free inquiry about the purposes of each. The university is not a church, but nor is it a nation state, corporation or military institution. It should seek to engage all these forms of social life by exploring assumptions, finding connections and by subjecting them to the "*universitas*" the whole that should render our common endeavor intelligible if it is not to be fragmented into competing "colleges" without any overarching purpose. How that "whole" gets defined is exceedingly complex, but it can only be found if we continue to ask the question, What is a well-lived life? Or additionally, What is a life worth living? We must connect those questions both to the histories students bring to the university, the history of that university, and where we think we are headed into the future.

2

Should Ethics Be Taught? Ethics in the Secular University

ROBERT J. HOWELL

NOT LONG AGO, A colleague approached me with scandalous news: our university's new curriculum might require courses in ethics. "Ethics!" he said, eyebrows raised, obviously worried this ethics business might be a toe in the door for Alchemy and Astrology. Not long afterwards, another professor alluded to the same scandal. "They think we should be teaching our students how to behave!" I wasn't clear who "They" were, but from my colleague's tone, I had no doubt that They wore dark cloaks and had designs on our students' souls. In both cases, I could only muster a sheepish smile; after all, I had a dark cloak hanging on the back of my office door. That's right: I'm one of Them. I admit it. I think teaching ethics and ethical thinking might be the single most important contribution contemporary universities can make. Nevertheless, one has to be careful about how one advocates this. The fact is, people often don't understand what it means to teach ethics. Does it mean we are pushing students towards or away from a set of religious beliefs? Are we encouraging them to see the world and its people in terms of the stark contrast between good and evil? Whatever it is we are doing, who do we think we are to teach such a thing? The gall!

In fact, these worries are based on a number of confusions, that have been to some degree encouraged within the academy. There are some valid concerns about the idea of teaching ethics, but to dismiss ethics from the curriculum because of these valid concerns is to throw out a very important baby with some admittedly dirty bathwater.

In what follows, I'd like to address a few of these concerns, in part by being clear about what teaching ethics is and what it is not. Once we get clear on what it is, I think a clear case can be made for its importance. I want to end by suggesting some ways that ethics can be integrated into a traditional curriculum that preserves the values of a secular liberal arts education.

The Secular University's Dilemma

Like most philosophers I use the terms "ethics" and "morality," as well as "ethical" and "moral," interchangeably. The study of ethics is, generally speaking, the study of what one ought morally to do and what is morally good. So stated, to talk of teaching ethics is apt to sound alarm bells in many areas. Two related questions immediately come to mind for the modern academic, and even the savvy student:

> *Question One*: Isn't the teaching of ethics and morals the province of religion? And relatedly,

> *Question Two*: Isn't the notion that there is a "capital M" Morality and an objective truth about ethics deeply suspect? Doesn't the very teaching of ethics presuppose the dubious thought that there is some mysterious Right way to act regardless of cultural background or circumstance?

These questions are deeply linked, because for many people it is inconceivable that there be an objective fact of the matter about what is right or wrong without a God to say that it's so. If ethics isn't grounded in God, then surely it is a matter of cultural norms that don't have objective standing. This way of thinking about things poses a dilemma for the secular institution that wants to engage in the teaching of ethics.

> The Secular University's Dilemma: either Morality and Ethics encode God's will (and thus have a religious backing) or they are merely a matter of cultural custom. Either way, teaching ethics in a secular university is inappropriate. If Ethics and Morality are really a way to sneak God into the curriculum, then the secular university is no longer secular: a central part of its teachings presuppose a religious point of view that might not be shared by many of its students and teachers. On the other hand, if ethics isn't backed by religion, it is a mere cultural construct and, again, to teach it as though it were objectively true would be intellectually

irresponsible and alienating to those students and teachers who don't share, and perhaps even want to critique, the social mores that are being enshrined as ethical precepts.

Faced with this dilemma, it is tempting either to say "so much the worse for secular institutions!" or to steer clear of teaching ethics altogether.

To me, it seems clear that both of these reactions are unacceptable. Regardless of the soundness of the reasoning behind the university's dilemma, and I think it is extremely suspect, as a practical matter it is undesirable, and perhaps even impossible, to keep ethical deliberations within the fences of religious institutions. It is undesirable because this ever-shrinking world is home to people of diverse cultures and religions and, inevitably, the question will arise of what we should do to, with, or for one another. If our conversations about ethical obligations bottom out in an ineliminable appeal to religion, it's hard to see how two groups with very different religious views can have a reasoned discussion on common ground. Unless these intercultural conversations are always to be backed by the possibility of violence, there must be a way we can reason with each other, across religious and cultural contexts. This, in my view, is where secular ethics comes in. A secular ethics is not one that shuns religion or even religious basis—there is nothing to prevent a devout Christian or Muslim from working in secular ethics. It's just that this sort of inquiry doesn't make essential reference to a particular religious tradition. If universities hope to produce the next generation of leaders, and they want those leaders to lead in a diverse world, they must teach their students how to reason about what they, their businesses and their countries should do in a way that is accessible to those from a different tradition.

If the above is right, there is excellent practical reason to teach ethics in a way that is independent of particular religious traditions. But this doesn't really answer the Secular University's Dilemma. One answer, of course, would simply deny its presuppositions. Many philosophers, myself included, think that not only does objective morality not presuppose divine commandments, but that divine commandments—if they are to be backed by more than godly might—presuppose objective morality. But these issues are tricky and a discussion of them would take us off track.[1] Instead, I

---

1. Of course this sort of discussion starts with Plato's *Euthyphro*, and continues through centuries of debates about divine command theory. A classic discussion sympathetic to divine command theory is Quinn (1978). A more critical discussion is in Mackie (1977), but the literature is voluminous.

will argue that there is something contradictory at the heart of the Secular University's Dilemma.

A university that was persuaded by the University's Dilemma to conclude ethics had no place in the curriculum would be deeply hypocritical. It would be hypocritical to say, at one and the same time, that ethics should not be taught in a secular curriculum because for some reason ethics is suspect. After all, what is the import of that claim that ethics should not be taught if it is not itself a claim about what it is ethically permissible for the university to do? The very claim presupposes the system it denies. Granted, by making a decision based on reasoning about what is permissible, one is not thereby teaching ethics. But that's not the point. The point is that there is no escaping questions about what one should do, and we make the decisions we make—whether as teachers, university administrators, or as students—because we think there is a right answer to such questions. What's more, we think there is a right way to reason about such questions. Perhaps we think we *should not* impose belief systems on those who disagree with us, or that we *should* have a curriculum that is open to all. If we shape our conception of the university based on such thoughts, we must think these shoulds and should-nots are pretty important. What sort of university would we be, then, if we thought such normative claims were so important but we then failed to teach our students how to think about such claims?

The point is that the question "should we teach ethics" answers itself. To the extent that we think this is the sort of question that has an answer, and to the extent we care about getting that answer right, we are already committed to reasoning about the sorts of questions ethics concerns itself with. Further, to the extent we think there are better and worse ways to think about such questions, we are likewise committed to the idea that there are better and worse ways to think about ethical issues.[2] Once we believe this, it would be perverse to think that we shouldn't teach these sorts of skills to our students. Unless, then, we think the question too silly to even think about answering, the answer to the question of whether we should teach ethics is a clear yes.

Ethical Thinking vs. Ethical Principles

An argument like the one above, which aims to show that even our reservations about ethics are ethical reservations, is unlikely to mollify those

2. The reasoning in this section is similar to that of Nagel.

who have such reservations. Teaching ethics can still sound imperialistic, as though it involved the handing down of wisdom from on high. Addressing this concern requires saying a little about what teaching ethics should look like.

In general, teaching ethics—or at least the kind of teaching I am advocating—is not a matter of drilling students on a list of principles they are to memorize and abide by. In the first instance, it isn't a matter of telling people how they should act at all. Instead it is a matter of teaching them how to reason about ethical issues. To this extent, teaching ethics is not unlike teaching science. Although in both ethics and science the ultimate goal is that our students find some truths that inform their beliefs and behavior, the more important thing in the end is that the students learn how to reason their way through particular sorts of problems. In science we want them to learn the method of hypothesis formation, experiment design, and empirical testing. We want them to see what sort of evidence bears on empirical hypotheses. In ethics, on the other hand, we want them to learn to seek a more general principle behind a moral judgment and to determine what else such a principle commits them to. We want them to learn what sorts of reasons bear on judgments about what one should or shouldn't do.

There are important disanalogies between ethics and science, of course. I'm not thinking simply about the fact that in science bad reasoning can lead to explosions. (Indeed, bad reasoning in ethics can lead to explosions too.) For the purposes of education, a different disanalogy is more relevant, and, I would argue, it suggests that teaching ethics is perhaps even more important than teaching science. (That being said, it would be a deep mistake to force a tradeoff between the two.) The disanalogy is this: one doesn't need to know the physics behind the combustion engine to drive a car as well as possible. Similarly, one doesn't need to understand the biology of the pancreas in order to benefit fully from insulin shots. We do, however, need to understand why what we are doing is the ethical thing to do if we are to fully reap the benefits of ethics. Unlike science, in ethics we are not really entitled to stand on the shoulders of giants. We must, each of us, understand it from the ground up.

To see this, consider the following thought experiment:

Suppose that there were an app, developed by those masterminds at Google, that told the user the moral thing to do in any situation. Just as Google Maps tells us how to get from Dallas to Houston, so Google Morals would tell us whether or not it was right to give to charity or to vote for a candidate who was the better of two evils. It wouldn't explain why, but it would generate the correct ethical answer for any query. Granted, imagining having such confidence in an app is a bit of a stretch, but for the moment let's set that concern aside. Even if we could rely on such an app, we should ask: is there something wrong with using it?[3]

On the one hand, clearly that the world would be a better place if people used the app. Most people don't even think in terms of what should be done very often, and when they do they are often too lazy—or too ill-prepared—to think seriously about what should be done. That's the nice thing about simple commandments or principles—they generate clear results about what one should do without requiring much thought of the agent. "Always give back what you owe" is pretty clear, and it sounds like a pretty good rule to follow. But as Socrates points out at the beginning of Plato's Republic, there are situations in which giving back what is owed seems the wrong thing to do. (If your neighbor lends you his gun, and then asks for it back when he is drunk and angry at his wife, don't give it back.) Google Morals has the advantage of principles—it gives answers without much thought—without its drawbacks—it will generate the right result even if odd situations in which our standard moral rules fail us. So, what would be wrong with using it? If we could, somehow, develop such an app, would we need to teach ethics at all? Yes.

The problem with someone relying on a Google Morals is that while they are doing the right thing, they do not understand *why* they are doing what they are doing. They will not be able to explain to others, for example, why they did what they did, and they will not be able to persuade anyone else that they should act the same way. If someone disapproved of their actions and challenged them, there would not be much they could say. This is important not only on the level of personal interaction. It is arguable that part of being a responsible citizen in a democracy is being able to explain why one is voting for certain sorts of policies or for people who support those policies. If I vote for a government to take away a substantial portion of someone's money or to restrict their liberties, you might think I owe them an explanation. It would be unfortunate if all I could do was point to my phone and say "google morals says."

The problem with something like google morals arguably goes even deeper. If someone were to act in a certain way just because Google Morals told them to do so, they would likely lack the emotional reactions that

3. Howell, "Google Morals," 389–415.

undergird many moral judgments. (Would we think someone moral who refrained from murdering a child because a computer told them not to, but they lacked the repulsion to child murder that makes it inconceivable to us?) One way to put the problem is that if someone relies on Google Morals to tell them how to act, they will act morally but will not be moral people. Their actions do not redound to their characters because their characters are not involved at all!

The reaction of most people is that a world where people did moral things but without understanding why, and without doing it because of their moral characters, is a deeply impoverished world. We get such a world, however, not only by relying on Google Morals. We get such a world by failing to teach ethics and by failing to teach people to develop that part of themselves that both intellectually and viscerally understands why something is right and something is wrong. This is why we need to teach ethics, but it is also why teaching ethics is not—and cannot be—simply a matter of teaching principles and rules. It is teaching a way of deliberating such that one understands not just whether a course of action generates profits or efficiency, but whether or not it should be pursued given the full range of its implications and consequences.

Teaching Ethical Inquiry

So if teaching ethics isn't a matter of handing over a book of principles, what is it? It might help to distinguish several different "parts" of ethical instruction. Philosophers tend to divide ethics into the following three categories, from more to less abstract:

1. **Metaethics:** The study of the nature of ethical judgments, ethical knowledge and ethical concepts. Metaethics isn't so much the study of what in particular is good, but rather what it even means to say that something is good. So, for example, in metaethics one might discuss whether or not there is such a thing as objective good and bad and whether or not that can be known.

2. **Normative Ethics:** The general study of moral systems and frameworks to determine what makes something good or an action the right one to take. Is the right action the one that maximizes pleasure, or must it take certain rights and duties into account? What generates such rights and duties?

3. **Applied Ethics:** The study of how to act and reason morally in particular, usually controversial situations. While normative ethics concerns the general theory behind the nature of morality, applied ethics
explains how that theory bears on particular situations or controversies. So, for example, what follows are some of the fields of applied
ethics and some of the questions they will consider:

- *Business Ethics*: Do CEOs have obligations to anyone but their
  shareholders? Are there limits to the sort of marketing that are
  ethical?

- *Medical Ethics*: Must one always gain patient consent for a medical
  procedure? What should one do when a patient is unable to consent? Is it ever permissible to "pull the plug" on a patient?

- *Environmental Ethics*: Is there any value to preserving a multiplicity of species? Do we have an obligation to avoid undue destruc-
  tion of natural resources?

- *Political Philosophy*: Is taxation permissible and for what reasons?
  Is there an obligation to participate in the democratic process?
  When is governmental regulation justified?

- *Parental Ethics*: What rights do children have? Is abortion permissible? What sorts of punishment of children are permissible?

- *Legal/Criminal Ethics*: How should one weigh the risks of punish-
  ing the innocent against the risk of leaving the guilty unpunished?
  Is capital punishment moral? Are laws always morally binding?

- *Ethics of Technology*: What is the nature of privacy and what
  lengths should we go to in protecting it? Should we pursue artificial superintelligence?

The list of issues and fields in applied ethics is extremely long, but
this sampling should make two things clear. One is just how pervasive and
important these questions are. Every domain, professional and personal,
will involve moral quandries that deserve serious thought. Our students
need to be able to think through them, but they also need be able to recognize when these, as well as new sorts of challenges arise. The ethical
dilemmas of tomorrow are likely not even on the radar today. The second
thing that should be clear is that applied ethics, including the ethics of
various professions, is not simply a matter of professional codes and legal

standards. Too often the ethical codes in a profession are about staying out of legal trouble, but don't address the deep moral controversies that come with the field. For every professional code of ethics there are (at least) two questions: should one always follow it, and if one follows it has one done all that is morally required? My suspicion is that the answer to both of these questions is no, but the main point is that these are questions our students need to be able to deliberate about and answer.

Given the general division between metaethics, normative ethics, and applied ethics, which one of these should be taught in the average university curriculum? Not surprisingly, my view is that we should aim to teach a little bit of each.

A natural thought, though, is that there is no need to teach anything but applied ethics. After all, what use is there in teaching our students something they will not apply? This thought, however, ignores some of the lessons of google morals. If all we cared about was getting the right ethical answers to individual problems, we might as well just google it. But, we saw that there was a value to having ethical judgments and actions stem from an integrated set of reasons and motivations within the moral agent. This is why even when the focus is on particular circumstances and application, there needs to be a background understanding of why certain considerations are at play in general. There needs to be a way, among other things, to discuss decisions with someone who disagrees with them, and often this will draw from normative theory. There are those, for example, who believe that actions should be pursued as long as they generate the greatest good consequences. This way of approaching things will often yield very clear policy recommendations but might well run the risk of ignoring individual rights. (It might be, for example, that genetically testing employees would save money and lead to a healthier workforce, but there are serious questions about whether this violates the employees' rights.) This is the sort of difference that is best addressed at the more theoretical level of normative ethics. While we shouldn't expect our students to become ethical theorists, they nevertheless need to understand what sorts of reasons are adduced in favor of these various theories and the fact that certain initially plausible ways of looking at things have serious drawbacks.

The same sort of reasoning explains why I think it is of benefit to teach metaethics as well. Just as ethical disagreements sometimes push one back from the questions at hand to consider more theoretical questions, so too certain disagreements force one to reconsider and defend the very presuppositions of the whole ethical project. It's not unusual, for example, to be debating with someone about what to do in a certain case, only to find out that they ultimately believe that there is no such thing as objective right and wrong. This sort of view comes in various flavors, from out and out nihilism to a more subtle cultural relativism, but the implications can nevertheless be profound. One could be debating very specific issues about the permissibility of drilling for oil or digging for diamonds in sub-saharan Africa, but if it turned out that someone believed that there are no ethical guidelines that transcended individual cultures, that will deeply change the way they think about these issues. Put another way, it seems of little value teach students the intricacies of applied ethics if they don't see any reason to believe there is such a thing as ethical truth in the first place. If that is what they believe, they are really just back to memorizing rules of a particular game, without seeing why we should do any more than pay them lipservice.

Though a curriculum that embraces an ethics education should teach a bit from all three general categories of ethics, it seems reasonable to give them different levels of emphasis. There will no doubt be many recommendations about how much emphasis each one deserves, but it's important to keep the following in mind: students often don't end up in the professions they prepare for, and the issues that face professions are constantly in flux. So, whatever the distribution of time, it is important that individual problems or controversies are used to teach the students to think about ethical issues in general, so that as their lives change and the contours of their professions evolve, they have the ability to apply their skills to new areas.

Ethics and the Curriculum

So, how does one bring ethics into the curriculum? While this question deserves serious empirical research to determine what best works in different populations of students, I will make some general suggestions and then briefly sketch some programs and initiatives we are implementing at Southern Methodist University with help and support from the Maguire Center for Ethics and Public Responsibility.

Make Ethics Interdisciplinary

Too often, ethics is seen as the exclusive purview of philosophy departments. Though it might be the case that much of the research work in ethics occurs in those departments, it should be emphasized that ethics instruction ought not be so contained. One reason is simply practical: your typical philosophy department simply cannot singlehandedly staff a part of the curriculum that serves every student. Perhaps the more important reason, though, is that there is really no more interdisciplinary a field than ethics. As we've seen, ethical questions arise across the curriculum and really appreciating those questions will require participants from many departments. If there is ever an area that should resist being siloed, it is ethics. At SMU, our attempt to encourage this outlook is represented by the fact that we have two university professors in ethics—The Maguire Chair in Ethics and The Elizabeth Scurlock University Chair of Human Values—who are not officially in a department but are instead under the provost. These distinguished professors are in a position to develop programs and ideas that span disciplines and schools. Addtionally, our university's ethics center is not under the purview of any dean but rather an at-large program of the entire university that reports directly to the provost.

The interdisciplinary nature of ethics should also be built into the curriculum. At SMU, we are currently working on a curriculum that develops this goal in two important ways.

1. The Civic and Individual Ethics Proficiency: Each student must complete a course that is tagged as developing civic and individual ethics. This course can be in any discipline, so long as it leads students to deliberate about ethical issues in that area. For example, a course in journalism that involved discussion of the First Amendment would qualify, as would a political science course that discussed the ideals behind the Constitution or a psychology course that discussed the ethics of research methods. The interdisciplinary nature of this tag leads students to see that ethical issues arise everywhere, but it also leads professors to reflect on places in their courses in which discussion of ethics might be appropriate.

2. The Freshman Seminar: This class focuses on three areas: critical thinking, writing and ethics. Critical thinking and writing skills are developed in the context of a morally significant issue or controversy. Students will learn to bring argument and empirical evidence to bear upon a topic of contemporary ethical importance. Professors from a range of departments and schools are encouraged to develop their own classes, but potential classes might discuss the ethics and science

of climate change, the nature of political revolution and civil disobedience, or the nature of revenge in literature.

Educate the Faculty

Because many faculty members haven't taken courses in ethics, and have themselves only rarely encountered systematic discussion of ethical arguments, they will likely feel unqualified and imposed upon if they are asked to help implement an ethics curriculum. (They might also have the reaction of some of my colleagues, that teaching ethics is inappropriate in the academy.) Seminars and workshops should be provided so that professors from various disciplines can share ideas and educate each other about the best way to have a discussion of ethics in the classroom. If incentives can be given for course development, all the better. SMU's Maguire Center for Ethics has done our university a great service, for example, by offering grants to professors who are willing to develop courses with an ethics component. They are then invited to a weekend retreat in which they refine course ideas. Professors with experience teaching ethics are invited to answer questions and in some case run brief seminars in ethics pedagogy.

Involve the Community

If serious and disciplined discussion of ethical issues is lacking in the university, it is all the more absent in the community at large. There are, of course, important outlets for this sort of discussion; churches and institutions like the Rotary Club come to mind. The university is uniquely well positioned, however, to host these discussions. Not only do they often have experts in many fields, including experts in ethics, as well as extensive facilities, they have professors with tenure. When it comes to discussions of ethics, this last point is important. Discussions of morality should not be mere preaching to the choir. People have strong disagreements about ethical issues, and to paper over those disagreements with a posture of academic unanimity is a mistake. It is important to articulate the appeal of even unpopular positions. But defending certain positions, which might be unpopular in a particular community, is a dangerous proposition if one doesn't have the sort of security tenure is meant to provide. The goal of tenure is to protect the freedom to articulate and develop views that might be threatening to those with power. That freedom is largely wasted if those views aren't ever given an airing—even if the result of giving them an airing is that they are roundly refuted. At SMU, owing to a partnership between the Maguire Center for Ethics, Dedman College and the Center for Presidential History, we have begun a lecture series called "The Third Rail." In that series, two professors are invited to debate and discuss two sides of an issue of ethical import. It has proven wildly successful, forcing us to bigger and bigger venues to accommodate community interest. Topics discussed include "Are We Too Dumb for Democracy?" "Political Discourse and Identity Politics," and "Hope or Alarm in the Age of Trump?"

Look to the Future

Ethics, and Philosophy in general, can seem like a stale disciplines focused upon unresolvable problems. This is partly the fault of the way we teach it. If we continue to teach and reteach the old debates, whether between Kant and the Utilitarians or between pro-lifers and pro-choicers, we will lose the attention of our students. As the world changes more and more quickly, ethical decision points are multiplying and our very sense of morality is changing. Take, for example, the relationship between personal privacy and technology. It has almost become commonplace to think that the right to privacy no longer exists and that to worry about data collection is useless paranoia.[4] Part of the reason for this is that too little thought has been given to articulating the value of privacy to those who will be developing the technologies that threaten it. Similarly, we are witnessing an explosion in artificial intelligence. There are those who see a future in which most of our jobs are taken by robots and computers. Perhaps this will happen, perhaps not. But it is a real possibility and we need to be thinking about what this does to our sense of desert, social safety nets, and self-worth. Some, including those at the top of the tech field—including Bill Gates, Elon Musk, and Ray Kurzweil—think artificial superintelligence poses an existential risk to humanity.[5] Perhaps they are wrong, but it would be foolish to dismiss the possiblity. What should we do in the face of this explosion? Meanwhile, other technological advances have allowed us to learn how to modify humanity in surprising ways. Psychopharmaceuticals have long offered us the opportunity to increase focus and decrease depression, but how long before other chemical modifications allow us to "enhance"

4. Johnson, "Privacy No Longer."
5. Bostrom, *Superintelligence*.

ourselves well beyond normal human capacities? Should we avail ourselves of these opportunities? Should we allow others to do so? CRISPR and other technologies are opening the possibility to make modifications in our very DNA. Is doing so permissible?[6]

Students will not fail to see the pressing relevance of the questions raised by emerging technologies, and their immediacy serves to highlight the crucial role ethics should play in our deliberations. Two classes at SMU, recently developed using grants from the Maguire Center, have proven successful in drawing students to just these questions: *Technology, Society and Value*, and *Neuroethics*. The former, an introductory level course, has continued to add sections since its inception and cannot keep up with demand. The latter fills whenever it is offered, and appeals to a wide range of students from pre-med to engineers. These are only two examples of ways ethics education can look to the future. More opportunities await and we will do our students and ethics in general a disservice if we ignore them.

Conclusion

It is often said that we should study history because those who do not are bound to repeat it. It is not often remarked that if we don't study ethics we won't know whether or not we *should* repeat it. Students flock to vocational programs because there is a chance that what they will learn can be brought to bear on decisions they make in the future. Very few flock to ethics, despite the fact that it is *guaranteed* that what they will learn will bear on decisions they make throughout their lives. As universities, we pride ourselves on developing the next generation of leaders. It is hard to imagine a more irresponsible goal than to produce a generation of leaders who haven't been taught how to think about what they should be leading others to do. If we are serious about these goals, therefore, its high time we brought ethics to the center of a collegiate level education rather than letting in languish as a curricular afterthought.

6. Buchanan, *Better than Human*.

3

Christian Ethics, the University, and the Broader Human Society

Charles E. Curran

THERE IS NO DOUBT that Christian ethics is related primarily to the church. It serves the church by its study of how the Christian message affects the way in which Christians are called to live and act. But Christian ethics is also related to the academy or university and the broader human society. This essay will consider the relationship of Christian ethics to the academy or university and to the broader human society.

Relationship to the Academy or the University

Christian ethics is the name usually given to this discipline in Protestant circles whereas moral theology is more often used in Catholic circles. In my judgment, Christian ethics is the more appropriate title today. Christian ethics is a type or species of religious ethics. The two general categories of ethics are philosophical ethics and religious ethics. Philosophical ethics bases its approach solely on human experience and reason, which are common to all human beings. Religious ethics involves sources that are proper to the particular religious community—e.g., Muslim, Jewish, Christian.

The particular sources of Christian ethics are the Bible and the Christian tradition, although most Christian ethics give a significant role to human sources of moral wisdom and knowledge. A well known and somewhat widely accepted understanding of the sources for Christian ethics is found in the Wesleyan quadrilateral. This quadrilateral was not explicitly developed by John Wesley, the founder of the Wesleyan and Methodist denominations, but was first proposed by Albert Outler, the well-known Methodist theologian who taught for many years at Southern Methodist University. According to Outler, the Wesleyan quadrilateral based on the writings of Wesley himself recognizes four sources for the discipline of Christian ethics—Scripture, tradition, reason, and experience. But not all Christian ethicists accept these four sources or understand them in the same way.[1]

With regard to the university, the primary reality is that Christian ethics is an academic discipline. It involves what is technically called second order discourse. This is likewise true of philosophical ethics. Here I make a significant distinction between morality and ethics. Most people would agree that human beings are called to act morally, although in honesty we all recognize that we often fail to live up to our own moral standards. The moral life is what all are called to live. Ethics as a second order discipline stands back from the lived reality of the moral life to study theoretically, systematically, reflexively, and critically the moral life. To some extent it is true that everyone who leads a moral life does invoke a somewhat systematic and critical perspective at times but not at the level of the academic discipline of ethics. Thus both religious and philosophical ethics are academic disciplines involved in this work of systematic, reflexive, and critical study.

An analogy might help to understand better the difference between morality and ethics. All of us human beings are called to have a good emotional human existence. Psychiatry is a second order discipline that stands back from the lived reality to study theoretically, systematically, reflexively, and critically human emotional maturity. Just as the vast majority of people can live a good emotional human life without ever having studied the second order discourse of psychiatry, so the vast majority of people can live good moral lives without having studied ethics. When problems arise in our emotional life, the psychiatrist can be helpful in diagnosing the problems and dealing with them. So too the ethicist is especially helpful in dealing not only with the theory of the moral life but also in helping to solve complex and difficult moral issues.

The analogy between ethics and psychiatry also helps to explain the role of the ethicist as such. Are psychiatrists the most emotionally mature, well-balanced human beings in the world? Without denigrating a particular

1. Campbell, "Wesleyan Quadrilateral," 154–61.

profession, all would generally agree that psychiatrists are not necessarily the most emotionally mature, well-balanced human beings. The same is true in an analogous way for ethicists. They are not better moral persons than other human beings. They are not even better at making moral decisions. The expertise of the ethicist is precisely in the academic and intellectual order. As second order discourse, the discipline of ethics deals with the theory of the moral life and also a consideration of practical issues, but even in the area of practical issues the professional ethicist is a help to people making decisions although such people can still make very good decisions without the help of ethicists.

Religious ethics just as philosophical ethics is a second order approach that studies the moral life in a theoretical, systematic, reflexive, and critical way. Such an understanding is the basis for the fact that Christian ethics itself is not monolithic. There is not just one theory of Christian ethics, just as there is not just one theory of psychiatry. Different academicians put together a systematic approach in many different ways. Too often there is a general feeling that Christian ethics is monolithic with only one approach. However, the reality is that in Christian ethics, as in any academic discipline, there is a pluralism and a multiplicity of approaches and methods.

Also, Christian ethicists disagree about specific moral and social issues. Some support the death penalty; others oppose it. Some support abortion; others oppose it. Some are pacifists; many are not pacifists but often disagree among themselves whether a particular war is justified or not. The fact of pluralism with regard to positions on specific issues is obvious to all.

Why is there such diversity on particular moral issues? It is easy to find agreement on very general moral principles. All can accept the fact that good is to be done and evil is to be avoided. All would probably agree that we should respect others. Christians all recognize the need to love our neighbor. But when you enter into specifics, there the diversity begins to appear. What is good? What is evil? What does it mean in the concrete to respect others? Who is my neighbor and what is the meaning of love? The reason for such diversity and pluralism is that in the midst of specificity and complexity one can never claim to have moral certitude. Logic reminds us that certitude is more easily found on the level of the general but cannot be present on the level of the complex and the specific.

Christian ethics as a discipline is generally helped by an academic and university setting. As mentioned with regard to the sources of moral wisdom and knowledge, most Christian ethicists recognize that their discipline must be in dialogue with other academic disciplines. Perhaps the best example here is that of Thomas Aquinas, one of the first theologians to systematically address the meaning of the moral life in a university setting. Aquinas was greatly influenced by the Greek philosopher Aristotle and incorporated many aspects of Aristotelian thought in the development of his own Christian ethics. Contemporary Christian ethicists are necessarily involved in dialogue not only with philosophers but also with the disciplines of political science, economics, and psychology. One cannot talk about the political and economic issues facing our society without being in dialogue with political science and economics. Likewise, a dialogue with psychology is very helpful in theorizing about the role of conscience in the moral life.

Christian ethics as an academic discipline should have a place in the university. Some years ago, there was a feeling that religion should not be in the university. Religion, however, for many people involves an important aspect of their life and how they should live their life. In some ways, the importance of religion in the Muslim world in the last few decades has made many realize that religion should be taught in universities in order to understand better how people live their lives. Today there is a general recognition that religion should be a part of the university curriculum.

History shows there has recently been a significant change in the home of Christian ethics. Until 1970 the seminary or theologate was the primary place in which Christian ethics existed. Since 1970, however, the college and university have also become home to Christian ethics. The discipline of Christian ethics has grown dramatically in the last fifty years because of this shift.

The role of religion in the university is not to proselytize but to explain. In my undergraduate courses in Christian ethics here at Southern Methodist University, I explain the first day that the purpose is simply to explain how Christians in theory and practice develop their ethical approaches with all the pluralism mentioned earlier. I insist that one does not have to be a Christian to take this class. Without a doubt, the vast majority who take the course come from the Christian tradition, but some explicitly mention they no longer practice this faith. Two of my best students over the years were not Christians. It was only on the final paper that one student told me she was Jewish but had taken the course to understand better the religion and ethics of a number of her good friends. One Muslim student who was one of the top students in the whole university took two classes from me. His major was political science, and he took the courses to understand better Christian social ethics and its role in the public life of the world.

There is, however, also something special that Christian ethics can bring to the university—raising the questions of ultimate human meaning such as the purpose of life, the realities of evil, suffering, and death. The university as a whole does not seem to deal that much with questions of ultimate meaning. Two years ago I went through our university catalog to see if such questions were addressed. I found one course in English literature dealing with death but nothing else. The university today discusses every variety of particular questions but definitely shies away from the ultimate questions of the meaning of human life and existence. Religion in general and Christian ethics in particular do raise such issues. One can, and many will, disagree with the answers proposed by Christian ethics to the ultimate meaning of human existence, but at least this discipline does raise such issues.

Christian Ethics Affects the Broader Human Society

Christian ethics not only has a role in the university but also has an important influence on the broader human society. Christian ethics deals with how Christians should live their daily lives. Christian social ethics discusses what a good social, political, and economic society should look like. The Bible itself provides the basis for recognizing the social role of the Christian tradition. In the Hebrew Bible, the prophetic tradition reminds the Jewish people of the importance of justice and the need to feed the hungry and come to the assistance of the poor. The prophet Amos condemns the people for oppressing the poor and taking advantage of the needy. As a result, God despises your feasts, your sacrifices, and the noise of your songs. Instead of these ritual practices, let justice roll like waters and righteousness like an ever flowing stream (Amos 5:24).

The New Testament has insisted on the twofold love command of Jesus—love of God and love of neighbor. The famous last judgment scene in Matthew 25 has the king representing God welcoming the blessed into the fullness of the kingdom. "I was hungry and you gave me food, I was thirsty and you gave me drink, I was a stranger and you welcomed me, I was naked and you clothed me, I was sick and you visited me, I was in prison and you came to me," Matthew 25. The recipients of the good news ask when they did these things. The answer came back, when you did it to the least of these, my sisters and brothers, you did it to me. Thus the Christian's love for God is known and manifested in the love for those in need.

The best way to show both the role of Christian ethics in affecting the broader human society and the great diversity and pluralism in the approaches of Christian ethics is to give a brief historical overview of this discipline. Here again many fail to recognize the great diversity and the different theoretical and practical approaches to life found in Christian ethics as it focuses on the broader human society.

Modern Christian social ethics only began in the late nineteenth century. In the historical development, one can distinguish in a necessarily schematic way more liberal approaches and more conservative approaches while recognizing the fluidity of these terms. In addition, it is important especially in the beginning to recognize the different theoretical approaches in the Protestant tradition and in the Roman Catholic tradition.

Early Liberal Protestant Social Ethics

Modern Protestant social ethics began in the late nineteenth and early twentieth century with the work of the Social Gospel movement. The leading figure in the Social Gospel movement was Walter Rauschenbusch (d. 1918). His first book on the subject was *Christianity and the Social Crisis* (1907),[2] and his last book was *Theology for the Social Gospel* (1917).[3] Rauschenbusch was influenced by liberal theology in Germany, the progressive movement in the United States, his pastoral experience with the working poor in the Hell's Kitchen area of New York City where he experienced first-hand the problems of the workers and the injustices they suffered in light of the industrial revolution, and a need to provide a Christian alternative to the Marxist approach to the social problems.

Rauschenbusch maintained that the teaching of Jesus in the New Testament and the prophetic vision of the Old Testament provide the moral principles for a more just society. Protestantism had put too much emphasis on the individual and on the past—what Jesus did in the past to save the individual sinner. He insisted on the centrality of the concept of the kingdom of God to change the social conditions of the present time. Immediately following the dedication in *Christianity and the Social Crisis*, he cites the words of the Lord's Prayer: "Thy kingdom come! Thy will be done

2. Rauschenbusch, *Christianity and the Social Crisis.*
3. Rauschenbusch, *Theology for the Social Gospel.*

on earth!" Rauschenbusch strongly opposed the capitalism of the day with its many inequalities and called for a much more cooperative approach to the economic order. He strongly defended workers and insisted on working together to achieve a greater justice for them. There is no doubt that the Social Gospel was a liberal movement that had an enormous effect on many clergy in the mainline Protestant denominations. Martin Luther King in 1960 maintained that Rauschenbusch left an indelible influence on his thinking. Despite his shortcomings Rauschenbusch gave to American Protestantism a sense of social responsibility it should never lose.[4]

The Social Gospel petered out after the 1920s. Many pointed out that the approach was too optimistic, and this became very evident in the light of the brutal realities of World War I and the economic depression in the United States and elsewhere. The approach of Christian realism succeeded the Social Gospel as the liberal approach to social justice in the period beginning in the 1920s and continuing into the 1960s. The most prominent figure in Christian realism was Reinhold Niebuhr (d. 1971). Christian realism recognized the role of sin in the world and the need to dislodge power with power. It was not enough simply to give good sermons and repeat the teaching of Jesus to bring about change, especially in light of the problems brought about in the United States by the industrial revolution.

The introduction to Niebuhr's 1932 book *Moral Man and Immoral Society: A Study in Ethics and Politics* explains his approach. His book is directed against the moralists both religious and secular who imagine that the egoism of individuals is being progressively checked by the development of rationality or the growth of a religiously inspired good will. Unfortunately, such an approach completely disregards the political necessities in the struggle for justice in human society by failing to recognize those elements in human collective behavior that can never be completely brought under the dominion of reason or conscience. Collective power, whether in the form of imperialism or class domination, can never be dislodged unless power is raised against it. Too often both secular and religious moralists have failed to understand the brutal character of the behavior of all human collectives and the power of self-interest and collective egoism in all intergroup relations. They do not see that the limitations of the human imagination, the easy subservience of reason to prejudice and passion, and the consequent persistence of irrational egoism, particularly

---

4. King, "Pilgrimage to Nonviolence."

in group behavior, make social conflict an inevitability in human history, probably to its very end.[5]

Niebuhr himself had been brought up in the school of Protestant liberalism associated with the Social Gospel. In his early life he also had been strongly attracted to socialism and communism and was a committed pacifist until the rise of Hitler. However, he confronted the realities of poverty and the exploitation of capitalism as a pastor in Detroit in the 1920s. The problems of the workers could be overcome only if they came together to use power to overcome the power of the capitalistic system and its leaders such as Henry Ford. In 1928 he began teaching at Union Theological Seminary in New York, which greatly enhanced his leadership in the theory and practice of Christian realism. In the late 1930s he gave up his pacifism and strongly supported the need for war against Hitler to overcome the evils of Hitler. Only power could overcome the power of evil represented by Hitler.

Niebuhr continued to have a most significant influence in the immediate post-war period. Niebuhrian realism had a great influence on US foreign policy. Yes, Niebuhr insisted on an important role for power, but his realism also recognized the limitations and dangers of power. He disagreed with the United States' insistence in World War II on the need for unconditional surrender by the Nazis. He strongly opposed the Vietnam War while strenuously supporting the Civil Rights Movement. Niebuhr called the Civil Rights Movement and the anti-war movements the two most important moral issues of the time. Activist liberal Protestant clergy became strongly involved in these two social movements in the 1960s.

Niebuhr's influence extended well beyond the church. He was truly a public intellectual who exerted an important influence on international relations and US policy and attitudes. No other Christian theologian has ever had the same influential role in both the theoretical and practical realities of international relations and American policies.

Catholic Social Teaching and Ethics

The same conditions that gave rise to the beginning of Protestant social ethics in the late nineteenth century—the plight of workers as a result of the industrial revolution and the challenge of Marxism—also occasioned the rise of what has been called "Catholic social teaching." This term today generally

---

5. Niebuhr, *Moral Man*. For the best development of his Christian realism, see Niebuhr, *Nature and Destiny of Man*.

refers to the Catholic teaching proposed by papal encyclicals and other hierarchical Church documents related to the social order. Pope Leo XIII in 1891 wrote the first of these encyclicals entitled *Rerum novarum* (the titles of these documents come from the first Latin words of the text).[6]

The methodology of this Catholic tradition differs considerably from the approach taken by the Social Gospel, which gave primacy to the role of Scripture. Leo XIII in an earlier encyclical and other writings insisted that Catholic theology and philosophy follow the approach and methodology of Thomas Aquinas. Leo then applied the philosophy of Aquinas with its use of natural law—human reason reflecting on what God has made can determine how God wants human beings to act—to the social problems of the day. *Rerum novarum* on the basis of this methodology strongly attacked socialism, recognized the legitimacy and the need for greater participation of all in private property, and defended the just wage and the basic human rights of workers, but Leo also recognized another important way to protect the rights of workers in the midst of the problems of the industrial revolution—the role of government and of law. If the general interest of any particular class suffers or is threatened with evils, which can in no other way be met, the public authority must step up to meet them. However, law must not go further than is required for the remedy of the evil or the removal of the danger. Thus, although he condemned socialism, his recognition of the need for government intervention and law to protect the rights of the workers opened up the consideration of the proper role of the state in social and economic life.

On the fortieth anniversary of *Rerum novarum* in 1931, Pope Pius XI issued his encyclical *Quadragesimo anno* (In the fortieth year) enlarging and building on the work of his predecessor in light of the beginnings of the economic depression. In the process, this document developed more explicitly the proper role of the state in economic life. The Catholic approach to the role of the state constitutes a middle position between the extremes of socialism on the one hand and capitalistic individualism on the other hand. To put the understanding of the role of the state in these documents in a more systematic way, one must begin with anthropology—the understanding of the human person. Catholic social teaching understands the human person to be both sacred and social. The sacredness

6. For the individual documents involved in Catholic social teaching, see O'Brien and Shannon, *Catholic Social Thought: The Documentary Heritage*. For commentaries, see Himes, *Modern Catholic Social Teaching: Commentaries and Interpretations*.

of the person comes from the fact that the human person is created in the image and likeness of God which later Catholic teaching saw as the grounding of the dignity of the human person and the basis for human rights. The human person, however, is not an isolated individual but the human person is social by nature.

On the basis of this anthropology, the papal encyclicals condemn the two extremes of socialism and individualistic capitalism. Socialism stresses the good of society but does not give enough importance to the individual; individualistic capitalism stresses the individual but does not give enough emphasis to society. *Quadragesimo anno* is thus opposed to both liberalism and socialism. Liberalistic capitalism is not vicious of its very nature, but it tends to forget about the human dignity of the workers, the social character of economic life, social justice, and the common good. *Quadragesimo anno* distinguishes between a radical form of communism and a more moderate socialism, which unlike communism condemns violence and to some extent moderates class warfare and the abolition of private property. But socialism cannot be brought into harmony with Catholic teaching. In this connection, *Quadragesimo anno* goes on to propose a more radical restructuring of society that does not see labor and capital pitted against each other but sees consumers, capital, and labor working together for a just economic society. Later popes, however, recognize that this solution could never be implemented in our world.

How does *Quadragesimo anno* then understand the positive role of the state in social and economic life? Here the encyclical appeals to the principle of subsidiarity. Subsidiarity comes from the Latin word *subsidium,* which means help. This approach sees society as embracing the natural societies like the family, all sorts of voluntary societies and associations in all aspects of social, economic, cultural, and educational life, and then the levels of government beginning with the local, then the state and the federal government. The higher realities should help the lower realities to achieve their proper goal and end and take action only when the lesser group's project involved is so large that the lesser social groups cannot achieve what needs to be done. In this view, the state is something natural, necessary, and good but limited. Pope John XXIII in *Mater et magistra* (1961) pointed out that in the growing complexity of modern life, there is a need for a greater involvement of the state to address the complex issues that exist in modern society.

Subsequent Catholic theology continued to recognize the need for an approach that is a middle course between the extremes of individualism and socialism. Property has both a social and an individual aspect. Ownership is somewhat instrumental and limited by the social good of property to serve the needs of all human beings. There are three types of justice—commutative justice regarding the relationship of individuals to individuals (the individual, however, can also be a business or corporation), as well as distributive justice, which governs how society should distribute its goods and burdens among citizens, and social justice, which governs how individuals should contribute to the good of society. There were more significant developments after the two early papal encyclicals in which Catholic social teaching continued to employ a middle approach between individualism and socialism.

Vatican Council II (1962–65) brought about some dramatic changes in Catholicism. For purposes of this essay, three aspects are most pertinent. First, Vatican II insisted on the primacy of Scripture in Catholic theology and life. Second, the council recognized the importance of ecumenism and dialogue with other religions such as Judaism and Islam. This ecumenism changed the understanding of Protestants from "heretics" to "separated brethren." These two aspects overcame the previous strong separation between Catholicism and Protestantism. In the area of theology and theological ethics, methods were no longer so diverse. Today Catholic and Protestant ethicians are in dialogue with each other and learn from each other. In fact in reading an article or a book, one many times has difficulty determining if the author is Prostestant or Catholic.

The third and most important substantive change involved the acceptance of religious liberty. The previous Catholic teaching insisted that the ideal was the union of church and state, but one could tolerate the separation of church and state in situations in which the majority of the population was not Catholic. The Catholic position insisted that the state should support and promote the one true religion (Catholicism).

The acceptance of religious freedom at Vatican II logically involved two other important changes. First, Catholic teaching now accepted the fundamental importance of freedom in human society. Pope Leo XIII had strongly opposed the modern freedoms of religion, speech, press, etc. Now Catholic teaching recognized that the dignity of the human person calls for a greater respect for the freedom of the human person in society. The Catholic teaching had also opposed the existence of human rights to protect human freedom, because freedom was always ordered to the truth. After Vatican II in the long papacy of John Paul II, the pope insisted on the importance of human rights in a just society. Commentators have pointed out that the Catholic acceptance of human rights was one of the most significant political developments in the latter part of the twentieth century. However, while accepting the political and civil rights protective of human freedom, Catholicism, in keeping with its emphasis on the social nature of human beings, also recognized social and economic rights such as the right to food, clothing, shelter, education, and healthcare.

Second, the acceptance of religious liberty implied the full Catholic acceptance of democracy. This development followed the growing emphasis on the dignity, equality, and participation of the human person in the life of society. For most of the twentieth century, Catholic scholars often referred to the indifference of the church with regard to the form of government provided that it was just. Pope Pius XII in 1944 gingerly recognized that a democratic form of government appears to many as a postulate of human reason. The document on religious freedom of Vatican II accepted the principle of the free society. Subsequent Church documents continued the strong support for democracy.

Entry of Conservative Protestants

The major change that occurred in Protestant life and even in the broader American public in the 1970s was the involvement of conservative Protestants in public and political life.[7] Conservative churches such as the Southern Baptists, fundamentalists, evangelicals (there is an important distinction between fundamentalists and evangelicals, because evangelicals do not stress the role of Scripture as infallible and the literal inerrancy of the Bible), and charismatic conservatives had emphasized the personal moral life and were not all that concerned about the role of the church in social and political life. But all that changed in the 1970s.

Beginning in the middle seventies Jerry Falwell, a Baptist minister and a Christian fundamentalist, abandoned the Baptist belief of the separation of church and state and began working for conservative Christians to have a greater influence on American public life. Thus, the Christian right started. In 1970 with the help of others, he founded the Moral Majority, heavily

---

7. For an overview of the development of the Protestant religious right, see Hunter, *Culture Wars: The Struggle to Define America.*

grounded in conservative Protestant positions emphasizing the political importance of the following issues—the traditional vision of the family, opposition to the anti-family media and the equal rights amendment, opposition to abortion and homosexual relations, and support for prayer in the public schools. This organization petered out in the late 1980s but its influence continued to be felt. Pat Robertson, a Protestant evangelical, founded the Christian Coalition in the 1980s. This group, which had a national following, issued voter guides to support particular political candidates. The group lasted into the twenty-first century. Together these two groups and others illustrated the strength of the Christian right in trying to change American public and political life.

The influence of the Christian right also had an impact on some members of the mainline Protestant churches who shared their views. There was also dialogue and even cooperation with the Roman Catholic Church, especially among Catholic bishops and others who strongly supported the traditional family and opposed both abortion and homosexuality. However, not all Protestant evangelicals supported the Christian right as exemplified by the journal called *Sojourners*. The Christian right primarily employed an activist approach and did not pay that much attention to theory. At most, the supporters of the Christian right appealed to the Bible for backing for their political positions. Consequently, there were few Christian ethicists who developed the theory of the Christian right but this movement strongly influenced American public life for decades.

Liberal Protestant Social Ethics after Niebuhr

The liberal tradition in Protestant social ethics continued after Niebuhr but in a different form. No longer would one person such as Niebuhr dominate the field. No Christian social ethicist has since been well recognized in American public life with regard to political and international relations. In addition, the United States after Niebuhr was no longer primarily a WASP society that was open to take seriously Protestant Christian ethics. Another reason was that after Niebuhr the number of Protestant ethicists (and Catholic social ethicists) grew very rapidly. Rauschenbusch and Niebuhr had taught in Protestant seminaries; but, as mentioned earlier, in the 1970s and later the primary home of Christian ethics shifted to the college and university. Consequently, there became many more trained Protestant ethicists than there ever were in the time of Niebuhr.

The liberal tradition continued after Niebuhr, but in a quite different form with many more scholars involved.

As a result, this short chapter will not attempt to do more than point out the most significant development in liberal Christian social ethics in the four or five last decades—forms of liberation theology. Here, too, with occasional different emphases the ecumenical working together of Protestant and Catholic social ethicists is present. Liberation theology in the strict sense had its origin among Catholic theologians in Latin America beginning with the work of Gustavo Gutiérrez but quickly also included Protestant thinkers.[8] Black liberation theology came to the fore among black Protestant theologians in the United States spearheaded by the work of James Cone.[9] Both Protestant and Catholic scholars contributed to the growth of feminist liberation theology and other liberation theologies.

Three methodological approaches form the basis for liberation theology. First, the biblical aspect underscores the special place for the poor and oppressed in the Judeo-Christian tradition. God has a special concern for the poor and oppressed. Liberation theologians often speak of God's preferential option for the poor and oppressed. Yes, God loves all the creatures that God has made, but God has a special concern for the poor. The Bible constantly reminds readers of this preferential option for the poor. In a true sense God has a prejudice in favor of the poor. Prejudice in our usual usage is a pejorative term, but in its original meaning, it is simply a prejudgment and in this case a prejudgment in favor of the poor. In a true sense God is not neutral.

The epistemological aspect is a second characteristic of the theory of liberation theology. Epistemology refers to human knowing. In this context, the question arises: who is the best knower? The American academy in general has insisted that the ideal knower is the objective, neutral, value-free person who is swayed only by the evidence. Science has made tremendous strides based on this methodological approach. The best judgments are made by people who strive to be objective in their approach. Think also of the characteristics we demand for people who serve on juries.

Liberationists respond there is no such thing as the objective, neutral, value-free knower. We are all conditioned and affected by particularities and limitations of our own upbringing, experience, and relationships. This explains why historically white people did not see or recognize the oppressive

8. Gutiérrez, *Theology of Liberation: History, Politics, and Salvation.*

9. Cone, *Black Theology and Black Power.*

situation of blacks or men did not recognize the oppressive situations affecting women. Since there is no such thing as an objective, neutral, value-free observer, everyone begins with one's own historically and culturally conditioned way of looking at the world. All must be willing to recognize their own limitations and conditioning. Liberation theologians justify their option for the poor and the oppressed on the basis of the Christian understanding that God is on the side of the poor and oppressed. Such a biblical understanding justifies the prejudgment in favor of the oppressed.

A third aspect of the method of liberation theology concerns the existence of structural sin. The Christian tradition has traditionally seen sin as an action of an individual person. But there exist in our culture and our world sinful structures that influence us even when we are not aware of them. I often remind women of a certain age (my age and even younger) whose professional and work world was limited to the roles of teaching, nursing, or secretarial work. Christians consequently must raise their consciousness to become aware of the sinful structures that continue to affect attitudes and actions. Then after having discovered these sinful structures, Christians are called to change and eliminate them.

There exist different emphases within black liberation theology. This paragraph will briefly summarize the approach of James Cone, who started writing extensively on the subject in 1968 and has continued to the present. His approach tends to be more radical than some others. Cone strongly condemns white Christians who have been responsible for slavery and the oppression and even murder of many black people. A white theology emphasizing God as the father and creator of all has stifled black self-determination. God identifies with the oppressed, and hence God is black. God's blackness is not an anthropological but an ontological understanding based on God's identification with the oppressed.

Feminist liberation theology sees patriarchy as the form of oppression. Patriarchy is the system in which males hold the power resulting in the subordination and oppression of women. There are two steps in Christian feminist methodology. First, the hermeneutic of suspicion calls for recognizing the role of patriarchy in many structures and cultural practices in our society. Take for example the marriage rite in which the father hands his daughter off to another male (her husband) who will take care of her. The second step in the method is the more difficult hermeneutic of recovery or retrieval. Most but not all Christian feminists want to shape a world in which all human beings and all God's creation will be properly protected and supported. Christian feminists have also strongly pointed out the patriarchy in the church. Some have gone so far as to declare themselves post-Christian feminists, because they conclude the Christian church is a thoroughly patriarchal society that cannot be changed.

Some black women scholars pointed out that the experience of white, middle class feminists was not their experience of oppression. They often experience oppression at the hands of black males. In the context of their twofold oppression, they developed what they called a womanist theology. In a further development, Hispanic women, mostly Catholic, have experienced a different kind of oppression which gave rise to a *mujerista* theology.

Recent Catholic Social Teaching

In the world of Catholic social ethics after Vatican II, the popes continued the tradition of Catholic social teaching. With regard to method, these newer documents followed the Vatican II approach of recognizing the important role of Scripture and of more theological considerations in addition to a modified natural law approach. Catholic social ethicists employed a more sophisticated and critical hermeneutic to these documents after Vatican II.

The US Catholic bishops in their two letters on peace and the economy in the 1980s followed the more liberal interpretation of Catholic social teaching with a more critical perspective on US domestic and foreign policy. A smaller but influential group of Catholic neoconservatives interpreted the papal documents as less critical of US policies. In addition as noted above, bishops and neoconservative ethicists joined forces with conservative evangelical Protestants in working for laws defending traditional family values and strongly opposing abortion and homosexuality. Somewhat independently of Catholic social teaching, Catholic social ethicists developed broader and deeper approaches to the discipline. Thus, Catholic social teaching became only a part of the broader Catholic social ethics approach which also showed the effects of the ecumenical dialogue.

With regard to content, Pope Paul VI (1967), recognizing that the social question was now worldwide, underscored the needs of the developing world, and stressed the destiny of the goods of creation to serve the needs of all while emphasizing human aspirations to equality and participation in political and economic life. In the first of his three encyclicals, Pope John Paul II emphasized the priority of labor over capital and incorporated to some extent the liberation themes of structural sin and preferential option for the poor. His 1987 encyclical criticized the opposing blocks of liberal capitalism in the west and Marxist collectivism in the east. After the fall of communism, his final social encyclical accepts the market economy but only within a strong juridical framework to protect the rights of all, especially the poor and the needy. Pope Benedict XVI in 2009 continued the tradition by opposing both a simplistic free market model and an interventionist big government solution. Pope Francis's encyclical *Laudato si'* in 2015 insisted on the need to protect our common ecological home while criticizing irresponsible development, global warming, and environmental degradation.

Conclusion

The second part of this essay has pointed out in a schematic, historical way the nature of the role and the different theoretical and methodological approaches of Christian social ethics as well as the disagreements among Christian social ethicists on the concrete issues facing society. This discussion focused on the differences between liberal and conservative approaches. In addition, there is a much smaller, more radical position related in Protestant circles to the Anabaptist tradition that is also exemplified in the Catholic Worker movement. The differences within the ambit of Christian social ethics are quite large but still they exist within the broader parameter of the Christian tradition and some general shared values common to that tradition.

The first part of this essay emphasized the academic nature of the discipline of Christian ethics. The role of Christian social ethics in contributing to the life of the broader human society in the second part of the essay also supports the presence of Christian ethics in the university. A discipline that greatly affects what occurs in this world should logically be found in the college and the university. In addition, the understanding of Christian ethics as described here shows why it is a true academic discipline.

4

STEM as a Calling

RICHARD O. MASON

Ethical responsibility . . . involves more than leading a decent, honest, truthful life, as important as such lives certainly remain. And it involves something much more than making wise choices when such choices suddenly, unexpectedly present themselves. Our moral obligations must . . . include a willingness to engage others in the difficult work of defining what the crucial choices are that confront technological society and how intelligently to confront them.

—LANGDON WINNER

IN MARY SHELLEY'S CAUTIONARY tale, the scientist Victor Frankenstein is obsessed with gaining scientific knowledge. Blinded by ambition, he isolates himself from his wife, family, and community—that is, from any sort of moral context and ethical questions about his work. He wants to shape mankind's future, and he conceives of and makes a creature, a unique living thing. But when Victor brings his creature to life, it turns out to be a "monster." Victor realizes his attempt is a disaster and rejects the creature, but it's too late: the monster has been unleashed on the world. Critically, the creature lacks any concept of morality or sense of responsibility. Although the monster is not initially violent by nature, Victor has failed to nourish or care for it, and it lashes out at others whenever it senses it is being rejected. The monster eventually destroys Victor's life by preying on those around him.

While the scientist's actions in Shelley's nightmarish story are extreme, at the very least, twenty-first-century scientists are likely to work on projects that are potentially fraught with ethical issues. If society fails to help them understand the importance of doing science within a moral context, then it fails them just as Victor Frankenstein failed first himself, his family and friends, and then even society.

Today more students than ever are preparing for careers, directly or indirectly, in fields that are, for the most part, subsumed under the acronym STEM. These roles in science, technology, engineering and mathematics are of many stripes, but for discussion purposes, let's collectively refer to them as STEMists. STEM, in its most comprehensive sense, is not housed or taught in any single organizational unit. Rather, it permeates many different curriculums and institutions. A recent *U.S. News & World Report* study found, "40 percent of bachelor's degrees earned by men and 29 percent earned by women are now in STEM fields. At the doctoral level, more than half of the degrees earned by men (58 percent) and one-third earned by women (33 percent) are in STEM fields."[1]

Underlying these trends—and perhaps a major causal factor—is the fact that we live and work today in a society that increasingly depends on scientific and technological knowledge. This is a major reason why in business, government, research and, importantly, entrepreneurship more and more jobs and careers rely on STEM knowledge. In large measure, how we live today—and certainly how we will live in the future—stems from STEM and its progeny.

More than a Job: STEM Is a Calling

Martin Luther's idea of a calling, or the need for "moral justification in worldly activity" is generally considered to be one of the most important social contributions of the Reformation. In *The Protestant Ethic and the Spirit of Capitalism*, the great German sociologist and philosopher "Max" Weber draws on this notion of a calling.[2] Weber, following Luther, proposes that the highest form of moral activity in which an individual can engage is to fulfill one's duty when participating in worldly affairs.

In an early Occasional Paper for the Cary M. Maguire Center for Ethics and Public Responsibility at SMU, theology professor Joseph L. Allen explored the conditions of "Politics as a Calling."

---

1. Bidwell, "More Students Earning STEM Degrees," para. 4.
2. Weber, *Protestant Ethic*.

Theologically, to have a calling involves both an outer and an inner dimension. Outwardly a calling is a certain kind of station or office in life. As Luther saw it, in order for any role or work to be a calling, it must be one that can be helpful to others if it is followed. Through it God calls one to serve the need and benefit of the neighbor, which is our duty in all life's relationships. Moreover, a calling is an office whose presence serves the common good, the well-being of the whole community, and not only the individuals within it. This outer sense of a calling has a certain objectivity, in that whether an office can serve the good of others depends on how it is related to people's needs, and not only on what any particular individual thinks about it.

Internally, whether an office is a calling depends upon the motivation with which one pursues it. Inwardly, then, one has a calling when she understands God has called her to this position, this work, specifically as a way of serving the need of the neighbor. If I hold a position that can outwardly speaking be a calling, yet do not subjectively understand it as a calling, then I shall not pursue it as such. For me it is simply a job.[3]

STEM work can be just a "job," simply a means of making a living or occupying one's time. Or, it can be a calling. The key difference is that in answering to a calling an individual must fulfill the obligations of his or her position in the greater world in a way that is acceptable by a higher moral power. Fulfilling one's calling is a major challenge.

A STEMist's Calling Requires Some Kind of Internal Court

The initial work of a STEMist, as moral agent, typically falls into the realm of individual ethics. Virtue, duty, and consequential theories of ethics such as those taught in basic ethics courses apply. Ethicist Joseph Herkert refers to this level of ethics as *microethics*.[4]

While this chapter doesn't attempt to explain the theories taught in basic ethics courses, the German philosopher Immanuel Kant provides a helpful way to think about the morality of individual actions: Kant compared one's conscience to an "internal court," in which reason holds "the

3. Allen, "Politics as a Calling," 1.
4. Herkert, "Microethics, Macroethics, and Professional Engineering Societies."

human being's duty before him . . . for his acquittal or condemnation in every case that comes under a [moral] law."[5]

This theory has useful practical implications. The metaphor of an "inner court" suggests that STEMists should periodically conduct a court in their minds, playing the roles of accuser, excuser, and judge: In what ways might what I am doing lead to untoward results? Harm the common good? In what ways might what I am doing lead to beneficial results? Promote the common good? On balance, what actions should I take to reduce harm and secure benefits?

STEMists can also use the inner court of their minds as a place to ask themselves a crucial question: Am I acting with appropriate humility? Because STEMists often provide society with valued—and valuable—knowledge and technical expertise, that expertise, in turn, becomes the source of extreme pride, even arrogance, that often culminates into a vice Aristotle called *hubris*. In *The Hubris Syndrome*, former UK Foreign Secretary David Owen describes hubris as the intoxication of power.[6] Acting out of hubris almost always leads to miscalculation and overconfidence and, in turn, it invariably leads to some form of sorrow. Investigative reporter Meredith Whitney estimates that "Hubris is the cause of management mistakes 90 percent of the time."[7] Thus, overconfident, STEMists tend to misjudge their capabilities, sometimes to the extent that, in the extreme, they lose contact with reality. They forget that humility is the antidote for hubris. This oversight inevitably leads to some form of a downfall.

Causal Chains and Organizational Ethics

Some STEMists, like reclusive monks, view themselves as independent, autonomous actors in the world whose only responsibility is to themselves and to their science. On the other hand, those who view their efforts as a calling recognize that they take actions that can shape a community's life and, accordingly, acknowledge that they have a moral duty to act for the common good. That is, such a person is a *moral agent*.

Although some STEMists practice on their own—fitting the myth of the lonely scientist in a dimly lit garret—most become members of an organization—a firm, a university, a research institute, a government agency,

5. Kant, *Metaphysics of Morals*, 160.

6. Owen, *Hubris Syndrome*.

7. Kolhatkar, "In Meredith Whitney We Trust?"

and the like. In 1937 the British economist Ronald Coase wrote an influential essay entitled *The Nature of the Firm* in which he explained why society at that time—largely in response to changes in social organization due to the industrial revolution—began to be comprised of a number of organizations instead of consisting almost exclusively of a multitude of independent, self-employed people who contracted with one another.[8] Coase focused on business, but the same analysis applies to scientific endeavors. An organization is formed when individuals from different backgrounds and varied interests come together on a common platform, specify a set of goals and objectives, and then work collectively towards accomplishing those goals and objectives. In the process, the individuals who become members of the organization must relinquish some of their personal interests in favor of that organization's values. The core challenge of organizational ethics is for its members to accede to its values as the organization responds to internal and external stimuli. *Organizational ethics* deals with three key requirements: choices made about what communal laws and moral guidelines should be prescribed and whether and when to follow them; choices made about coping with economic and social issues outside those required by law; and choices made about the conflict between a member's self interest and those of the organization. A common ethical issue a STEMist faces as a member of an organization is to bring into synch the personal motivation to use one's talents and knowledge for one's own creative purposes with the demands place on him by the organization.[9]

Beyond the organizational level is the *systemic* level. Major innovations are not the product of one genius' efforts alone. They are the product of the work and ideas of a string of geniuses, organizers, thought leaders, and many hardworking yeomen, all of whose efforts culminated in the new outcome. Along this line, the polymath anthropologist Margaret Mead argued that major innovations of social and technological magnitude are not just the result of a single person's genius, as important as genius may be. Rather, full-blown innovations emerge from "a cluster of interacting individuals who within the special conditions provided by period and culture make choices which set a direction—a channel—in which events tend to

---

8. Coase, "Nature of the Firm," 386–405.

9. Organizational ethics is well treated in books of business ethics. For two among many see, Velasquez, *Business Ethics: Concepts and Cases*, and De George, *Business Ethics*. For a useful book related to the topic of this essay, see also Allinson, *Global Disasters*.

flow until other points of divergence are reached."[10] Such actions set into motion a *causal chain,* in which one result leads to another and another and another, until they reach some external limit. As a given chain unfolds, one result leads to another and so on, as actions cascade until they reach some limit. Within the context of this network of complexity, a moral agent is morally responsible and accountable for his or her actions and, importantly, the consequences they bring about as they are propagated along the causal chain. Business ethicist Richard De George explains:

> *Causal responsibility* is an ingredient in both moral and legal responsibility. The causal chain sometimes is a long one. If I give a command and a number of people transmit that command until it is finally carried out, both the ones who carry out the action and I (the one issuing the command) are responsible for it, though each is responsible in a different way in the causal chain. Usually, we are most concerned with the proximate cause in the chain, with the person doing the action in question. Yet, especially in questions of agency, the originator of the chain [and all of the interceding contributors] also bears responsibility for the action [however distant their efforts might be].[11]

The scientist, the engineer, the technologist, the entrepreneur and other STEMists all take actions that release or contribute to such causal chains. Thus, they bear some moral responsibility for the final global outcomes.

Initiating a causal chain creates a *cone of causation* that culminates in some final outcome. One implication of this process is that the final outcome is the product of "many hands." Theoretical physicist Robert Oppenheimer led the effort to create the atomic bomb but about 130,000 people, laborers as well as scientists and engineers, worked on it during the nearly six years it took to complete the Manhattan Project. All 130,000 participants bear some moral responsibility.

Ethicist Dennis F. Thompson, has questioned the prevailing tendency in political contexts to assign moral responsibility to just one individual. The selected party is often someone who, for some reason, stood out in the context, as Oppenheimer did in creating the atomic bomb. Often overlooked are the crucial members who work at other levels of the organization. He goes on to observe,

---

10. Mead, *Continuities in Cultural Evolution*, 249.

11. De George, *Business Ethics*, 111.

Because many different officials contribute in many ways to decisions and policies of government, it is difficult even in principle to
identify who is morally responsible for political outcomes. This is
what I call the problem of many hands.

. . . The criteria for personal responsibility I adopt are common to a wide range of moral theories: *they hold us responsible for
outcomes insofar as we cause them [that is, participate in the causal
chain] and do not act in ignorance or under compulsion.*[12]

The two conditions Thompson cites to exempt one from moral responsibility—compulsion and ignorance—require further refinement.
The compulsion must be so forceful that an average person occupying
that role could not resist it. That is, one should not give in too easily.
The ignorance should be "invincible" in the sense that a person in that
situation had no reasonable way available to him to obtain the relevant
knowledge and understanding. Otherwise, the ignorance is "culpable."
Culpable ignorance refers to the lack of knowledge or understanding that
results from the omission of ordinary care to acquire such knowledge or
understanding.[13] That is, a person did not know, but a typical person in
that role should have known.

Moral Malleability and the Uncertain
Consequences of Science

A fundamental property of STEM and the processes and products it facilitates is that they are *morally malleable*. STEM knowhow can be applied in
ways that are good or in evil, right or wrong, or just or unjust outcomes
depending on one's moral perspective. Frequently, the outcome is morally
dappled. Whatever the moral implications, every participating STEMist
bears some moral responsibility for the outcome.

The Pulitzer Prize-winning journalist Thomas Friedman makes
a crucial point that the ultimate outcomes of revolutions in scientific
knowledge are uncertain. Unanticipated and unwanted events are likely
to occur, generating major ethical issues today and creating even more
in the future. Friedman examines two planetary forces that may affect
scientific outcomes: Market Forces, as they have contributed to globaliza-
tion, and Mother Nature, which has been negatively impacted by climate

12. Thompson, "Moral Responsibility of Public Officials," 905–16.

13. For a discussion of culpable ignorance, see Smith, "Culpable Ignorance," 543–71.

change and biodiversity loss. In his view, there will be winners and losers resulting from a conflict among these forces. On the one hand, society will realize an immense bounty in the form of dazzling personal technology (think iPhone and Instagram), advanced commercial and governmental infrastructure, and near-boundless access to the cultural items that enrich our lives. Amid this bounty, however, is the specter of wrenching change. Professions and occupations of all kinds from doctors, to lawyers, to truck drivers will be forever upended. Companies will be forced to transform or die. Recent economic indicators reflect this shift: fewer people are working, and wages are falling even as productivity and profits soar. Perhaps most wrenching, however, are the unknown and unintended consequences that derive from turning these new scientific ideas and technology loose. Each of the individual STEMists who participated in producing the new technology bears some of the moral responsibility.

Thompson describes an ex-post analysis that is conducted by decomposing the causal chain back down to its individual roots. Under this scenario, we assume the deed is already done, and the central question is: "Who is to Blame?" In contrast, in this chapter I am proposing that STEMists must also perform an ex-anti moral analysis. They should hold an "inner court" debating the moral implications of their actions, and make an attempt to *anticipate* what ultimate dangers or harms their work might help to cause, and then make an effort to attenuate, if not eliminate, them. This is an essential requirement to make STEM a calling.

Acclaimed software engineer David Parnas serves as an exemplar for moral anticipation and action. On March 23, 1983, President Reagan announced the Strategic Defense Initiative (SDI), popularly known as "Star Wars." The purpose was to protect the US from ballistic missile attacks. The project was to be implemented by means of new, and untested, developments in sensors and networks that would feed observational data into a newly envisioned supercomputer. Parnas was appointed to the SDI's prestigious managing organization and research advisory board. About three months into the project, Parnas resigned, giving as his reason, "SDI cannot meet its goals." Given the current state, he claimed, it was impossible to write reliable software for a project of this scope, complexity and vulnerability. It could not be trusted to prevent a nuclear attack. Hence, he maintained it would be unethical for him to continue to work on it.[14]

---

14. Parnas, "Software Aspects," 1326–35.

This need to evaluate actions as they affect the common good requires an ethics at the systemic level. Brown University Ethicist John Ladd observed that issues at this level were best described as "macroethics."[15] An inquiry into macroethics begins at the highest level: What is good or evil, just or unjust for our universe and planet? From there it incorporates concerns for society at large and humankind as a whole.

Look before You Leap: The Precautionary Principle

Parnas's ethical response is a good illustration of the "Precautionary Principle." By one account, PP was originally proposed in 1982 as part of the World Charter for Nature that was adopted by the United Nations General Assembly. The basic idea, however, has a long history. Hippocrates, who lived in the fourth century BC, advised, "As to disease, make a habit of two things—to help, or at least *do no harm*." There are also sayings in the common lore such as "Look before you leap," "Better safe than sorry," or "Be careful." Concerned about the possible dangers of genetic modification (GMOs), Nassim Taleb, a philosopher of probability, and his associates defined the principle as follows: "The Precautionary Principle states that if an action or policy has a suspected risk of causing severe harm to the public domain (affecting general health or the environment globally), the action should not be taken in the absence of scientific near-certainty about its safety."[16]

Using the Precautionary Principle is especially important to STEM fields, largely due to the possibility that mishaps will occur, occasioned by limitations of the existing state of knowledge, the likelihood of error, the horse type blinders induced by focusing on a narrow set of values and interests, and the vast complexity of the target environment.

One important precautionary approach to scientific inquiry and technological development is to take a *pause for reflection*. That is, "Relax. Take a deep breath. Think it through. Access your inner court. Ask yourself, 'What can go wrong?'" When risk and uncertainty are high and the stakes are large, it is probably a good time to stop working for a while, to take stock of the situation and to make an effort to gain a broader ethical perspective on it.

---

15. Ladd, "Quest for a Code," 154–59.
16. Taleb et al., "Precautionary Principle," 1.

Contemporary Knowledge Revolutions

Speaking at Hiroshima, Japan, on May 27, 2016, US President Barack Obama focused on one major challenge when he observed: "The scientific revolution that led to the splitting of an atom requires a moral revolution as well." He might well have added that so, too, do the revolutions brought about by computer science, nanotechnology, and genetics. About the middle of the twentieth century, these four powerful scientific innovations took hold and are now materially changing our understanding of the world in which we live, while at the same time, posing fundamental questions about human nature itself. Who are we? What is our role as human beings in the universe? Will the human species survive? To better understand both the causes and effects and threats of these innovations, it helps to start by viewing them through the lens of Goethe's poem, "The Sorcerer's Apprentice."

At the beginning of the poem, an old wizard is called away from his workshop, leaving his apprentice with the chore of mopping clean the shop's spacious floor. As he swabs away, the apprentice soon grows tired of fetching water pail by pail. So he casts a spell on his mop instructing it to do the work for him. Unfortunately, the apprentice is not yet fully trained in the magic nor in its appropriate application. The broom takes on a life of its own, pumping out more and more water, and before long the floor is flooded. The neophyte apprentice concocts a plan and splits the broom in two with an axe, but each of these just-formed pieces transforms itself into a whole new broom and these new brooms each take up another pail and continue to fetch and spill water, only now at twice the speed. Almost immediately the two new pieces divide again making four, and then eight, and so on exponentially. Fortunately, just as it seems that all is lost, the old sorcerer returns and, because he knows the relevant magic, he quickly is able to break the spell and bring things back into control.

The poem helps illustrate the cumulative effects of major scientific revolutions—atomic energy and weapons, artificial intelligence, nanotechnology, and genetics. As Friedman observes, the effects of these revolutions are pushing us into a new era he calls the "Age of Accelerations."[17] This age reflects what he refers to as the "tectonic movements" that are reshaping our world today. An important feature of these innovations is the uncertainties and risks they evoke. Vitally, each possesses a dangerous *amplifying factor*. Like the apprentice's broom, they can self-replicate by

17. Friedman, *Thank You for Being Late.*

initiating chain reactions. And, once the process has begun we don't know much about how to stop it. So far, this modern day Goethe phenomenon has no masterful sorcerer to control it.

Moreover, as observed above, these innovations—like all innovations—are morally malleable. Their dual-use characteristic means that they can be, and have been, used for both good and bad and even, in the extreme, evil. Importantly, the ethical concerns raised by these innovations are very much with us today. If anything, they are growing more difficult to deal with as every day passes.

Information and Communication Technology (ICT) and Artificial Intelligence (AI)

The modern complement to an atom is the *bit*, the basic unit of information used in computing and digital communications—the fundament of ICT. Because bits have only one of two values, usually zero or one, they can be implemented physically by means of a two-state device. In *Being Digital* Nicholas Negroponte, then head of the MIT Media Lab, wrote that the evolving relationship between atoms and bits was becoming increasingly important.[18] Atoms, he observed, make up physical stuff, whereas bits are more ethereal. Importantly, these bits are becoming more central to our everyday way of life. Presciently, Negroponte pointed out that while atoms were the basis of the old economy of manufacturing, railroads and trucks, and "bricks and mortar" stores, bits have become the driving force behind a new, digitized economy and society—institutions that today include things such as social networks, mobile apps, virtual reality, cloud computing, 3D printing and of increasing significance, artificial intelligence (AI) and the Internet of Things (IoT).

When Friedman writes about these scientific revolutions, he is influenced by MIT professors Erik Brynjolfsson and Andrew McAfee's 2014 treatise[19] in which the authors explore how digital technology is transforming our work and our lives. The push for ICT and AI is all about replacing human labor and, increasingly, human cognition with software-driven machines.

Brynjolfsson and McAfee argue that Moore's law and its correlates are the socio-technical driving force. The "law" derives from the observation

18. Negroponte, *Being Digital.*
19. Brynjolfsson and McAfee, "Second Machine."

66

made by Intel cofounder Gordon Moore in 1965 that the number of transistors per square inch on integrated circuits had doubled every year since their invention. Moore's law predicts that this trend for exponential growth in computing power will continue into the foreseeable future. As of this writing, the law is still at work.[20] Computing power along with memory and digital storage capacity has in fact been doubling about every two years. This new power greatly expands the world's capacity to automate and to perfect previously human tasks.

As ethical controversies go, ICT and AI have not fared much better than atomic energy. Philosopher Nick Bostrom believes that although machines are currently far inferior to humans in general intelligence, society is well on its way to "superintelligence," defined as "any intellect that greatly exceeds the cognitive performance of humans in virtually all domains of interest."[21] Many thought leaders believe that superintelligence will beget "the Singularity," "a future period during which the pace of technological change will be so rapid, its impact so deep, that human life will be irreversibly transformed." "The key idea underlying the impending Singularity," according to inventor-futurist Ray Kurzweil, "is that the pace of change of our human-created technology is accelerating and its powers are expanding at an exponential pace."[22]

Concerned about the social and moral implications of an impending Singularity, billionaire entrepreneur and Tesla CEO Elon Musk warned at an MIT symposium in April 2015 that, in his view, AI and machine learning[23] are "our biggest existential threat."[24] He argued that AI constitutes a "Faustian Bargain," a kind of agreement in which humans abandon their own spiritual values or moral principles in order to satisfy what is perceived to be their

20. It would appear that based on traditional scaling approaches when a relation of one atom per memory cell is reached Moore's law will end. But, researchers are exploring micro-architectural restricting and other methods to extend its application life much further.

21. Bostrom, *Superintelligence*, 22.

22. Kurzweil, *Singularity Is Near*.

23. In 1959 IBM's Arthur Samuel defined machine learning as science that gives "computers the ability to learn without being explicitly programmed." Its basic premise is to develop algorithms that can receive input data and apply statistical analysis to predict an output value within an acceptable range. That range usually referring to the limits of human capacity.

24. Musk repeated his concern at the National Governors Association meeting in July 2017, stating that AI "is the biggest risk that we face as a civilization."

limitless desire for knowledge, power, wealth, and perfection.[25] AI, Musk claimed, is "potentially more dangerous than nukes." A cadre of other scientists and technology leaders, including theoretical physicist Stephen Hawking and Microsoft cofounder Bill Gates, echoed Musk's concern.

The considerable progress that has been made in endowing technology with human-like cognition is what underlies the "existential threat" Musk fears. "We may hope that machines will eventually compete with men in all purely intellectual fields," Alan Turing declared in 1950.[26] In the fall of 1955, scientists started to develop what is now considered the first machine to compete with human cognition: an artificial intelligence program called the Logic Theorist. That AI program eventually proved 38 of the first 52 theorems in chapter 2 of Russell and Whitehead's landmark work in formal logic *Principia Mathematica*. Turing's insights also inspired John McCarthy and others to host the Dartmouth Summer Research Project on Artificial Intelligence in 1956. About 20 researchers participated, each of whom would eventually launch the field of AI. Early efforts involved teaching machines how to play games like checkers and chess as well as proving mathematical theorems. One harbinger of things to come was Geoffrey Clarkson's "A Model of the Trust Investment Process" derived from his PhD work at Carnegie-Mellon University in 1961 and drawing on concepts developed by Newell and Simon. Using the hardware and software of the day, Clarkson was able to successfully simulate the "procedures used in choosing investment policies for particular accounts, in evaluating the alternatives presented by the market, and in selecting the required portfolios" that a trust investment officer at a medium-sized national bank did. Heretofore, investment decision-making, like proving theorems in logic, had been considered a decidedly human activity. Now, that nominally human task had been supplanted. Beginning in 1965, four scientists developed Dendral, an expert system (or, intelligent assistant) that could help chemists in identifying unknown organic molecules by analyzing mass spectra and drawing on a selected knowledge base of

25. According to German folklore Faust made a contract with the Devil by exchanging his soul for worldly gains. Faustian bargains are by their nature tragic or self-defeating for those who makes them, because what is surrendered is ultimately far more valuable than what is gained in return, whether or not the bargainer appreciates that fact at the time. Goethe popularized the legend by portraying Faust as a dissatisfied intellectual— STEMist?—who yearns for "more than earthly meat and drink" during his lifetime.

26. Turing, "Computing Machinery and Intelligence," 433–60.

chemistry. Dendral performed as well as chemical experts at this task and was eventually used in industry and academia.

In one disconcerting application at Campbell Soup, researchers developed an expert system to capture Aldo Cimino's forty-six years of knowledge about the soup sterilization process. Cimino was the person on call for problems with caldrons around the world and was about to retire. The new program replaced him and he became known as "The man whose brain was drained." Soon, however, the rule-based approach to expert systems, as exemplified by Dendral and most previous systems, hit its application limit, creating a lull in further development and giving rise to what has been called the "AI Winter."

"AI Spring" began in the 1990s as research on machine learning and data-driven approaches replaced rule-based and knowledge base-driven approaches. AI researchers began creating programs for computers that could analyze large amounts of data and draw conclusions—or "learn"—from the results. This was followed by developments in neural network learning applications that have resulted in many remarkable accomplishments. Among the many highlights in applications of machine learning one recently stood out. On May 23, 2017, *The New York Times* reported,

> It isn't looking good for humanity. The world's best player [a nineteen-year-old Chinese national named Ke Jie] of what might be humankind's most complicated board game was defeated on Tuesday by a Google computer program [AlphaGo]. Adding insult to potentially deep existential injury, he was defeated at Go—a game that claims centuries of play by humans—in China, where the game was invented. . . .
>
> "Last year, it was still quite humanlike when it played," Mr. Ke said after the game. "But this year, it became like a god of Go."[27]

One of the arenas in which AI is playing an expanding role is the development of self-driving or autonomous vehicles (AVs). AVs should reduce traffic accidents and reduce the stress of driving, but programming them also requires a resolution to a moral quandary. Will the driver's self-interest or the public good or some other set of values predominate?

Meanwhile, the peoples of the world are getting "hooked up." Digital connectivity has become international. One indicator is that in 2015, the International Telecommunication Union estimated that approximately 3.2

---

27. Mozur, "Google's AlphaGo," paras. 1–2, 5. See also Silver and Hassabis, "AlphaGo: Mastering the Ancient Game."

billion people (about half of the world's population) would have access to the Internet by the start of 2016. This widespread connectivity potentially is enriching the lives of its many users. At the same time, it has also exacerbated the impact of several ethical issues. At risk—especially with social media applications such as Facebook, LinkedIn, Twitter, and Instagram—are treasured life-sustaining values such as safeguarding an individual's privacy, providing fair access to valuable information, protecting intellectual property, and ensuring that the information users receive and rely on to make decisions is valid and accurate. Also, there are nefarious uses. We are learning that the enhanced communication capability the Internet provides has proven to be a useful tool for terrorists and con artists.

One application of the Internet that has expanded recently is the Internet of Things (IoT). IoT involves the interconnection of sensors and computing devices that are embedded in everyday objects—such as cameras, thermostats, baby monitors, DVR players, televisions and refrigerators—that can send and receive data to and from other sources. In many cases, IoT can be used to perform statistical data mining so as to anticipate human behavior. In other applications, IoTs can be remotely controlled. That is, they can start performing tasks without human intervention. At least two ethical quandaries have been posed about these possibilities:

- Right to privacy: Is it possible to avoid the IoT? As we move around in our daily lives, should we now assume that our lives or our behavior are being monitored at all times?

- Social contract: Does the IoT constitute the ultimate utilitarian approach to society? Are we monitoring the lives, or specific aspects of lives, of everyone in order to reduce the risk to each of us?[28] Or, are we making things worst?

The IoT is vulnerable. On October 21, 2016, a malicious perpetrator unleashed a Mirai botnet[29] consisting of 100,000 infected devices and launched a distributed denial of service (DDoS) attack against Dyn, Inc., a subsidiary of Oracle that offers domain registration services, email, and products to monitor, control, and optimize online infrastructure. As a result, Dyn's systems were unable to connect customers' domain names to their web addresses, effectively curtailing all service. In all, about seventy

28. Covert and Orebaugh, "Ethical Challenges of the Internet of Things."

29. A network of private computers infected with malicious software and controlled as a group without the owners' knowledge.

websites were affected. They represent a kind of "who's who" of popular services, including Amazon, CNN, Fox News, *The Guardian*, HBO, Netflix, *The New York Times*, PayPal, Reddit, Spotify, Swedish Government, Twitter, Visa, and Wired. Dyn worked quickly to restore service, responding basically within a day. However, the attack demonstrated how attackers can (and likely will) leverage insecure IoT devices to wreak havoc against the Internet as a whole and its users in particular. In an article in *Foreign Policy* entitled "The Internet of Things is a Cyberwar Nightmare," the authors conclude, "The attack exposed the clear reasons for concern about the coming age of an Internet of Things, in which ever more household devices are connected to the web. What's less immediately clear [and should be of concern for STEMists] is what should be done to ensure the Internet's most likely future iteration remains safe."[30]

One outcome of digitization and networking is a substantial restructuring of the global economy. On May 6, 2017, *The Economist* featured a story entitled "The world's most valuable resource is no longer oil, but data." Eliciting shades of the old "robber barons" of the late nineteenth-century industrial era, the editors argued that the new data economy demands a new approach to antitrust rules. Five companies now control the majority of the economic power: Amazon, Apple, Facebook, Microsoft, and Alphabet (Google's parent company). Effectively they form an oligopoly, resulting in a market structure in which a small number of firms control a majority of the market for goods and services. The threat is that these companies, if they are unregulated and allowed to run free, will attain excessive market power. They may engage in price fixing, control the availability of supply, make exclusive deals, require customers to buy a packaged or "bundled" set of products instead of item by item, or set and enforce a standard price across all markets. In the process, at least three important values associated with perfect (or effective) competition would be compromised: capitalist justice—benefits distributed according to the value of an organizations contribution; economic efficiency, and respect for negative rights—respecting a duty not to interfere in certain activities of individuals who hold those rights. A contemporary example is the right to privacy and individuality. A recent article in the *Washington Post* reports on new efforts to "dig even deeper into our lives":

30. Stravridis and Weinstein, "Internet of Things."

> Google kicked off its annual developers conference Wednesday by outlining a broad vision of how it thinks artificial intelligence will shape the way we communicate, travel, work and play.
>
> Chief executive Sundar Pichai said that improving artificial intelligence is Google's top strategy in its continuing goal to organize the world's information.
>
> Using AI, Gmail will now suggest phrases for your replies, based on its interpretation of your conversation. Google Photos will figure out which of your snapshots are best for sharing, and it will use facial recognition to figure out who should get those photos. A program called Google Lens will analyze your photos and be able to remove obstacles, such as a chain-link fence, that obscure your shot. Google Assistant will also be more proactive, now nudging you to leave earlier if the traffic to your next appointment is bad, rather than waiting for you to ask about it.[31]

Patrick Moorhead, the principle analyst at Moor Insight and Strategies, sounded a minor alarm: "Many of these new features in Google Assistant, Photos, and Home add value but also require a lot of personal voice, photo, video and location information. Google has the most personal information [and] does the processing in the cloud, so I think right now they have the richest consumer AI capabilities."[32] Can we entrust Google with this power?

Nanotechnology

Nanotechnology is the branch of technology that involves the manipulation of individual atoms and molecules at the tiny nanoscale of a nanometer, or one billionth of a meter. Nanotechnology promises to be a highly disruptive technology, yielding many remarkable benefits while at the same time exposing society to enormous, even existential, dangers.

Gene-Editing, Gene-Therapy and Epigenetics

In 1953, James D. Watson and Francis H. Crick discovered the double helix structure of DNA, elevating the field of genetics and the human genome into the scientific and popular forefront. About five years later, Crick

---

31. Tsukayama, "Google's Focus on AI," paras. 1–3.
32. Tsukayama, "Google's Focus on AI," para. 6.

formulated what he called the "Central Dogma of molecular biology." His theory proposed that genes encode chemical messages that build proteins which proteins ultimately result in an organism's form and function.[33] They energize the body and give it life. Crick's dogma also suggests that "DNA is destiny." Once an organism inherits its DNA and genes, according to Mendelian and Darwinian mechanisms, it is pretty much stuck with them for life—an assumption that was soon to be challenged. The completion of the Human Genome Project in April 2003 provided another powerful tool for understanding human genetics. The project sequenced some 3.2 base pairs of nucleotides[34] that are allocated to about 20,000 genes and distributed to 23 pairs of chromosomes and located in about 37.2 trillion cells within the human body. It also perfected technologies for sequencing genomes.

Researchers never really accepted Crick's supposed proposition that the human genome was immutable. Given the results of explorations begun during the 1950s, they became emboldened to try to find ways to change genes so that organisms, especially humans, were not forever the prisoners of their genetic inheritance. Among the new techniques that were uncovered and developed are gene therapy, gene editing, and epigenetics.

Gene therapy involves introducing selected DNA into a patient in order to treat a specific genetic disorder or disease. Typically, DNA is extracted from a source that has a normally functioning gene. The new healthy DNA is then introduced into a mutated or abnormally functioning gene in order to correct the effects that are causing the disorder. On September 14, 1990, in Bethesda, Maryland, a four-year-old girl became the first human being to be treated in an approved gene therapy trial. She had suffered from a rare and severe immune deficiency disease called adenosine deaminase (ADA) deficiency. ADA is a genetic disease that leaves its victims defenseless against infections. The girl's genome lacked a gene that regulates the production of an enzyme needed by the human body to keep its immune cells alive. During the procedure, a sample of her white blood cells were removed, and some normal genes for making ADA were inserted into these cells. The corrected cells were then injected into her body. The procedure worked as hoped, and the girl's health improved significantly. She maintained a normal white blood cell count as well as measurable levels of the ADA enzyme; both had been almost nonexistent prior to the treatment.[35]

33. Technically, "DNA is transcribed into RNA is translated into Proteins."
34. The base pairs in DNA are adenine-thymine and guanine-cytosine. A, T, G, C.
35. Kuo and Kohn, "Gene Therapy."

This and subsequence successes encouraged researchers to attempt gene therapy for other diseases such as cystic fibrosis and sickle-cell anemia. The implication was clear. Human beings who were born with certain genetic disorders were no longer prisoners of their inherited genes.

As the pace of research picked up, the research community became more concerned with the ethical issues the new gene therapy posed. In a book with far reaching implications, bioethicist LeRoy Walters and attorney Julie Gage Palmer developed a moral framework within which to deliberate on the ethics of a proposed genetic intervention.[36]

Type of Cell Targeted

Purpose of Intervention	Somatic	Germ Line
Prevention, treatment, or cure of a disease	1	2
Enhancement of capabilities or characteristics	3	4

From an ethical perspective, all interventions must of course be carefully evaluated on the basis of a risk verses benefit analysis. Although they may involve substantial risk, interventions in category 1, such as that of the girl with ADA, generally carry the lesser ethical burden than those in the other categories. They seek to repair a deficiency formed at birth. Nevertheless, gene therapy suffered a major set back in September 1999 when eighteen-year-old Jesse Gelsinger died during a gene therapy trial intended to treat ornithine transcarbamylase deficiency. OTC is a rare metabolic disorder that prevents the body from getting rid of ammonia, thereby allowing it to build up and enter the blood steam causing harm throughout the body, especially the brain. This was a category 1 trial. Jesse had OTC from birth. During treatment he suffered from symptoms that had never been seen before. An FDA investigation uncovered several instances in which the trial's risks versus its benefits had not been properly assessed. As a result the Gelsinger family sued the hospital and the US government suspended all other gene therapy research that was going on at the University of Pennsylvania. This had a chilling effect on all gene therapy research.

Category 2 interventions raise deeper ethical issues. Being germ line, the new DNA is therefore inheritable and potentially will effect all of the patient's future generations. In addition to raising issues such as informed

36. Walters and Palmer, *Ethics of Human Gene Therapy.*

consent, inequality, access and unintended consequences, changing the human germ line raises knotty questions about transgressing natural or divine laws. Interventions for the purpose of enhancement are even more ethically problematic. A category 3 intervention might, say, involve improving the height, intelligence, athletic ability or eyesight of an individual. But would the result give some unfair advantage to the recipient? It might be the means toward producing a controversial "designer baby."

Interventions in Category 4 raise the specter of eugenics and attempts at creating a "master race," concerns long considered to have deep moral implications. With respect to each of these categories there are several ethical questions that should be addressed:

- To repeat, do the potential benefits of the intervention outweigh the potential risks? Are the parties well informed about the risks and benefits and consent to be exposed to them?

- Do alternatives exist? Is gene therapy really needed? Is it the best available course of action?

- Is the trait that is being targeted normal or does it constitute a disability, disorder or disease? How sever is the abnormality? Who decides?

- Who pays? Will high costs make the intervention available only to the wealthy?

- Will the results of the intervention create new social divides and provide a basis for discrimination?

The controversy over gene therapy is now being augmented by ethical concerns over newly developed techniques of gene-editing. Gene-editing is a method that can be used to precisely and efficiently modify DNA within a cell. The entire August 2016 issue of *National Geographic* was devoted to "The DNA Revolution."[37] The articles in this edition reported on some of the ways in which our newly found scientific ability to economically edit genes enables us to efficiently alter the code of life. In the process, the new gene-editing technology, called CRISPR/Cas9, has given society unprecedented power over important aspects of life and the natural world. "With new gene-editing techniques, we can transform life—but should we?" the editors ask. Among the many ethical issues raised is how CRISPR/Cas9, developed by UC Berkeley Professor of Chemistry and Cell Biology Jennifer Doudna and others, should be used. In *A Crack in*

37. Specter, "DNA Revolution."

Creation: Gene Editing and the Unthinkable Power to Control Evolution,[38] Doudna and Samuel Sternberg describe the tool's functioning: An enzyme called Cas9 is programmed to latch onto any selected twenty-letter sequence of DNA. At that point the enzyme cuts the double helix, splitting the DNA strand in two. The interveners then supply a snippet of the new genetic material they want to insert, making sure its ends match up with the cut strands. At this point, the cell's repair mechanism responds to fix the cut and, in the process, pastes in the new DNA. The organism's genetic makeup has now been changed.

CRISPR/Cas9 is currently the cheapest, simplest, and most effective way of manipulating DNA. Thus, there are few barriers, other than possessing the necessary technical knowledge, to its being used. The tool's proponents believe that it can be applied, among other things, to cure HIV, heal some genetic diseases, and treat some forms of cancer. In addition, it potentially can be used to perfect crops and, thereby, help address the world's hunger crisis. Since it is in its infancy, the full range of the consequences of using CRISPR/Cas 9 in the real world is far from being recognized. It is possible that even the tiniest change in DNA when let loose out of the lab could have a myriad of unanticipated and unintended consequences.

For example, in November 2018, Jian-kui HE, a Chinese scientist, announced that his lab had "created" the first gene-edited babies, designed to be naturally immune to HIV (the human immunodeficiency virus). This claim triggered widespread criticism over the scientific and ethical legitimacy of HE's genetic experiments. In accordance with an international consensus China's guidelines and regulations had banned germline genome editing on human embryos for clinical use. HE's human experimentation not only violated these Chinese regulations but also breached other ethical and regulatory norms. Among the norms potentially violated are questionable scientific value, unreasonable risk-benefit ratio, illegitimate or inadequate ethics review, invalid informed consent, and regulatory misconduct.[39]

What Are the Ethical Implications for STEMists?

In November 2001, President George W. Bush created the President's Council on Bioethics. Leon Kass, a noted bioethicist and University of

---

38. Doudna and Sternberg, *Crack in Creation.*

39 Li et al., "First Gene-Edited Babies," 32–38.

Chicago professor of social thought, was appointed to head the 20 plus member Council. The late 90s and early 2000s had become a period of scientific controversy, especially concerning the ethics of stem cell research. Previously, Kass had argued that the country needed to have more discussions about science and technology and that these discussions should address not only how biotechnologies work, but also, and most importantly, what these innovations meant for humanity. Following Kass's leadership, the Council prepared to debate the new science's implications for humanity and for the flourishing of life.

In preparation for the first meeting, William F. May, then Cary M. Maguire Professor of Ethics and Director of the Maguire Center of Ethics at SMU, made an unusual proposal by requesting that the Council members discuss Nathaniel Hawthorne's short story "The Birthmark." It turns out that Hawthorne's story also serves as a good example for STEMists of the harms that can be inflicted by undertaking science without careful thought.

In this provocative and cautionary tale, Aylmer, an accomplished scientist and a dedicated perfectionist, had married a beautiful woman named Georgiana. The narrator tells us that they enjoyed a deep and abiding mutual love. In Aylmer's eyes, Georgiana was physically perfect, but with one troubling exception. Georgiana had a minor blemish—a small red birthmark the shape of a hand—located on her cheek. Alymer becomes obsessed with removing this tiny flaw. So, being a scientist, he devises a concoction that when ingested he predicts will rid Georgiana of her birthmark forever. Hawthorne observes: Aylmer "was confident in his science, and felt that he could draw a magic circle round her within which no evil might intrude."

But Alymer was mistaken. He gives Georgiana the potion, she swallows it, and quickly it courses through her body. Hawthorne recounts that as the brew takes effect Georgiana turns to Aylmer and with "more that human tenderness" lovingly confides in him: "My poor Aylmer, you have aimed loftily; you have done nobly. Do not repent that with so high and pure a feeling, you have rejected the best the earth could offer. Aylmer, dearest Aylmer, I am dying!" The birthmark fades completely, and as it does Georgiana fades away too.

For Professor May, the story "throws light on two powerful human experiences: the desire for perfection and the struggle with the un-elected marks that go with our birth." And, he goes on to say,

> It may not be too much of a reach to say that modern science exhibits the two sides of love suggested here. On the one hand

science engages us in beholding. It lets us study and savor the world as it is. On the other hand science and the technologies it generates engage us in molding, in the perfecting, in the project of transforming, amending, and perfecting the given world.[40]

The quest for human perfection—to make life better, easier, more encompassing, less demanding—is deeply rooted in human nature. The Greek philosopher, Aristotle, advised his son, Nicomachus, that the highest thing humans can aspire to is a good and flourishing life, an ideal goal he called *eudaimonia*.[41] At least since Aristotle's time, human beings have turned to science, technology, and engineering as instruments to aid them in this pursuit—but with mixed results. Clearly, most people today lead enriched lives due to the many benefits that new developments in knowledge and technology have brought us. At the same time, as a result of relying too extensively on the products of science and technology, humankind has also been confronted with many pitfalls and, indeed, existential dangers. In many cases advances in science and technology have started to push society down a *slippery slope*.[42] The initial adoptions seem innocuous, or harmless or even laudable. But, as subsequent consequences unfold, society evolves into something significantly different, a new state that most often conceals emerging bad consequences within the good.

Hawthorne's story itself offers a philosophical perspective:

> It was the fatal flaw of humanity which Nature, in one shape or another, stamps ineffaceably on all her productions, either to imply that they are temporary and finite, or that their perfection must be wrought by toil and pain. The crimson hand expressed the ineludible grip in which mortality clutches the highest and purest earthly mold, degrading them into kindred with the lowest, and even with the very brutes, like whom their visible frames return to dust. In this manner, selecting it as the symbol of his wife's liability to sin, sorrow, decay and death, Aylmer's somber imagination was not long in rendering the birthmark a frightful object, causing him

---

40. Quoted in Whitaker, "Neoconservative Nathaniel," para. 9.

41. Aristotle's father and grandfather were also named Nicomachus. Nevertheless, tradition has it that his classic *Nicomachean Ethics* was intended as instruction for his son.

42. A slippery slope, or thin end of the wedge, argument asserts that once one form of an action is accepted, other forms—usually negative—will inevitably follow.

more trouble and horror than ever Georgiana's beauty, whether of soul or sense, had given him delight.[43]

"The Birthmark" may be read as an allegory relevant to our modern STEM-based technological world. The science and technologies of genetics, AI and robotics, nanotechnology, and atomic science have all been proposed—and in fact are being used—as tools for "molding, in perfecting, in the project of transforming, amending, and perfecting the given world." An ethical STEMist seeks to apply the extant body of knowledge for many purposes: to produce a better world, to streamline life, to simplify human activities, to make them easier, to increase productivity, to overcome burdens, to eliminate undesirable flaws, and, in general, to produce the "good life." An unethical, or merely unreflective, STEMist engages in these pursuits often for some personal satisfaction and ignores the possibility of producing evil or, at least, outcomes that are bad for some unsuspecting parties. Both outcomes are possible and the perpetrating STEMist, being a contributing "hand," is partially, if not wholly, responsible for the results.

Another moral of Aylmer's story is that all scientific endeavors—qua purposive social actions—result in some unanticipated or unintended consequences. In the real world, omniscience is an unattainable ideal. Yet many STEMists, like Alymer, or Mary Shelley's Victor, or the Sorcerer's apprentice, become enamored with what they believe to be their mastery of a special body of knowledge.

Like Alymer, even a presumed perfectionist is not always perfect. Errors can, and almost inevitably, will be made. It is usually just a question of how severe they are. The real world is complex, and vast, and as Hobbes observed it's often "nasty, brutish and short." Errors can be made at any point in a STEM-based process: in a flawed overall estimate of the situation and resulting problem formation, in not acquiring an adequate amount of relevant data, in drawing faulty inferences from the data, in making poor decisions in formulating a course of action, or, in the neglectful execution of the chosen course of action. Often errors occur because the acting agent has developed a form of tunnel vision and attends only to a limited set of convenient factors that he or she assumes are the only ones that are pertinent to the situation. Thereby ignoring other possibilities.

Attending to just a single interest can also constrict an acting agent's perspective. Alymer was so intent on removing the birthmark that he failed to consider the possibility of other consequences. Actions are not taken in

43. Hawthorne, "Birthmark," para. 8.

a vacuum—social, organizational, psychological, or biological. Rather, they are taken in the context of many spheres of interest. Moreover, once taken, actions ramify. Their effects are not restricted to a single area but have second, third, and n^{th} order consequences as the causal chain unfolds. Given the prevailing nature of risk in implementing new STEM results, an increased interest has been taken in applying "The Precautionary Principle." A famous pause for reflection taken in the development of recombinant DNA technology serves as a good illustration.

Recombinant DNA is DNA that has been formed artificially by combining constituents from different organisms. In the winter of 1970, Stanford biochemist Paul Berg and a postdoctoral researcher, David Jackson, successfully joined the entire genome of a Simian vacuolating virus 40 (SV40) with a piece of DNA from the bacterial virus Lambda bacteriophage and added three genes from the bacterium *E. coli*. As a result, Berg and his associate are arguably the first scientists to create a new molecule containing DNA from two different species. An outcome of this type is frequently called a *chimera*. In Greek mythology, a chimera is a fire-breathing female monster with a lion's head, a goat's body, and a serpent's tail. The mythical version resided in Asia Minor, where it ravaged the lands with its breath of fire. The mythical chimera was an entirely new entity and, hence, its actions were largely unpredictable. Berg began to wonder whether research that involved crossing over between species might get out of control in this manner. Would it unleash wild chimeras? He was alarmed soon afterward by an unexpected event. In June 1972 one of his colleagues, Janet Mertz, attended a course on animal cells and viruses at Cold Spring Harbor. During the course, she relayed some of her plans to make chimeras using SV40 and *E. coli* genes. The experiment she planned involved inserting a cancer-causing gene from a monkey virus into a bacterium that lives in humans.

Following Mertz's presentation, one of the instructors, virologist Robert Pollack, called Berg to discuss his ethical concerns about the dangers inherent in her project:

> I posed to her the simple question, whether she had thought about the fact that she was bridging evolutionary barriers that had existed since the last common ancestors of bacteria and people, by putting a viral genome from a primate virus into a bacterium, and whether that might jump a species barrier and cause someone to

develop colon tumors from transformation of their colon lining as this bacterium established itself in their gut.[44]

For Berg, the frightening possibility of "bridging evolutionary barriers that had existed since the last common ancestors between bacterium and people" presented far too great a risk to have Mertz continue her experiment—and others like it—until they had engaged in some deeper reflection and had developed the necessary controls.[45]

During the early 1970s, many other scientists also worried that hybrid molecules created by recombinant DNA experiments could result in dangerous new organisms that could pose a threat to public health. Still others were deeply concerned about ethical issues related to the possibility of engaging in genetic engineering, especially as it might be applied to humans. This confounding situation led the National Academy of Sciences to ask Paul Berg to head a committee that in July 1974 took the unusual move of calling for a voluntary *moratorium* on certain types of recombinant DNA experiments until the hazards could be evaluated.[46] Seven months later, Berg organized the International Congress on Recombinant DNA Molecules, which was held in February 1975 at the Asilomar Conference Center in Pacific Grove, California.

In an essay for *Nature* entitled "Meetings That Changed the World: Asilomar 1975: DNA Modification Secured," Berg reflects on what the conference accomplished:

> Today, the benefits of genetic engineering, and the risks and ethical dilemmas that it presents, are part of everyday public discourse, thrashed out in newspaper columns and by politicians and commentators everywhere. In the early 1970s, it was a very different picture. Scientists were only just learning how to manipulate DNA from various sources into combinations that were not known to exist naturally. Although they were confident that the new technology offered considerable opportunities, the potential health and environmental risks were unclear.
>
> The people who sounded the alarm about this new line of experimentation were not politicians, religious groups or journalists, as one might expect: they were scientists. They called for a worldwide moratorium on the work, followed by an international conference of experts at which the nature and magnitude of the

44. Pollack, "Bridging Evolutionary Barriers."

45. Mukherjee, *Gene*, 209.

46. US National Library of Medicine, "Recombinant DNA Technologies," para. 3.

risks could be assessed. At that gathering, the International Congress on Recombinant DNA Molecules, held at the Asilomar Conference Center in Pacific Grove, California, in February 1975, it was agreed that the research should continue but under stringent guidelines. The conference marked the beginning of an exceptional era for science and for the public discussion of science policy.[47]

Berg describes the moral quandary that beset the scientists. They ultimately focused on a proposed policy to assign a risk estimate to each of the different types of experiments envisaged and to apply safety guidelines of varying levels of stringency according to the degrees of risk they were able to assess. As a result of Asilomar, leading biologists decided among themselves what restrictions should apply to various types of genetic manipulation (although at that time they focused primarily on laboratory safety and had not yet considered some of the wider social concerns.) Gene splicing recommenced in 1976. By this time, the restrictions proposed by the scientists at Asilomar had become the basis for regulations and laws in many countries.

Just as STEMists should hold "internal courts" with their consciences to evaluate the moral implications of what they are doing, they should also participate in an "outer court" with their peers and stakeholders.[48] The Asilomar experience suggests a model for implementing such an outer court for developing precautions with respect to scientific research and technological development:

1. Call for a moratorium to take stock of the situation.

2. Hold a conference including interested stakeholders as well as involved STEMists to identify and debate the ethical issues.

3. Draw on the results of the conference to develop a set of guidelines for safety and other protections. Containment methods should include physical, biological, social and psychological guidelines.

4. Create an advisory committee with enough resources and authority to monitor activities and enforce the guidelines.

---

47. Berg, "Meetings that Changed the World," 290.

48. A stakeholder is any individual or group that is affected by or who can affect the outcome of an entity's activities. See Mason and Mitroff, *Challenging Strategic Planning*, 43. Also Freeman, *Strategic Management*.

Taking this "Look before you leap" mentality is an important responsibility for STEMists as they pursue their calling. Hawthorne, reflecting on Aylmer's predicament, draws this moral: "The momentary circumstance was too strong for him; he failed to look beyond the shadowy scope of time, and, living once for all in eternity, to find the perfect future in the present."[49]

Some Final Thoughts: Bill Joy's Warning

In the April 2000 issue of *Wired* magazine, Bill Joy, who was then Chief Scientist at Sun Microsystems, published an article entitled "Why the Future Doesn't Need Us." "Our most powerful twenty-first-century technologies—robotics, genetic engineering and nanotech—are threatening to make humans an endangered species," he warned. Scientists need to remember their complicity in past societal evils and change accordingly:

> The experiences of the atomic scientists clearly show the need to take personal responsibility, the danger that things will move too fast, and the way in which process can take on a life of its own. We can, as they did, create insurmountable problems in almost no time flat. We must do more thinking up front if we are not to be similarly surprised and shocked by the consequences of our inventions.[50]

Since Joy gave notice of the dangers of STEM-generated activities, science, technology and engineering have only accelerated in their accomplishments and created more threats to the common good. Consistent with Joy's warning, Jennifer Doudna recalls that as she realized that the newfound power of the discoveries she and her colleagues were working on might be used deliberately, unconsciously or accidentally not only for good but also for evil, she experienced a kind of epiphany. In effect she describes how her career moved from being a job to a calling:

49. Hawthorne, "Birthmark," para. 90.

50. Joy, "Why the Future Doesn't Need Us," para. 141. Joy is here referring to a group of Manhattan Project scientists who were troubled by the use of atomic bombs against Japan and who soon after the war founded the Atomic Scientists of Chicago (ASC). Albert Einstein, a founder, wrote "The unleashed power of the atom has changed everything save our modes of thinking, and thus we drift toward unparalleled catastrophe." ASC publishes *The Bulletin of the Atomic Scientists*, which devised the Doomsday Clock in 1947. The Clock conveys man-made existential threats to humanity. The apocalypse occurs at midnight. The Clock currently stands at two and one half minutes to midnight.

I wasn't used to asking myself these sorts of [ethical] questions in my day-to-day life as a professor and biochemical researcher. Although I recall writing on my application to graduate school that I was interested in scientific communication, in truth I much preferred working in the lab and trying new experiments to thinking about the theoretical, long-term implications of my research and trying to explain them to nonscientists. And as I got more deeply involved in my field, I spent increasing amounts of time talking with specialists and less time talking to people outside my immediate circle of experts. In this way, I fell into a common trap; scientists, like anyone else feel most comfortable when surrounded by others like themselves, people who speak the same language and worry about the same issues, big and small.

Two years after my colleagues and I published the article that described CRISPR as a new gene-editing platform, though, I was finding it impossible to ignore these big-picture questions and stay inside my familiar scientific bubble. As scientists used CRISPR to edit genes of more and more animals, and as they continued to expand the tool's capabilities, I realized it would not be long before researchers somewhere tested CRISPR on human eggs, sperm, or embryos with a goal of permanently rewriting the genome of future individuals.[51]

Doudna goes on to discuss several concerns: various philosophical, practical and safety issues that result from the introduction of heritable changes into the human genome; her apprehension about how by means of a series of reckless, poorly conceived experiments scientists might do great harm; and, her fear that since CRISPR is so effective and relatively easy to use it might be abused or employed for nefarious purposes. She recalls a disturbing dream in which a colleague asks her to teach someone about how to use gene-editing technology. The colleague takes her by the hand and leads her into a room. There sits Adolf Hitler (with the face of a pig).[52]

The students who employ STEM knowledge must have the ethical training necessary to become masters of the knowledge domains they concentrate on. Crucially, in addition, they must be able to reflect on its impacts at a macro or systemic level, as well as at an organizational level and at their own individual level. To fail to do so is grievous. They almost certainly cannot rely on a sorcerer's return to bail them out—or the rest of us, for that matter.

51. Doudna and Sternberg, *Crack in Creation*, 197–98.
52. Doudna and Sternberg, *Crack in Creation*, 199.

5

Using the Humanities to Explore
Professionalism in Medical
and Law Schools

Thomas Wm. Mayo

I. Traditional Ethics Instruction
in Professional Schools

I STARTED WORK ON this essay with a different topic in mind: teaching ethics in professional schools, namely law school and medical school. The enterprise is relatively straightforward in both places. Both professions have codes of ethics with rules that can be taught and memorized. For lawyers, it is the *Model Rules of Professional Conduct* of the American Bar Association (ABA),[1] made all the more important for students because it is the focus of the Multistate Professional Responsibility Examination, which all but three states require for admission to the bar. In medicine, the principle ethics code is published by the American Medical Association (AMA),[2] which is—like the ABA—a voluntary professional association whose ethics rules are binding on members but membership in which is not required for licensure. In addition, significant codes have been promulgated by other professional groups, most notably by specialty societies such as the American College of Physicians, the American College of Obstetricians and Gynecologists, and the American College of Surgeons, to name a few. As for pedagogy, the posing of hypothetical cases that illustrate the rules and more hypotheticals

1. American Bar Association, *Model Rules*.
2. American Medical Association, "Code of Medical Ethics Overview."

85

that push the boundaries of the rules is the time-honored tradition in both pre-professional settings.

"Time-honored" might be a stretch. The curricula of both law and medical schools included, until about forty to fifty years ago and with some notable exceptions, little about ethics. After the Watergate scandal, which involved at least fourteen lawyers associated with the Nixon White House (from the President, Attorney General, and White House counsel on down),[3] the ABA insisted that legal ethics be taught in law schools that it accredited. That requirement was satisfied in some law schools with a dedicated course on the subject. Other schools adopted the "pervasive method"—similar to the "embedded ethics" approach adopted by some medical schools and de-scribed by Camp et al. elsewhere in this volume—which instead sought to include legal ethics in courses across the curriculum.

There is reason to believe that when everyone on the faculty is expected to include ethics in their syllabus, few will do so. One might also wonder whether a single-semester course in ethics is significantly better than no dedicated course at all, though I will leave that debate to someone who has taught legal ethics in law school (and I am not that person). A majority of law schools in the United States now offer a stand-alone course in legal ethics, with a minority of schools still relying on the pervasive method to establish compliance with the ABA's accreditation standard. Apart from compliance concerns, there is much to be said for a school to embrace both approaches to teaching ethics simultaneously, as Deborah Rhode has argued.[4]

Medical schools were equally slow to embrace the teaching of medical ethics, but society nonetheless marched on ahead. The history of "bioeth-ics" as a field and as a profession is complex and often hotly disputed,[5] but a few key developments deserve mention. In 1969, the Hastings Center was created to explore the ethical issues created by ongoing revolutions in biology and medicine.[6] Driven by these technological revolutions and a massive influx of public and private research financing, human-subject re-search blossomed after World War II. In 1979 the National Commission for the Protection of Human Subjects of Biomedical and Behavioral Research

---

3. American Bar Association, "Lawyers of Watergate."
4. Rhode, "Ethics by the Pervasive Method," 31–32.
5. Evans, *History and Future of Bioethics*, xi–li.
6. Callahan, *Roots of Bioethics*, 24–29.

issued the Belmont Report,[7] which addressed principles and protections for human-subject research.

During the same postwar period, technology and money (including primarily the expanded availability of health insurance) had an equally powerful impact on the practice of medicine. This led the President's Commission for the Study of Ethical Problems in Medicine and Biomedical and Behavioral Research to publish from 1978 to 1983 a dozen influential reports, not only on research protections but also on such important non-research topics as making medical decisions and withholding and withdrawing life-sustaining treatment.[8] Medical schools came to realize that ethical issues deserved a place in their curricula, which led to the same "embedded vs. stand-alone" debate that law schools were engaged in after Watergate.

Academic ethics instruction in medical and law schools tends to be rule-based, perhaps because the rules are viewed as authoritative and more or less binding on practitioners. Of course, the rules are sometimes not all cut and dried. In some instances they are precatory and in others they may create significant room for individuals' conscience-based judgments. Things, in short, can get complicated quickly.

A term that sums up this complexity, as well as informing it and challenging it, is "professionalism." Professionalism, properly understood, seeks to identify the values that responsible practitioners bring to their relationships with patients, clients, families, and society. As Professor William F. May has explained, "Case-oriented quandary ethics, as taught in professional schools, deals chiefly with discrete dilemmas: Should I pull the plug or not? Should I withhold the truth or not? . . . All such professional dilemmas pose the question, what shall I do?"[9] As May observes, there is a deeper vein of inquiry that runs under professionals' ethical dilemmas: "Behind many of these dilemmas lie the deeper questions of professional identity. Who am I? Whom shall I be? . . . What am I? A mix of technician plus entrepreneur? A careerist . . . ? Or something more?"[10]

The first paragraph of this chapter set up a false dichotomy, or at least a true dichotomy in a false manner. Professional ethics is a robust discipline that embraces inquiry into both "What shall I do?" and "Whom

7. Department of Health, Education and Welfare, "Belmont Report."

8. The President's Council on Bioethics, "Being Human."

9. May, *Beleaguered Rulers*, 6.

10. May, *Beleaguered Rulers*, 7.

shall I be?" The type of course I want to describe does not deal chiefly with discrete dilemmas, the bread and butter of professional ethics instruction. Although quandary ethics is not banned from this classroom, it takes a back seat to an exploration of May's "deeper questions of professional identity." And it does this not through codes or rules or other tools of quandary ethics, but rather through the humanities.

II. Exploring Professionalism Through the Humanities

A. Learning from Students

My decision to use novels, poems, plays, and short stories to explore issues of professional identity was catalyzed by two student encounters.

One of these encounters was in my "Bioethics and Law" class. I had assigned a poem—"My Death," by Raymond Carver[11]—to introduce the unit on death and dying: the poem works well in this class, for a couple of reasons.

"My Death" is a fine example of a patient making a seemingly inexplicable decision to die fully supported by technology, in a hospital hooked up to wires and tubes. This usually leads the class to a discussion about the end-of-life choices the students believe most people would make for themselves. Or the choices their relatives might have made for their own deaths. Or the choices they did not make for their own deaths.

In addition, the poem gives us a chance to consider the concept of "choice" at the end of life. For millennia, people didn't have clinical choices to make. Technology offered little in the way of options. Whether death came slowly or suddenly, there was not a lot to negotiate over or to discuss. Today, on the other hand, technology has given us choices, and we have ways of communicating those choices that make them more or less binding on our family and our treating physicians. Reading Carver's poem, we can almost forget, or take for granted, that over the past fifty years, choice has entered for the first time into the end-of-life equation.

One year, however, the classroom discussion of "My Death" took an unexpected turn. A third-year student, fresh from his summer clerkship with a law firm, raised his hand and stated, "I get this whole 'medicine is both an art and a science' thing. But what does that have to do with law? I've seen the practice of law. It's just plumbing, not art." My first reaction

11. Carver, "My Death," in *All of Us*, 122–23.

was that the student's remark might have been unfair to plumbers. On further reflection, though, I despaired that the creativity and joy of practicing law was entirely missing from this student's experience (both in his law-school classes and in his summer employment) and that he did not see the profession as one that offered opportunities to exercise one's moral imagination for the benefit of a client.

The second student encounter was actually two encounters, about a month apart. I was starting my second year of teaching, and two students from my previous year's Civil Procedure class separately came by my office to catch up on their summer activity. Both students were despondent over the prospect of two more years of law school. The first year had left them wondering if they had made a vast mistake choosing a career in the law.

Both students had been undergraduate English majors, and each had given up reading anything for pleasure during the pressure-cooker first year of law school. I suggested that quitting an activity that had given so much pleasure for the previous four years of their lives was tantamount to losing an arm or a leg, a fairly radical alteration of the person they were. Remembering my own law-school encounter with a "Law and Literature" course, I suggested that the students might want to take such a course, perhaps the sooner the better. We then discovered that a course in which the readings were of primary works of literature did not exist at our school.

After some discussion, we cobbled together a reading list with civil disobedience as the unifying theme. Later that year we met once a week in an oxymoronic "group independent study" to discuss Sophocles's *Antigone*, Thoreau's "Civil Disobedience," Hannah Arendt's *Eichmann in Jerusalem*, Martin Luther King's "Letter from Birmingham Jail," and a handful of other titles now lost beyond the dim reaches of my memory. We finished with John Irving's *The Cider House Rules*, which had just been published and was favorably reviewed on the front page of the *New York Times Sunday Book Review* by my undergraduate Shakespeare teacher, Benjamin DeMott. In its simplest terms, the novel is about Dr. Larch, a physician who offers pregnant women in Maine their choice of an abortion or an adoption in an era when abortions were illegal, and the orphan-protegé whom Lark had groomed to take over his work after he died. The novel is rich with history, medical fact, and characters and events that stay with the reader long after the book is finished. Even ten or more years after *Roe v. Wade*, the novel offered us much to discuss about disobedience of the law (in contrast to the doctrine of "civil disobedience") and was a vehicle for discussing universally illegal medical practices (in 1985) such as physician-assisted suicide and active euthanasia.

The semester went better than I could possibly have hoped, and for a number of years after that, I enrolled eight law students in the spring of their third year for the same experience of independent study together. Gradually the focus of the class shifted toward bioethics-and-law-oriented readings, still limited to works of literature. Over time, fourth-year medical students joined the third-year law students. Eventually the faculties at both my law school and the nearby state medical school formally approved my "Law, Literature, and Medicine" seminar, which is described later in this chapter.

B. Literature-Based Courses in Professional Schools: A Brief Encounter

Lawyers and physicians have both embraced the humanities as part of their respective professional canons. This has been true across centuries, and there is probably no turning back the clock nor is there any observable desire to do so. The medical canon includes the writings of physician-authors such as John Keats, Mikhail Bulgakov, Anton Chekhov, William Carlos Williams, Oliver Sacks, and Richard Selzer, as well as countless non-physicians. For lawyers, the canon includes Carl Sandburg and extends through Charles Dickens and W.H. Auden to Scott Turow and John Grisham. The place of the humanities in law and medical schools, however, appears to be a more recent phenomenon, is less widely accepted, and is probably less secure.

The use of literature in medical school has been aided by the appearance of literary anthologies, including those put together by The President's Council on Bioethics,[12] Richard Reynolds and John Stone,[13] Richard Gordon,[14] and Peter and Renata Singer,[15] to name only a few. Anthologies of law-related literature are less numerous. Fine examples include collections edited by Shapiro and Garry,[16] Thomas Morawetz,[17]

12. The President's Council on Bioethics, "Being Human."
13. Reynolds and Stone, *On Doctoring.*
14. Gordon, *Literary Companion to Medicine.*
15. Singer and Singer, *Moral of the Story.*
16. Shapiro and Garry, *Trial and Error.*
17. Morawetz, *Literature and the Law.*

and Thane Rosenbaum.[18] A unique member of this club is the collection of short stories about criminal justice by the late Norval Morris, written in the persona of Eric Blair, the birth name of George Orwell, and set in pre-independence Burma.[19]

The body of works *about* the humanities and law or medicine is densely populated, occasionally entertaining, usually quite turgid, and predictably theoretical. Titles worth reading include those by Paul Heald,[20] Professor Austin Sarat and others,[21] Brooks and Gewirtz,[22] Lenora Ledwon (an interesting blend of anthology and extensive commentary),[23] and Bankowski and del Mar (unique discussion of non-textual arts and the law).[24] Medical ethics and film are treated extensively and quite helpfully in books edited by Henri Colt and others[25] and by Sandra Shapshay.[26] A persistent critic of the idea that literature has any unique value to contribute to our understanding of the law and lawyers' lives in the law is retired Judge Richard Posner.[27]

Against the backdrop of this avalanche of writing of and about the humanities and the legal and medical professions, in 2018 Professor Thomas Morawetz produced a valuable guide to the past and future justifications of the humanities—broadly defined to include "hybrid (or hyphenate) courses on philosophy (jurisprudence), law and literature, and legal history, in the law school curriculum."[28] With a few word substitutions here and there, his discussion could apply equally to the value of the humanities in medical school.

As Morawetz describes the traditional argument for the humanities, they "enhance 'perspective' and analytical skills [including] logical analysis, abstract conceptualization, psychological understanding, appreciation of good writing styles, and empathy."[29] His critique of these justifications is

18. Rosenbaum, *Law Lit.*

19. Morris, *Brothel Boy.*

20. Heald, *Legal Problem Solving.*

21. Sarat et al., *Law and the Humanities.*

22. Brooks and Gewirtz, *Law's Stories.*

23. Ledwon, *Law and Literature.*

24. Bankowski and del Mar, *Moral Imagination.*

25. Colt et al., *Picture of Health.*

26. Shapshay, *Bioethics at the Movies.*

27. Posner, *Law and Literature.*

28. Morawetz, "Self-Knowledge," 137.

29. Morawetz, "Self-Knowledge," 137–38.

that they are both overfamiliar and insufficiently unique to the humanities. Further, "they do little or nothing to address the question of the *relative* importance of this kind of learning in law school."[30] In addition, he writes, these justifications fail to address such questions as whether law school is the time or place for this type of education and whether law students are even capable of adapting their behaviors and patterns of thought changed through exposure to the humanities.

Morawetz argues a more modern three-part case for the humanities might begin with the following. The first argument would identify at least one goal that is particularly beneficial to law students and not likely to be achieved through other law school experiences. The second argument would be a somewhat general account of the "skill-set" justification identified above. A third argument (and one that appears to be tightly bound to the first two) would "give examples of ideas and experiences that students are likely to have only in the context of [humanities] courses and to make evident their formative importance." Morawetz ties these three ways of justifying the humanities in law school together by identifying them with two goals of legal education: the instrumental goal of becoming a better lawyer and the far less recognized goal of making one's life better by "addressing rather than avoiding the question 'Who am I?'"[31]

Morawetz's discussion of the three-part case to be made for the humanities in law school not only harkens back to Professor May's discussion of the deeper questions of professional identity and obligation, but also to James Boyd White's *The Legal Imagination*, a pioneering casebook in the field of law and literature. Boyd's brief discussion of the justification for including the humanities in law school is also perfectly consistent with Professor May's analysis: "The effort of the book is not to reach conclusions, even tentative ones, but to define responsibilities. The hope is not that a systematic view of life will be exposed, but that the student will come to some new awareness of his place in the world, of his powers and obligations. . . It might be summed up by saying that the student or other reader [can] ask: 'Where do I go now?' He is asked to collect himself for the moment and imagine his future."[32]

Both law school and medical school offer an explicit curriculum as well as what is often called a "hidden curriculum." (The hidden curriculum

30. Morawetz, "Self-Knowledge," 138.

31. Morawetz, "Self-Knowledge," 140.

32. White, *Legal Imagination*, xxi.

may not be unique to these two professional schools.[33]) Both versions of professional school education, implicitly and sometimes overtly, stress a separation, bordering on denial, of self-knowledge in the service of the professional's fiduciary duty to promote the interests of her client or patient. Morawetz observes that "a dose of jurisprudence and a slug of law and literature" probably cannot do much to cure the things that can go wrong in the life of a lawyer (or physician) but concludes with the "hope that self-reflective lawyers [and doctors] may be in a better position to affect these circumstances for both personal and social benefit."[34]

III. Law, Literature, and Medicine: An Experiment

A. Tonic, Not Cure

The student encounters described earlier in this chapter can now be understood more clearly against the arguments put forward by May, Morawetz, and White. The experience my two Civil Procedure students had with literature in their pre-law-school lives must have seemed entirely divorced from the cases, statutes, and law review articles they read in their first year of law school. The first-year curriculum in particular makes no concerted attempt to relate its content to the particular analytical, narrative, and writing skills exemplified by literary texts. In addition, the opportunity to develop empathy and self-knowledge is typically lost to the analysis of doctrine and learning to "think like a lawyer."

It turned out that the Bioethics student spent his summer, as many students do, copying pleadings out of generic "form books" and plugging in the blanks of the forms with the details of the case that was assigned to him. There is still room in such work for moral imagination, empathy, and the development of narrative skill. It is the rare student, however, who will look for these nuggets within the arid pages of a form book, let alone treat the exercise as an opportunity to develop self-knowledge.

In my earliest years of teaching law, I plead guilty to this stunted view of the possibilities for professional growth and self-reflection, particularly in my first-year classes of Civil Procedure, Constitutional Law, and Torts. "Law, Literature, and Medicine" was intended as tonic for my youthful oversight, even if "cure" was unlikely and in any event too late.

33. Hariharan, "Uncovering the Hidden Curriculum."
34. Morawetz, "Self-Knowledge," 153.

Before describing this course and its rationale further, a caveat is in order. The writers I have discussed above subscribe to an aspirational view of "professionalism" but are by no means blind to the dark side of this tradition. In selecting a physician, W. H. Auden's father warned him "to shun the sadist, the nod-crafty, and the fee-conscious."[35] On the law side, Sandburg wonders, "Why is there always a secret singing / When a lawyer cashes in?" and "Why does a hearse horse snicker / Hauling a lawyer away?"[36] A response to Sandburg is suggested by Rosenbaum's section titles: "Lawless Law," "The Law Made Low," "The Law Laborious," "The Lawyer as Lout," "The Law and the Loophole," "Layman's Law," and "The Law and Longing."[37]

As self-regulating professions, both law and medicine have shown a tendency to be self-protective of their autonomy and financial security even to the point of sacrificing the principle of fidelity to their clients and patients. For writers like May, Morawetz, and White, the humanities in general and literature in particular point students and practitioners alike to a broad understanding of who they are and where they are headed as professionals, an understanding that situates them in service to clients and patients and to society at large. Private and public obligations become an important part of self-reflection and self-knowledge, and literature and the arts provides a path to this understanding.

B. "Law, Literature, and Medicine" Described

I have described this course in considerable detail elsewhere,[38] and the description that follows is intended to hit the highlights of that description.

The broad goals of "LawLitMed" are explained to the students early in the semester:

1. to give future lawyers and doctors some insight into one another's profession, as well as to give them a chance to develop their own ways of talking to one another;

2. to give each group a chance to gain insight into their own profession's values by taking a look at another profession;

35. Auden, "Art of Healing."
36. Sandburg, "Lawyers Know Too Much."
37. Rosenbaum, *Law Lit*, vii–ix.
38. Mayo, "Twyla Tharp Goes to Law School."

3. to introduce students to the study of literature as a way of gaining exposure to human experience and the ethical dilemmas of daily practice through the writings of master story-tellers;

4. to underline the importance of a humane and humanistic professional education and outlook—to develop students' sensitivity to the human dimension of their professional lives;

5. to introduce students to the notion that most of the information they will deal with in their professional lives is organized and transmitted in narrative form—judicial opinions, client and patient stories (in the form of complaints, histories, etc.), and practical, clinical information (what worked the last time it was tried—in court or with a type of patient). In that vein, it is useful for students to sharpen their narrative skills by reading and discussing great stories; and

6. to introduce students to a form of professional, case-based moral reasoning that resembles casuistry (as distinct from the dominant traditions of reasoning from first principles (deontology), consequentialism, and virtue ethics).

Throughout the semester, the readings are presented for class discussion by student teams that consist on one student from each school. This is particularly true of the medical and legal anthologies, for which the students also select the class-discussion pieces from a longer list of possibilities. The major exception to this approach is in the first two weeks, when my co-teacher (from the medical school) and I model an approach to promoting class discussion that we hope the students will emulate: lots of open-ended questions and relatively few, if any, opinions from the discussion leader in order to open up as wide a space as possible for class participation.

Week 1. The readings for this week are heavily didactic, including essays on narrative medicine, literary imagination and legal rhetoric, and the creation of a safe public space to discuss the students' private responses to the literary assignments. We close with poems by Carl Sandburg,[39] Billy Collins,[40] and John Stone[41] to give the students a taste of what is to come.

---

39. Sandburg, "Lawyers Know Too Much."
40. Collins, "Introduction to Poetry."
41. Stone, "Truck."

Week 2. Invariably, the faculty lead the discussion of readings selected from the two anthologies, *On Doctoring*[42] and, in recent years, *Law Lit*.[43] The class again watches and learns some of the rhetorical techniques we use to prompt discussion without being excessively directive.

Weeks 3–13. Students and occasionally faculty lead discussions drawn from the anthology readings, as well as selected novels, plays, short stories, and poetry. One play—Margaret Edson's extraordinary *Wit*[44]—has become a staple. And one novel—John Irving's *Cider House Rules*—has made the list every year since 1985. Throughout the semester, the students have obligations in addition to leading class discussions. They are encouraged to journal, a recommendation that was watered down from a requirement, so few if any write into a journal for the class. All are required to write poems around Week 4 and Week 10. Some years the students are also required to write two monologues about the same death (fictional or real) from medical and legal perspectives but without explicitly identifying the profession of each speaker.

The readings rely pretty heavily on poetry. This is partly for the convenience of relatively short pieces that address important issues with concision. An unexpected bonus is a function of most students' lack of experience, at least since high school, in reading poetry. Little or nothing in law or medical school prepares them to discuss a poem. Forced to lead a discussion about an assigned poem, the students' professional personae drop away and they are eager to receive help from the rest of the class. There is nothing like a good poem to create a collaborative learning environment.

Week 14. In lieu of a final paper or exam, all students are required to create a work of art, which are presented during the final class. For many, "creating art" is an enormous psychological burden with which many struggle throughout the semester and all seem to become comfortable with by the end. The one constraint imposed on their creativity is that their projects must relate in some fashion to the issues discussed in class during the semester. Given the vast breadth or our discussions, this turns out to be not much of a constraint at all.

The final projects are the capstone event of the semester. The unstated intention behind the requirement of an art project is to model empathy, which is a major goal of the entire semester. The students have to imagine

---

42. Reynolds and Stone, *On Doctoring*.

43. Rosenbaum, *Law Lit*.

44. Edson, *Wit*.

how a reader, viewer, or listener will respond to their work when they encounter it for the first time. Getting into the head of that imaginary reader, viewer, or listener requires them to get out of their own headspace and see this encounter through the senses of another human being. Most of the projects will never win a prize for technical skill, but the projects are impressively imaginative and rewarding: collections of poems or stories, paintings, drawings, sculptures, mosaics, an interpretive tap on the five stages of grief, a French horn concerto—composed and performed—on the same subject, many photo-essays, and more.

IV. Wrapping Up

The success of our empathy project is difficult if not impossible to measure. As teachers in this unusual course, we make a leap of faith and hope for the best. We have been privileged to witness students work hard to answer the subtextual questions "Who am I" and "Where am I headed?" We have seen personal growth toward a greater understanding of the professional lives they are about to enter beyond anything our traditional doctrinal or empirical courses offer. Some semesters we feel as though we have caught lightning in a bottle, but the experience has repeated itself so many times and for so many years, we are in truth no longer surprised at the result. Professor Morawetz's list of traditional reservations—Is professional school the appropriate place for this kind of education? Can twenty- and thirtysomethings really be transformed in a meaningful and lasting way over a mere fourteen weeks?—is still relevant. But the leap of faith beckons, and the responses of the students encourage us each year to take that leap with them.

6

Embedded Ethics in Medical Education

MARY CAMP, ALEXANDER COLE,
AND JOHN SADLER

Introduction

HISTORICALLY, ETHICS EDUCATION IN medical schools has been segregated into distinct courses, electives, or modules, which in a relatively brief period, provide an intensive but insular experience, typically didactic in nature. We argue that this style and format of delivery, while well-intended, sends the wrong implicit message to medical students. This implicit message is that ethics is for limited times and places, and very specialized and constrained clinical problems. In contrast, we argue that ethics education should be distributed across many, even most, preclinical and clinical experiences in medical education, embedded in other courses, training, and foci of interest—from genetic basic science to the day-to-day work of each of the major clinical specialties—internal medicine, surgery, pediatrics, psychiatry, family medicine, neurology, and obstetrics/gynecology. We review emerging trends in ethics medical education, which embeds ethics considerations and deliberations into other courses, thereby sending the message that ethics is part of the everyday practice of medicine.

I. Background: Medical Education and the Challenge of Learning Clinical Ethics

Medical education in the United States is a distinct form of adult education. Medical students typically undergo a four-year doctoral degree program which they enter after achieving a four-year college, or undergraduate, degree. A single class of medical students undergo a largely standard four-year doctoral program, culminating in the MD or DO degree. Granting that students may take electives and selectives during their education, the curricular expectations are otherwise similar across the country. The students must pass a series of nationally-standardized, progress examinations in order to be eligible for licensure to practice medicine. After receiving their medical degree, few go on to practice without additional training. The vast majority take medical specialty training, as "residents," resulting in the broad array of medical specialists we encounter today—from family physicians, to ophthalmologists, to psychiatrists, to cardiologists and many more. The four-year MD/DO degree is intended to present the core knowledge, skills, and attitudes of medicine which all physicians, regardless of specialty, should possess.

Ethics education for medical students is a late twentieth century phenomenon. Historians attribute the growth of medical ethics scholarship, practice, and education to the mid-century development of potent therapies which posed never-before questions about the value and meaning of the new medical technologies: examples include organ transplantation, artificial ventilation and cardiac life support, artificial insemination, birth control, "test-tube babies," and the explosive growth in the care of older adults with dementia. Prior to this time, considerations in medical school which today we would identify as "ethics" and "professionalism" were given, at most, informal mention under terms such as "medical courtesy."[1] The first reports about US medical ethics education appeared in the 1970s. Following an earlier 1973 report, Veatch and Sollito reported in the *Journal of the American Medical Association* a survey about the provision of ethics teaching in medical schools.[2] Of the 112 extant medical schools of the time, 107 schools responded, and of those 97 endorsed some sort of curriculum in medical ethics. In addition to subject matter, Veatch and Sollitto collected information on the format of ethics education delivery,

---

1. Veatch and Sollito, "Medical Ethics Teaching."
2. Veatch and Sollito, "Medical Ethics Teaching."

which is the primary interest of this chapter. Their informal classification of forms of curricula included (a) required courses (6/97 schools), (b) elective courses (26/97), (c) ethical perspective incorporated into other courses (69/97, with 19 of these offering no other ethics content), (d) issues incorporated into other courses (58/97), and (e) special programs (conferences/lectures; 56/97).

This diversity of approaches, with variations, persists into the present day. The questions addressed in this chapter focus on how best to educate medical students into being the humanistic, morally thoughtful clinicians the public, and all of us, desire. Towards this goal, we consider medical ethics education in the larger context of socializing medical students into the physician role, and we examine emerging trends and innovative interventions to enhance ethics education for medical students.

II. The Problem: How to Socialize Students into Ethical Medical Practitioners?

The medical sociologist and educator Fredric Hafferty provides a useful analysis of the socializing function of medical education, in the context of the late-twentieth century movement towards ethics education and the 'professionalism' movement within American medical schools.[3] Hafferty places the historical/social motive for these trends in education in the concept of 'nostalgic professionalism'. For Hafferty, nostalgic professionalism refers to the mid-1980s awareness of physicians and medical educators having lost a sense of the fundamental altruistic, trust, and service values of medicine, in the face of the rampant commercialization and commodification of health care. Hafferty documents carefully the evidence for this concern about lost traditional medical values through considering calls from national organizations like the American Association of Medical Colleges, widespread examination of both coursework to students (the formal curriculum), what is considered but not formally taught (the informal curriculum) and what is not intended to be taught, but is modeled through faculty actions and behavior (the hidden curriculum). A large part of this effort to recover these values of altruism, trust, and service in American medicine were the interconnected trends of medical ethics education and training in professionalism; the latter particularly aimed at inculcating students with these traditional medical ideals. Professionalism, as Hafferty

3. Hafferty, "Professionalism and the Socialization," 53–78.

describes, ultimately depends upon a transformation of the student's self-identity, assimilating into everyday practice values like altruism, trust, and service to the public. Such transformation, like all socialization enterprises, possesses particular characteristics: professionalizing students is iterative, requiring repeated exposure and expectation by teachers and role models; it flourishes in stressful environments as students incorporate physicianly self-images in the face of adversity; it has a tacit quality, as students learn to *be* or exemplify these values, behaviors and practices as part of themselves, but with little explicit awareness of their transformation; and pedagogically, the need for multiple frameworks, experiences, expectations, and repeated exposure for students to assimilate the ethical/ professional physician self-image.

While the professionalism movement was focusing on students' identities and core values, medical ethics, the older educational trend in medical education, was often preoccupied with transmitting particular contents, or factual knowledge about the field.[4] Only later, with the evolving cross-pollination of the two trends, did medical ethics education start focusing on developing physician identity and core values.[5]

III. Fitting Ethics Medical Education into a Socializing Rubric

While the literature above provides a compelling case for socialization as a pathway to ethical and professional identity formation, the practicalities of implementation present several challenges. First, this conceptualization relies on medical education as the primary vehicle by which socialization happens.[6] This process involves inculcating a set of values, all the while helping students transition from "outsiders" to "insiders" of a nuanced culture and complex group identity that involves a unique

---

4. Doukas et al., "Perspective," 334–41; DuBois and Burkemper, "Ethics Education," 432–37; Eckles et al., "Medical Ethics Education," 1143–52; Fox et al., "Medical Ethics Education," 761–69; Goldie, "Review of Ethics," 108–19; Musick, "Teaching Medical Ethics"; Veatch and Sollitto, "Medical Ethics Teaching," 1030–33.

5. Birden et al., "Teaching Professionalism"; Brooks and Bell, "Teaching, Learning and Assessment," 606–12; Campbell et al., "How Can We Know," 431–36; Carrese et al., "Essential Role," 744–52; Mattick and Bligh, "Teaching and Assessing," 181–85.

6. Hafferty, "Professionalism"; Holden, "Professional Identity Formation."

language, code of conduct, and social hierarchy.[7] That is a tall order for any curricular intervention.

Second, as noted above, in addition to the "formal" curriculum that transmits intended educational content, students encounter the "hidden" curriculum in which they experience the gritty realities of medical practice, as well as less-than-ideal trainee and physician behavior that may not align with the ethical principles taught in previous didactic courses or educational settings.[8] These experiences, whether intended or not, become part of the longitudinal socialization process by which students develop professional identity.[9] Martimianakis et al. refer to the hidden curriculum as the "real teacher" that displaces the formal curriculum in teaching students "what is 'actually' valued in medical education and medical practice."[10] In a recent position paper by the American College of Physicians, the authors propose ethics education, carried out through a "strong ethical culture" as well as "ethical competency," as a primary method to combat the negative impacts of the hidden curriculum.[11]

While students experience the hidden curriculum throughout medical school, its impact may be the strongest during the clinical years, when students rotate to different clinical sites where they will interact, for a limited period of time (one month to a few months), with a variety of preceptors (both faculty and residents), hospital or clinic staff, and patients. This setting includes a greater degree of variability and unpredictability corresponding to the vagaries of medical practice. In one representative study of students' reflective writing, students described their clinical learning experiences as haphazard, which contrasts with more structured and deliberate didactic curricula.[12]

Additionally, students often perceive the clinical learning environment as competitive and hierarchical, with students ranking as the least powerful members of the treatment team.[13] This hierarchy serves a purpose,

7. Cohen et al., "Identity Transformation in Medical Students."

8. Hafferty, "Beyond Curriculum Reform"; Lempp and Seale, "Hidden Curriculum"; Gaufberg, "Hidden Curriculum."

9. Holden, "Professional Identity Formation."

10. Martimianakis et al., "Humanism, the Hidden Curriculum," 59.

11. Lehmann et al., "Hidden Curricula, Ethics, and Professionalism," 507.

12. Lempp and Seale, "Hidden Curriculum."

13. Lempp and Seale, "Hidden Curriculum"; Cohen, "Identity Transformation in Medical Students"; Camp and Sadler, "Moral Distress"; Gaufberg et al., "Hidden Curriculum."

in that the team members with the most training and experience have the most decision-making authority in patient care. In an ideal training setting, students experience a safe and supportive environment in which they can raise and discuss ethical concerns with more experienced supervisors, for the betterment of their learning and patient care.[14] However, in many instances, students do not raise ethical concerns with supervisors, or they feel powerless to address these dilemmas.[15] While students may avoid ethics discussions for a variety of reasons, one particularly challenging reason may be student concerns about academic performance. Students may fear that areas of ethical questioning would be perceived as a lack of knowledge, unprofessional behavior, or another bad mark against the student. In our study of medical student reflective essays, one student commented that "I am a medical student. I am held hostage by a grade."[16]

Medical education literature on the hidden curriculum often dovetails with the related concept of 'moral distress', in which one identifies the ethically correct course of action but is prevented from carrying it out.[17] Originally studied in nurses, this phenomenon has since been identified across medical professionals, including medical students.[18] Wiggleton completed a web-based survey in which medical students responded to a series of ethically troubling scenarios.[19] Students reported that they had experienced nearly half of these scenarios, and around one third of the scenarios were associated with moral distress. Lomis et al. analyzed 192 case descriptions written by third year medical students and reported medical student moral distress involving problems within a team, access to care, allocation of resources, negative role models, or the students' own regret about inaction.[20] In a study of 802 medical student reflective essays, Camp and Sadler reported that 34 percent of the essays described student moral distress.[21] The moral distress essays were statistically associated with ethical themes involving the students' low rank on the training hierarchy,

---

14. Lehmann et al., "Hidden Curricula, Ethics, and Professionalism."

15. Parker et al., "Clinical Ethics Ward Rounds."

16. Camp and Sadler, "Moral Distress," 3.

17. Jameton, "Dilemmas of Moral Distress," 542–51.

18. Chiu et al., "Experience of Moral Distress"; Hilliard et al., "Ethical Conflicts and Moral Distress"; Kälvemark et al., "Living with Conflicts."

19. Wiggleton et al., "Medical Students' Experiences of Moral Distress."

20. Lomis et al., "Moral Distress in the Third Year."

21. Camp and Sadler, "Moral Distress."

disputes with team members or patients, witnessing insensitive care, and ethical disagreements with supervisors. In a survey of 1,853 medical students, Feudtner found that most students had done something in medical school that they believed was unethical, and 67 percent felt "bad or guilty" about it.[22] The authors considered this an indication of "ethical erosion" in the context of clinical educational experiences. Consistent with theoretical frameworks about the socialization process, multiple studies indicate that positive role models provide valuable resources for medical students in their ethical and professional development.[23] While some of the studies above indicate that factors in the training environment lead to the hidden curriculum and student moral distress, others postulate that broader structural and organizational factors underlie the professional and ethical challenges in medical care and training.[24]

Physicians face increasing pressure for productivity and efficiency, spending more time with electronic medical records and less time with patients, resulting increased frequency of physician stress and burnout.[25] Doukas suggests that social injustice inherent in the financing and delivery of healthcare prevents physicians from fulfilling ethical obligations to patients.[26] In this sense, learning to manage the ethical challenges of the hidden curriculum may equip students to manage the inevitable and insidious ethical challenges of a career in medicine. This is not to say that unprofessional or unethical behavior should be encouraged in training settings, but rather, that it may be recognized and used as part of the training experience in a productive way.[27]

Therefore, ethics education has the combined challenge of providing students with a baseline knowledge of ethical principles, instilling ethical values in professional identity, countering negative messages of the hidden curriculum, and preparing students for ethical conflict inherent in broader systems of care. In order to approach these broad and weighty objectives, we propose that ethics curriculum should also be broad in scope

22. Feudtner et al., "Do Clinical Clerks Suffer Ethical Erosion?"

23. Camp and Sadler, "Moral Distress"; Cohen et al., "Identity Transformation"; Gaufberg et al., "Hidden Curriculum."

24. Martimianakis, "Humanism, the Hidden Curriculum"; Lehmann et al., "Hidden Curricula, Ethics, and Professionalism."

25. West et al., "Physician Burnout."

26. Doukas et al., "Transforming Education Accountability."

27. Martimianakis, "Humanism, the Hidden Curriculum"; Lehmann et al., "Hidden Curricula, Ethics, and Professionalism."

and longitudinally designed to reach students at their ever evolving developmental level. In the next section, we describe relevant frameworks for ethics education, as well as some curricular interventions intended to meet the complex needs of medical trainees.

IV. Innovations in Integrated/Embedded Medical Ethics Education

Integrated, or 'embedded', curricula aim to incorporate the achievement of specific educational goals involving a set of related knowledge and/or skill sets into a larger educational framework. The methods and goals of curricular integration are varied, but Muller et al. describe conventions of curriculum design in the context of medical education: "it typically refers to interdisciplinary block courses in pre-clerkship years that bring together basic, clinical, and social sciences into one course, or weave longitudinal curricular themes across the curriculum."[28] The overall goal of a medical school curriculum, as an example, may be to train students in the scientific, professional, social, and ethical foundations of the practice of medicine and prepare them to practice as physicians under supervision during their next phase of training. For much of the twentieth century, curriculum design in medical education followed this methodology; students attended discrete courses on a variety of disparate topics with minimal attempts to explicitly link concepts, clinical themes, or practice conventions across subjects. Vidic and Weitlauf summarize the potential pitfalls of this approach: "in the absence of an integrated framework for the discipline-, course-, or subject-limited approach to instruction, the student's progress toward gaining an appreciation of medicine, as not being a simple sum of integral disciplines but an integrated function of all of them, is actually diminished and critically retarded."[29] Increasing recognition of these potential weaknesses, along with evidence from pedagogical research that demonstrate concrete advantages associated with an integrated educational approach, has resulted in a push for interdisciplinary integration in medical education curriculum design.[30]

---

28. Muller et al., "Lessons Learned," 778.
29. Vidic and Weitlauf, "Horizontal and Vertical Integration," 233.
30. Mann, "Thinking about Learning."

Ethics and professionalism education has followed these trends.[31] Parker et al. noted that longitudinal education based on "thematic links" is necessary to provide a sufficient ethics education to medical students.[32] These efforts, however, have been frustrated by unresolved basic questions about curricular design in ethics education. A survey of ethics syllabi from US medical schools showed that individual medical schools have little in common with respect to course objectives, methods of teaching, methods of assessment, and specific content areas to be addressed.[33] The ultimate aim of a clinical ethics curriculum is itself elusive, with goals ranging from the abstract (e.g., developing virtue) to the more concrete (e.g., familiarity with ethical principles directly related to patient care activities).[34] Current conceptualizations of ethics education typically incorporate concepts of professionalism and, often, aim to socialize students into the medical community by internalizing ethical principles and professional behaviors assumed to be fundamental to the practice of medicine.

Nevertheless, attempts have been made to operationalize integrated ethics curricula in medical education. These attempts often say little about specific pedagogical methodologies—for example, should ethics education be taught in formal lectures, in small groups, or via case-based discussions? Instead, they emphasize the importance of educational themes which are weaved throughout a medical school curriculum. Here we review some of these design innovations and, when available, describe educational outcomes associated with these attempts. We conclude this section with a brief summary of some newer methods of educational delivery of ethics/professionalism content.

Horizontal Integration

David Brauer and Kristi Ferguson define horizontal integration as "integration across disciplines but within a finite period of time."[35] In medical education, a commonly encountered application of horizontal integration is the "systems-based" curriculum of pre-clinical education. In this model,

31. Fox et al., "Medical Ethics Education."

32. Parker et al., "Teaching of Medical Ethics."

33. DuBois and Burkemper, "Ethics Education"; Lehmann, "Survey of Medical Ethics Education."

34. Musick, "Teaching Medical Ethics."

35. Brauer and Ferguson, "Integrated Curriculum."

content from courses that were once separated and taught in by scientific discipline (e.g, anatomy, physiology, etc) are, instead, taught together in the context of a specific organ system. To use the cardiopulmonary system as an example, students may study the large-scale structure of the heart and lungs (anatomy), then the cellular anatomy (histology), then the normal functioning of the heart and lungs in a living human (physiology), and, finally, how abnormal functioning of the heart and lungs can result in disease (pathophysiology) over the course of a multi-week curricular module. This approach intends to provide a cognitive framework with which to contextualize factual knowledge—increasing competency and knowledge retention. Using this approach, surveys of students reveal increased satisfaction with their educational experience.[36]

Implementation of horizontal integration within medical ethics education is, perhaps, the oldest attempt at explicit integration within the pre-clinical curriculum. Erich Loewy described a curricular design that incorporated medical ethics into an organ systems-based pre-clinical curriculum as early as 1984.[37] Using this model, ethical issues relevant to the current organ system module were discussed in both formal didactic and small group settings. Chin et al. describe a similar and more recent implementation of a horizontally integrated curriculum at National University of Singapore's Yong Loo Lin School of Medicine.[38] They found improvements in students' self-assessment of ethical knowledge, though behavioral outcomes (for example, being able to obtain informed consent from a patient) were mixed.

Vertical Integration

Vertical integration, by contrast, "represents integration across time" and, in the context of medical education, attempts "to improve education by disrupting the traditional barrier between the basic and clinical sciences."[39] In contrast to horizontal integration, vertical integration presents a challenge to curriculum design due to the traditionally sharp divide between the pre-clinical and clinical curricula. In non-ethics education, this design is most evident in attempts to provide early and

36. Klement et al., "Anatomy as the Backbone."
37. Loewy, "Teaching Medical Ethics."
38. Chin et al., "Evaluating the Effects."
39. Brauer and Ferguson, "Integrated Curriculum," 314.

frequent contact with patients, with these encounters forming the basis of education on physical examination skills, clinical knowledge, and basic science knowledge. Exposure to ethics concerns may be added to the discussions of these patient encounters. Reported benefits of this design include "earlier clinical exposure" and improved "perceived preparation for post-graduate training" on the part of students.[40]

Goldie et al. describe the implementation of a three-year, vertically integrated medical ethics curriculum at the University of Glasgow.[41] This curriculum utilized a variety of teaching methods, including small group discussions and plenary sessions, to teach a gradually expanding knowledge base over the duration of the curriculum. Each year, students were presented with a series of medical ethics case vignettes with several pre-written "resolutions" to the ethical issue presented; the proportion of students that chose the response considered to be the consensus response, as determined by a panel of medical ethicists, was used to assess the impact of the curriculum. A significant increase in the number of consensus answers provided by students occurred after the first year but remained flat the following two years—a surprising (and disappointing) finding for the authors. Parker et al. describe a four-year curriculum implemented at the University of Queensland centered on problem-based learning techniques with gradually increasing complexity over the four years; the goal, they state, is to "answer the demand for a framework in which to consider ethical matters, but in a way that does not impose a theory to be applied mechanically."[42] Details about this implementation are sparse, however, and no educational outcomes from the curriculum were published.

Spiral Integration

Spiral integration, as the name implies, incorporates both horizontal and vertical integration over the entire course of the medical curriculum, resulting in a longitudinal, interdisciplinary approach to teaching. Ronald Harden at the University of Dundee describes the spiral curriculum as "one on which there is an iterative revisiting of topics, subjects or themes throughout the course. A spiral curriculum is not simply the repetition of a topic taught. It requires also the deepening of it, which each successive

40. Brauer and Ferguson, "Integrated Curriculum," 315.
41. Goldie et al., "Impact of Three Years' Ethics Teaching."
42. Parker et al., "Teaching of Medical Ethics."

encounter building on the previous one."[43] More concretely, he describes the key features of a spiral curriculum as revisiting "topics, themes, or subjects on a number of occasions during a course" and, with each iteration, "the topics visited are addressed with successive levels of difficulty" with "new information or skills . . . related back and linked directly to learning in previous phases of the spiral."[44] Advantages of this curricular design, he argues, include reinforcement of knowledge, particularly knowledge presented early in the curriculum; a gradual increase in the complexity of content taught, resulting, ultimately, in achievement of high level educational objectives; and emphasis on a logical sequencing of material due to the inherent dependency of later portions of the curriculum on concepts taught earlier.

Richard Cruess at McGill University in Canada described the implementation of a four-year professionalism curriculum—which included explicit education about medical ethics—that incorporated many of these principles.[45] Explicit faculty development related to the professionalism curriculum "allowed for institutional agreement on definitions and characteristics, methods of teaching and evaluation, and the thrust for curricular change."[46] The professionalism curriculum was centered on a course "running in a longitudinal fashion throughout all four years of undergraduate medical education" utilizing a variety of teaching methods, including formal didactic lectures, small-group discussions, and case-based discussion. Importantly, teaching activities were "appropriate to the level of instruction" and, over the course of the curriculum, incorporated repetition of key principles to ensure understanding and retention.[47] Concepts and cases discussed in the curriculum become more sophisticated over time and were tailored to be relevant to student experiences at their level of training. The curriculum finished in the final year with a series of seminars on ethically complex topics relevant to graduating medical students (e.g., self-regulation, conflicts of interest, and the social contract). Woven throughout the curriculum are mentorship experiences with faculty members selected to serve as student mentors and periodic assessments throughout the curriculum.

43. Harden, "What Is a Spiral Curriculum?," 141.

44. Harden, "What Is a Spiral Curriculum?"

45. Cruess, "Teaching Professionalism," 177–85.

46. Cruess, "Teaching Professionalism," 180.

47. Cruess, "Teaching Professionalism."

Holden et al. present their own version of a spiral curriculum, embedded within a larger project of curriculum reform within the statewide University of Texas Health Science System.[48] Holden and colleagues formulated the task of medical socialization as 'professional identity formation' through constituting a vision of physician professional identity (scientific, moral, practical) and then formulated curricular opportunities within their system to implement and reward progress towards this idealized professional identity process. The outcomes for this approach are yet to be determined, though at least one other major institution has taken up the "professional identity formation" rubric.[49]

Regardless of the integration philosophy implemented, training in clinical ethics and professionalism requires methods and techniques for placement of curricular material within these broad rubrics or philosophies of education. In the case of clinical ethics education, some of these methods and techniques have included case analysis,[50] ethics questions integrated into clinical simulations,[51] reflective essay writing and discussion,[52] team-based learning modules,[53] and ethics in standardized patient encounters.[54]

V. Conclusion

We take as given that the public, as well as medical educators, want to create empathic, morally conscientious physicians. Contemporary ethics and professionalism education appears to be converging on a process which socializes students into professional identities that not only include scientific and interpersonal skills, but on inculcating young doctors into habits of thinking and practice which represent virtuous professional identities, instead of providing students with segregated ethics didactics isolated from everyday practice. Implementing these new approaches to ethics education have been challenging to medical educators. In addition to planning where and when to place ethics considerations in a social-developmentally astute manner, educators must contend with superimposed trends

---

48. Holden et al., "Professional Identity Formation."
49. Gaufberg et al., "In Pursuit of Educational Integrity."
50. Huijer et al., "Medical Students' Cases."
51. Ogden et al., "Clinical Simulation."
52. Lomis et al., "Moral Distress in the Third Year."
53. Chung et al., "Effect of Team-Based Learning."
54. May et al., "Ten Year Review of the Literature."

within American medicine at large which emphasize efficiency, productivity, efficacy, economy, and freedom from error. These latter trends within American medicine have contributed to unprecedented reports of moral distress and physician burnout.[55] Whether American medical education will succeed, or not, in promulgating ethically conscientious, professionally composed young physicians is an open question, given the challenges in outcome assessments of large-scale curriculum reforms, as well as the challenges of an encompassing, efficiency-driven medical system which too often undermines conscientious, humane medical practice.

55. Zuger, "Dissatisfaction with Medical Practice."

7

Sacred Spaces for Ethical Inquiry: Communicating Ideas on University Campuses

RITA KIRK AND C. R. CRESPO

UNIVERSITY CAMPUSES ARE DISTINCTIVE spaces. They bring together students from various backgrounds, place them in common housing where they are to find ways to live together, provide organizational space for like-minded groups to coalesce, challenge their thinking through course work and exposure to ideas, engage them in the topical issues of the day, encourage them to think, speak, test, and act on their ideas, identify them as "world changers," and then, in all their diversity of thought and background, expect them to convey the appropriate corporate identity that neither offends future employers, elicits unfavorable media scrutiny, nor harms the identity of those who require "safe spaces." As one scholar puts it, "Higher education can increase productivity; but it can also simply screen, or select, for the kinds of intellectual, social and personal characteristics required for the high-remuneration, high-status jobs that may be available."[1]

The "life of the mind"—where ideas are tested and created—is more suited to the monastic environment of its founding than the social media environment of today. When testing ideas, reading what some might regard as heretical concepts, or debating highly controversial subjects, the current educational environment is infested with media-grabbing headlines. Movements are formed and often quickly die but the sting of words said in anger and the reputational damage done to individuals and institutions

1. Johnstone, "Financing Higher Education."

are scars left behind. Navigating the public discourse about knowledge is, at best, difficult. We often wonder what it would be like to be the press secretary for Galileo when he announced his thesis that the sun—not the earth—is the center of the universe? Today, just as then, knowledge that challenges immutable truths is not only the subject of elites, but Tweets and Facebook posts. Rather than nuanced debates with in-depth treatises being tested, debates are more likely to be framed as headlines with reactionary responses. Communication of ideas, then, is something that universities must consider. How we treat facts and distinguish them from opinion is at the core of intellectual pursuits. Yet an even larger question for consideration is the impact of collective ethics, those that define our culture and inevitably affect the work we do.

News Consumption and the Ethical Norms of University Life

Public arguments deserve the highest level of ethical practice within the university and the stiffest critique. Yet in an era that champions carefully honed personas, rip-and-read reporting, and editorialized news, the models for effective communication do not embody a public ethos designed for intellectual understanding nor authentic communication practice. The facts are clear. A 2018 Pew Center study reported one in five Americans get at least some of their news on social media—with two out of ten doing so often and almost half of Americans receiving their news from television.[2] That, in itself, is not problematic but the lack of depth and the uncertainty of source credibility certainly is. A 2018 survey of 11,000 college students found that today's students are "multi-modal," meaning that they receive news from various places, with 67 percent of the respondents reporting they receive their news from five different places or "pathways." Ninety-three percent of students report they receive news from discussions with peers, while 70 percent learned of news from discussions with professors. Social media was the second highest source reported for news with 89 percent and to a lesser degree, online newspapers (76 percent), news feeds (55 percent), and podcasts (28 percent).[3] More than two-thirds of the students reported the "sheer amount of news was overwhelming" and half agreed it was "difficult tell the most important news stories on a given

2. Gottfried and Shearer, "News Use across Social Media Platforms."
3. Head et al., "How Students Engage with News."

day."[4] Most students simply do not have the time nor tools to conduct fact checks, nor the time and inclination to research in-depth the headlines and conversation snippets that flash in front of them through the day. However, the fact that 70 percent of students receive their news from professors provides a unique opportunity and a special responsibility on the part of the professor. Colleges and universities are certainly organizations at the forefront of teaching such skills, which must be viewed as one of the primary educational challenges of this era.

One example of a university professor fact-checking historical references and the mistreatment of facts in breaking news and the issues du jour is Princeton Professor of History Kevin Kruse. Kruse is followed by just over 300,000 Twitter users and on any given day tweets and retweets responses to breaking news headlines with historical perspective. For example, he's provided historical accounts on everything from America's long history of protesting the National Anthem to other times of intense civil unrest in the US. He provides prospective and quickly dispels "half-truths" and misused historical events.[5] He reminds us of the inconvenient truths that history provides. Kruse is bringing the level of thought and research you would see in a college classroom to the Twitter-verse. And despite responding through Twitter, a medium not known for careful thought, he "take[s] the time to find primary sources and work over his sentences."[6] However, even extraordinary scholars and historians have difficulty keeping up with today's news cycle. To state the obvious, social media, and the rise of pundits and the twenty-four-hour news cycle has changed the way we engage with news and each other and possibly changed or at least expanded the responsibility of the professoriate.

While many might prefer the idyllic university model of a quiet, contemplative space for learning, the university of today is producing and responding to explosions of knowledge that outdate textbooks before they are written and outstrip our moral questioning on the potential implications of that knowledge both on our ethics and even our cultural identity. For example, when physicists at Southern Methodist University (SMU), as part of a multi-university consortium, won the 2013 Nobel Prize for their discovery of the Higgs boson, few might have anticipated that the discovery's nickname, "the God particle," would stir such rapid

4. Head et al., "How Students Engage with News."
5. Pettit, "Kevin Kruse."
6. Pettit, "Kevin Kruse."

moral controversy. Headlines abounded: "Will the 'God particle' destroy the world?";[7] "'God particle' searchers still need a little faith"; "God and the God Particle";[8] or "Did God discover the God particle?"[9] Perhaps the lesson learned is that the need to boil down complex studies into sound-bites skews the public understanding of ethical issues at stake? There is no doubt that journalists have a special responsibility to move beyond the soundbite, and most of them do. Physicist Leon Lederman coined the term, "God Particle" when writing a book on the potential of the Higgs boson discovery. Lederman half-joking used the term as a placeholder title for a book, never expecting the publisher to use it. The 2012 Higgs boson discovery and the wide-spread use of the particle's nickname fanned the flames of the years–old science versus religion, creationism versus evolution debate, muddying the waters of the impact of the discovery. Though this is but one example daily headlines demonstrate that it is not unusual. It stands to reason that now more than ever university faculty and administrators are unfortunately obliged to consider the potential for "spin" and whether or not taking discovery and scholarship out of the university and into the news cycle is worth the price of admission.

The Classroom

So where is that space where students and scholars come together to *think*—to think outrageous thoughts about governance, science, art, or philosophy? Should we expect students to follow their professors on Twitter? Maybe. But, at least one of those spaces is supposed to be the classrooms and hallways of higher education. The pressure to be culturally sensitive and to suppress thoughts until they have a chance of being accepted by our peers is detrimental to the exploration process. So, how do we test ideas that are never uttered? Thinking is seriously limited in an era when communication has the power to be pervasive, intrusive, and gloriously inaccurate. A single utterance made in the pressure of the moment may be all it takes for a media storm to arise. Moreover, the backlash from others can be so extreme that is affects our assessment of self, leaving us wondering, are we really as morally bankrupt as our critics claim?

7. Urry, "God Particle."

8. Giberson, "God and the God Particle."

9. Chopra et al., "Did God Discover the God Particle?"

Most of us realize that many times we don't know we think something until we hear ourselves say it. At that point, we may choose to never utter the thoughts again because it sounds outrageous even to ourselves. On the other hand, there may be a kernel of knowledge that will germinate into something that proves useful or beautiful. Take for example a discussion in an undergraduate class on the removal of Confederate statues and symbols. It's reasonable to imagine two perspectives in the classroom: 1) the student who feels strongly the statues are historical artifacts that should not be removed and 2) the student who feels the statues are symbols of slavery and white supremacy and should be removed. How does each of these students wade through their own reasoning without fear of instant judgment from their peers? There is no doubt they are aware of how quickly they could become a meme or the subject of a Tumblr post or their classmate's group text. I suspect many of their responses are colored by this fear of online humiliation. Research Professor Brené Brown argues that teachers have an ethical duty to create spaces in their classrooms where students can freely express their thoughts and struggle with new ideas. Brown says, "We must be guardians of a space that allows student to breathe and be curious and explore who they are without suffocation. They [students] deserve a place where they can rumble with vulnerability and their hearts can exhale."[10] This means even when their reasoning is flawed and their ideas are not fully developed, we must provide a space where they can work out their ideas.

So how does this translate to the classroom? First, the traditional eighteen- to twenty-two-year-old is already searching for ways to sort through the overwhelming amount of news and information they receive. They are struggling to navigate what is and is not news and what is and is not worth their attention.[11] We have an opportunity in the class discussions to help them navigate these turbulent and cloudy waters, even at the risk of wading into controversial topics. Second, on the intellectual front, universities are in the business of fact finding and knowledge creation. If invented stories are perceived as real and valuable as those constructed in the multi-modal and multi-social world, then finding authentic voice and opinion are more difficult for students to achieve. Whose thoughts are these? How are they borne out of the arc of experiences you have had? Third, if confirmation bias, the tendency to interpret new evidence as confirmation of one's existing beliefs, is more important to students than questioning normative

10. Brown, *Dare to Lead*, 13.
11. Head et al., "How to Engage with Students"

thinking, then rote memorization becomes more valued than independent thinking, thus hampering the paradigm shifts that advance human understanding as well as the development of our next great inventions. Fourth, young people are encouraged in the social media world to seek normative understandings that do not challenge their comfort. This means that they avoid face-to-face encounters in general by retreating to the safety of their online universe. Finally, students are always in the ever-present now. There is no space for them to be alone with thought. Each of these has an impact on the way universities teach and reach young people.

Observe how in 2018 and 2019 issues in dispute include banned books and banned speakers, contraception, artificial intelligent design, immigration, net neutrality, opioid addiction, Russian hacking, sexual harassment, police brutality, and LGBTQ+ rights, to name a few. Rather than being educated on the arguments—and their ethical implications—in the classroom, undergraduate students frequently shy away from topics that might cause intellectual or emotional discomfort or might negatively affect others' impressions of them for taking an unpopular position. Raging debates should be normative, respectful, and informative in higher education but too often they are not. We have forgotten how to speak to each other and consequently we are unable to understand points of view different from our own. Interestingly though, Stanford Professor Robb Willer, who studies sociology, psychology and organizational behavior, found in a 2017 study that "people who were given the opportunity to judge each other's morality were more likely to cooperate and trust each other in a group than those who could not make such evaluations."[12] According to Willer, "Generally, people think of moral judgements negatively. But they are a critical means for encouraging good behavior in society."

Issue debates are critical but so are a host of social issues that expand the boundaries of the academy. As a microcosm of the larger social structure, universities also explode in media firestorms when some people find the mere expressions of ideas as an assault on their values. In recent months, a Black Lives Matter group argued for safe spaces. Neo-Nazi groups posted hate messages on campuses and left nooses suspended from trees. Public angst over what should be done with Confederate memorials spills into discussions of the endowed spaces on campus by people whose historic values are not in sync with current thinking. Uncertain of their future,

12. Shashkevich, "Moral Judging Helps People Cooperate." See Simpson et al., "Enforcement of Moral Bounderies."

students identified as "dreamers" have marched for immigration reform. Campuses erupt over sexual abuse by trusted doctors and coaches. Tragic events have emerged from the unintended consequences of people who thought they were within the boundaries of reasonableness, such as when a fraternity that bans alcohol forces pledges to drink large amounts of water, not realizing that it would cause death by drowning. Each of these groups have had encounters where the expressive function of shouting is more satisfying than reasoned disputation. And there are consequences for such isolating disagreements. Social scientist Arthur Brooks attributes today's climate of polarization not to incivility or intolerance, but rather contempt. Brooks argues that persuasion is impossible if we question the motives of and hate the person with whom we are arguing. [13] Further, if the research is telling us that students are overwhelmed by news and information and surrounded by a culture of contempt, then it's easy to see how students choose to ignore one another or simply disengage. Opening the space for vulnerability in the classroom is crucial to overcoming this sense of deluge, contempt, and disconnection.

Universities may make the bold claim that constraints be damned, but that is not the world in which we live. In fact, many colleges and universities are in constant struggle to make sense of their organization and audiences. Often the issue debates or uncomfortable topics spill out of the classroom and into the public sphere. Consider for a moment the myriad of constituencies the general counsel's office of a university has to consider when investigating accusations of inappropriate or "triggering" language used in a classroom context. The argument of academic freedom does have the power it once did. Those universities who do not consider the impact of public response do so at great risk to their reputations, their rankings, and their perceptual place in the hierarchy of public trust. According to the 2018 Edelman Trust Barometer, Technical Experts and Academic Experts received the highest ratings for being "very/extremely credible" in their yearly, worldwide survey on trust.[14] Maintaining credibility permits the universities to be the go-to source of facts for news outlets and the public at large, and validates its professorate and their considered judgments. Credibility gives faculty latitude for the discussion and exploration of controversial topics. Universities can hardly afford to

---

13. Brooks, "Our Culture of Contempt."
14. "2018 Edelman Trust Barometer Report."

lose such credibility for if they are seen as just one more opinionated out-let they are unlikely to be valued by society.

So where does that leave the big and often comfortable debates, the ethics discussions? How do we create sacred spaces for disagreement, academic discovery, and reflection without losing our ability to influence the greater community? The simple truth is that we can provide the tools for questioning, rethinking positions, challenging assumptions, responding to criticism, and adopting behavior change. When students (and often faculty) enter a university, they enter an established culture. That is somewhat peculiar in an organization that has a constant roil of new and graduating students, and an influx of faculty who often move across universities in the span of a career. Such constant churn results in an ever-evolving sense of identity that quite likely changes over the generations. But change is slow. The larger the organization, the slower the change. We love the analogy of Edinburgh town planner and social activist Patrick Geddes who made this observation in 1918 about the pace of meaningful change:

> But growth seems slow: and people are all out for immediate re-sults, like immediate votes or immediate money. A garden takes year and years to grow—ideas also take time to grow; and while a sower knows when his corn will ripen, the sowing of idea is as yet a far less certain affair.

There is a sense that universities must be places where thinking is both fast and slow. There must be a plodding, methodical approach to discovery and yet a sense of urgency to the implications for such dis-coveries. Moreover, there must be a culling of the weeds in the garden, whether as an invasion of an idea that has not borne fruit or the pruning and reshaping of ideas based on an idea's maturation. In most cases, this culling is a result of direct challenges to current thinking—thinking that often rejects such dissent.

The Ethics of Dissent

When you change the way you look at things, the things you look at change.

—GERMAN PHYSICIST MAX PLANCK, widely known
as the founder of Quantum Physics

Ethical agreement might be an easier if we had a small community based on a singular purpose with strict consequences for violations. Some of our founding communities in the United States tried to implement such communities. John Winthrop's famous *City on a Hill* sermon preached on board the *Arbella* en route to the new world is an example of that statement of intention. The Puritans, though they tried, certainly were not able to sustain that original purpose. And neither are we. Try as we might, circumstances change. People change. And progress changes us.

Although challenge to authority is difficult to accept as a leader, institutional change is often driven by it. Universities are no exception. Certainly, we can point to campuses of the 1960s and 1970s as hotbeds of protest. Yet today we are similarly stressed with protests about human rights, extremism in all its forms, and conflicting viewpoints on politics. Much as the institution might like to contain such protests to specific areas and limit the public exposure to reasoned discussions over protests, that is beyond to control of the university. Instead, the university must grapple with what to do when institutional challenges occur. After all, conflict is often a necessary ingredient to progress.

At the heart of this is an even deeper question: What drives the university's leadership? Is it rankings? Research? Enrollment? All of the above? Today's administrators face daunting challenges of reduced federal and state funding combined with heightened expectations for measurable outcomes. It's easy to see how the "ethical and moral development" of the student gets lost in the quest for four-year graduation rates, retention goals, and post-graduation job placement. In modern times, the state boards of regents and university trustees seem to be the dominant voice. Yet the academy, from which we derive the idea of academic studies tracing back to Plato's *akadēmeia,* is really about the creation of knowledge and the education of the whole student, mind and soul.

After all, faculty and student affairs personnel are the ones who have direct contact with students. Academic freedom is a term that stands in opposition to the mistaken presumption of the general public who assume that university presidents and provosts are the equivalent of CEOs and vice presidents in business—those who have direct authority others in the organization. University leadership, then, must not only respond to the larger societal concerns but to the professorate whose research and teaching are the core of the university's mission. The point is that current universities have an inherent tension between the governing boards who must financially protect the university guard it against outspoken critics, and the faculty whose jobs are at the very heart of the university's mission: professors and researchers who relish in the full-throated expression of new and sometimes controversial ideas. Often, it seems, universities find themselves in trouble whenever they begin to value financial support and rankings over ideas and ethical leadership within their campus community.

Historically, we can point to at least three times in history when notable institutional change occurred because of this loss of public favor. The first example is the prominence of the medieval university in the sixteenth century in England. [15] At the beginning of that century, monasteries were entwined in society ranging from the relationship with the court of Henry VIII to the education of the younger sons of wealthy patrons. Yet by 1539, the parliament approved the confiscation of monastic properties, their vast wealth transferred to the crown and their properties used to by the King as favor for an expanded class of supporters. A second example would be the fourth and fifth centuries where Buddhism prevailed throughout parts of China, India, and central Asia. Under the Tang Dynasty, Buddhism was the state religion and while it led to a cultural flourish of science, the arts, and philosophy, these institutions eventually became viewed as self-interested, self-sustaining institutions focused on the accumulation of wealth. That power they led to their dissolution. Simon Marginson notes,

> When these institutions stand for nothing more, nothing deeper or more collective, no greater public good, than the aggregation of self-interest (like the monasteries in China and England, that accumulated vast social resources but came to exist only for themselves and those who used them) then the institutions are vulnerable. Self-interest can be channeled in other ways. The institutions disappear and their functions are picked up elsewhere.[16]

We may be seeing such patterns developing in the US now. Churches, often thought to be the primary institution of moral purpose, have experienced declining attendance. An article in *Religion News & Ethics Newsweekly* notes, "Today more than 20 percent of all Americans say they do not identify with any particular religion. And the drop in affiliation is especially evident among young adults." Those young adults, of course, are the primary population for universities. So, if they do not get their moral compasses reaffirmed there, where else might they turn? As discussed in

15. Marginson, "Higher Education and Public Good."
16. Marginson, "Higher Education and Public Good."

other chapters of this book, there are a variety of places but among those are institutions of higher education.

Historically, three departments in the university have been tasked with moral instruction: theology, philosophy, and the university president. At face value, that is problematic. Not all universities have theology departments. In 2019, the Association of Theological Schools found ninety-eight theological schools were affiliated with a college or university.[17] Philosophy departments moved away from moral instruction years ago in favor of teaching logic and disputation. In both cases, enrollments are declining: "When adjusted for total enrollment, numbers from the National Center for Education Statistics show a 20-percent drop in philosophy and religion majors from 1970 through 2009."[18] The job of university president holds little resemblance to its past. In higher education's early days, in addition to managing the faculty and facilities, the president was a member of the faculty and taught courses. At certain institutions, the president held the responsibility of teaching the capstone course on moral development. This was a fundamental part of the student's education. Since then, our institutions have grown larger and more complex and calls for specialization and credentialing have only grown louder. There have been some claims that universities are not places where moral consideration are important, a claim we firmly reject. From business organizations to pulpits, repeated alignment of our moral compass is required. We believe in the soul of an organization, a resolute sense of character and confidence about what you stand for, and research suggests that, "a bedrock sense of values and identity is critical a critical element in long-term success.[19] We believe our students and faculty know when an organization's commitment to values and ethics is authentic and when the organization is serving a greater good.

Assuming for a moment that Plato is correct, the academy should be a place to educate leaders through reflection and contemplation. If we are to presume that higher education has some benefit in preparing graduates to be leaders in community, government, and industry then might we assume that *Mens Conscia Recti*—A Mind Conscious of Integrity—is a viable goal? Certainly, we can. But where are those lessons learned? The answer should be: everywhere. Teaching and reflecting on the ethical implications of choices and decisions should permeate every field of study

17. Association of Theological Schools, "Commission on Accrediting," 13.
18. McIntyre, "Making Philosophy Matter."
19. Bolman and Deal, *Reframing Organizations*, 388.

and every part of the mind. Yet we must not be so naïve to assume that the casual mention of a single case study in a course is sufficient. Indeed, there is a proper place for the study of ethics as its own field, and one that should be required of each student.

Higher education is a unique organization of learned scholars and neophytes. It faces all the challenges for financial survival other businesses would face yet it is also largely populated by young people who are testing their independence, away from the structures of family and community where reinforced values are ever present. No surprise to those who work in higher education, those choices can be far from wise. Instances of hazing are too often a routine matter, occasionally resulting in death or near–death outcomes, to say nothing of the psychological damage that may be inflicted. Underage drinking, drug use, little to no sleep, poor eating habits, increased stress and anxiety, and a desire by adults to protect students from poor decisions that have the potential to ruin the rest of their lives each contribute to a culture where ethical lapses are easily made. And that is the environment where higher ordered learning is to take place.

The Great Narrative: Learning from Mistakes

While a university has a dynamic culture, it can still have certain immutable characteristics that are similar to other universities. These often stem from a university's founding. Religious schools in particular may be established to provide education with certain viewpoints privileged over others. With such foundations come the essential story of life repeated in many diverse ways: the story of our beginning. At SMU, for example, each year's opening convocation takes place in the historic McFarlin Auditorium and the ceremony ends with the lowering of the Ovilla fire curtain. McFarlin Memorial Auditorium's genesis can be traced to a stormy Sunday in Ovilla, Texas.

Courtesy of Southern Methodist University, Hillsman S. Jackson.

A Presbyterian farmer, Benjamin Porter McFarlin, spent that Sunday helping a neighbor whose wheat crop had to be harvested to save it from the threatening weather. For this unselfish act McFarlin was "churched" (banished) by his congregation in return for working on the Sabbath day. McFarlin promptly offered a traveling Methodist minister the land and money to build a new church in Ovilla. The minister stayed and McFarlin became a Methodist.[20]

It was that group of Methodists who eventually founded Southern Methodist University. In honor of that founding event, the auditorium's fire curtain was painted with a pastoral scene that shows a modest frame building among the tree-lined lane with the word "Ovilla" at the bottom. The curtain is lowered once a year at opening convocation. Students are told that the purpose is to remind us of the lasting value of friendship. Yet today, if you polled current students and asked questions about our founding, this lesson might be lost on them.

Such story-telling is important. Stories establish a model of who we are and what we value. They are symbolic. Critically, these stories must have a sense of place and purpose, which conveys a sense of authenticity and uniqueness. Within most every institution, these stories summarize what happened 'in the beginning' and projects a future embedded in that common

20. Southern Methodist University, "McFarlin Auditorium."

past. A powerful Genesis story can be harnessed for the common good of an institution or community. Ethical discussions must be targeted to specific audiences, be embedded in our culture, our ethical claims must be repeated and repeatable, and, they must be able to withstand challenges.

Stories are both comforting and critical. Comforting because children often first learn about life's lessons through story telling. Learned again as an adult, they are replicable patterns of communicating what a culture believes about itself. Whether it's the story of a family's generational journey, myths about leaders like George Washington, or fanciful works like *The Little Prince* that instruct us on our behavior toward others, stories are dynamic, repeatable, and unifying. They are critical in that they give meaning to events. True or not, they tell us how to interpret our history and guide our future.

But having a religious foundation is not the only way to define an ethical university culture. Ethical stances are often determined by the organization's response to some challenging situation. In the play *Eqqus,* the psychologist instructs the audience, "We need a story to see in the dark."

Often, universities have moral stories built on the character developed as a result of some immoral or unethical act. Perhaps today, in light of the horrible stories of sexual abuse affecting Penn State football, we forget that it was in fact because of the football team a phrase was coined to speak to the university's ethical and moral commitment: *We Are Penn State.* According to legendary Penn State player Wally Triplett this is how the legend was born. The phrase was coined during the era of segregation when integrated teams in the north typically benched their black players when facing southern schools. In 1946, Penn State was faced with a situation where they would have had to bench star player Triplett in the match against the University of Miami. The team voted that they "would play all or none." There was no compromise, so the match was cancelled. Two years later, in 1948, Penn State was invited to post-season honors against Southern Methodist University at the Cotton Bowl. Again, Penn State was expected not to field black players. The team voted again, and this time, team captain Steve Suhey asked, "Are we going to have to have this meeting [about what to do] again?" and then added, "We're Penn State. There will be no more meetings."[21]

Important to this story is that while the myth of origin was, indeed, pulled from an actual event, the myth was created years after the event

21. Spiegel, "Origins of We Are Penn State Cheer."

took place. According to Lou Prato, Penn State football historian, Penn State cheerleaders first used the chant in 1976 and was not fully adopted by fans until 1981. Yet today, the call of "We are" demands the response "Penn State"—a call and response that has now been imbued with meaning. In the wake of the recent Sandusky revelations of sexual abuse, Penn State was rocked once again. Yet the ability of that phrase to unify supporters in a way that rejected the unseemly depictions of the university and brought attention to Penn State's ethical core resulted an identity that fans and alumni could claim as their historic center.[22] Regardless of the egregious behavior of a few, the core held an identity separate and apart from the scandal.

There is another lesson to be gleaned from this tragedy. As the saying goes, one ethical act doesn't make you "ethical" but one unethical act can brand you forever. That's a lesson that applies to individuals as well as organizations. Sometimes, that is a good thing. It creates a climate of "never forget" and "never repeat" the mistakes of yesterday. After all, humans are learning creatures and there is some comfort that we can learn from our mistakes and find a path to restoration. That's the redemption story.

That redemption story is also a part of the SMU legacy. In 1987, SMU was the first and only university to receive the "death penalty" in football. After being an undefeated team in 1982, and winning a second Southwest Conference championship in 1984, the bombshell dropped. SMU had been paying student athletes and the scandal ran from students to alumnus to members of our governing board. The first round of NCAA sanctions occurred in 1985 and after a series of events, the university was given the death penalty in 1987. Football at SMU for the next two years was literally nonexistent. The question arose as to whether SMU should restore football at all? In the end, the problem wasn't sports. It was ethics. As our ethics center benefactor and founder Cary Maguire once said to me, this wasn't limited to a couple of people. Somewhere along the line we had adopted a culture that enacted the premise that the only thing that matters is results. The decision was made to restore the program and, critically, to change the culture. Since then, we have had to learn how to talk about who we are again. It is has been slow but steady. What we know is that we should have been practicing our ethics as much as our athletic prowess.

Each university has its stories. They account for mistakes as well as lost opportunities. Yet at the heart of these narratives is a claim of what

22. See Milewski, "We are Penn State." See also Foley, "Penn State History."

could be—an umbrella idea that provides cohesiveness in an otherwise discordant community.

Conclusion

If we believe that ethics is indeed at the heart, *or soul*, of higher education, as we do, then there are several practices that we must adopt.

First, given that higher education admits a new class of young students each year, the process of addressing ethical issues is continual. There is never a time when the university does not need to be in the business of ethics education. Just as in childhood, lessons are rarely taught in a one-and-done episode. Lessons must be incessantly taught. They must be publicly reinforced. And the community needs to both know the established norms and reinforce them in the narratives that we tell and the spaces that we help to create.

Second, ethics must be modelled. From the residential hall director who oversees as student's conduct in university housing to advisors and professors, from the staff that serve students to the administration who leads them, and from the president to the board of trustees, no one is exempt. We must consider that students watch and model what they see. If their professors constantly remark that the only thing that counts is results, if the seminal lesson is that shortcuts are efficient, or if someone's power or prestige permits wink-and-nod leniency that others do not get, students will take note. The continual reinforcement of ethics must permeate the university as a whole and not simply focus on the students' academic experiences.

Third, the university must constantly help students see, verify, and interpret the data, events, and perspectives arising from conflicts so that they more wisely make decisions. Our perspective changes when we begin to assess the role of the university as an agent of moral reinforcement, and perhaps sometimes even change. We should remember that there are times when just looking at an event changes our interpretation of it. How do we see a vehicle manufacturer that cheats on emissions tests? How will we look at a company who sacrifices the health of thousands by raising the "fair market value" of a life-saving drug to such heights that patients cannot afford it?[23] How do we assess the impact companies, *or countries*, manipulating financial performance to influence reported earnings? It is

23. Bolman and Deal, *Reframing Organizations*.

naïve to believe that these catastrophic ethical lapses are the result of a few "bad actors." Rather, they are the result of a culture that prioritizes financial gain over the common good. Further, errors in judgment may not always be well-considered; they can be made unwittingly. Taking the time to evaluate policies and practices from an ethical lens is part of the responsible organization's charge.

Finally, we must create these sacred spaces of ethical inquiry across campus and especially in our classrooms. There has to be a place for reasoning together even if we arrive and differing conclusions. To do that requires the teaching clear argumentation, the testing of premises, and the evaluation of arguments in light of the public good. These are not new areas of study, rather they are time-tested elements that are a part of higher education. Perhaps they are even more important today than in any previous era. Argumentative reasoning and effective debate must be central to our ethical journey. Further, administrations must not only permit but encourage the rigorous debate required.

Ours is a laudable task and a challenging job. Yet either our ethics matter and require action or they just don't really matter at all. Founding Maguire Ethics director Bill May notes most poignantly, "A university does not fully discharge its duties to its students if it hands out knowledge—and the power that knowledge yields—without posing questions about its responsible uses." If we did that, and nothing more, ethics would indeed be proven to be at the heart of higher education.

8

The Founding of an Ethics Center

WILLIAM F. MAY

Preface

WHEN ACADEMICS WRITE ON the "conception" of something, you can be fairly sure that they have in mind its intellectual underpinnings. In large part this chapter will deal with just that for the Cary M. Maguire Center for Ethics and Public Responsibility at Southern Methodist University (SMU). But, at the outset, I want to recognize the "conception" of something in the sense of the indispensable agent at its birth. Cary M. Maguire, president of the Maguire Oil Company and a trustee of SMU, generously gave the funds to establish first the Maguire Chair in Ethics at the university in 1985 and later to found the Maguire Center in 1995. Yet again, in 2017, he pledged the splendid, enabling gift of $2 million to endow the directorship of the Center. Those three gifts by a determined man led to an institution at SMU that will outlast his life and mine.

I admire Mr. Maguire for those gifts, but I also want to express my own personal gratitude for a professional relationship that spans now more than three decades. Throughout, I have seen in Mr. Maguire, not just the agenda of a philanthropist, but a sustained and substantive interest in ethics. At the same time, however, he never sought to influence what I taught or wrote as the holder of the Maguire Chair or to shape the content of programs offered in my service as the first director of the Maguire Center for Ethics and Public Responsibility. He has shown a great respect for academic freedom. He fully honored the complexities of support and flourishing for a free university in a free society. My great respect and thanks to Cary Maguire for that.

Introduction

Clearly, the Center did not begin at SMU, like some orphan left on the university's doorstep. Before the Center's founding in 1995, the SMU Board of Trustees had already declared ethics to be one of its priorities for the 1990s. At an earlier defining moment in its history, the Master Plan of 1963, the university affirmed the formation of the citizen as one of its three defining goals. The mature citizen, I take it, is someone who has acquired the art of acting in concert with others for the common good. The goals of ethics and citizenship connect.

The provost at the time of the Center's founding, Ruth Morgan, gave just the right pre-natal name for this project in its vision statement, "The Center for Ethics and Public Responsibility." Following Aristotle, she wanted to bring together the two activities of ethics and politics. Ethics is the pursuit of the good; and politics, the pursuit of the common good. They are the two sides of the same coin in the formation of citizens and their leaders.

In shaping citizens, SMU believed then, and still believes now, that a university does not fully discharge its responsibility to its students and the community at large if it imparts knowledge (and the power which that knowledge eventually yields) without posing questions about its responsible uses.

The Corridors to Power

Traditional societies transmitted power largely on the basis of family and blood. Modern societies convey power chiefly through knowledge, a knowledge often acquired at a university. Through education, the young acquire substantial power in life as lawyers, doctors, accountants, engineers, business leaders, academics, religious leaders, politicians, media specialists, artists, labor leaders, and community organizers.

Yet, while professionals exercise great power and often enjoy the vast material privileges of a ruling class, they feel beleaguered. They do not see themselves as power-wielders. They feel marginal, insufficiently appreciated, suspect, harassed, often under siege. Patients, clients, and various publics respond to them ambivalently. The society grows restless with these knowledge-bearing rulers. Lay people contest professional authority. The doctor, from one day to the next, can plummet from hero to defendant in a malpractice suit. The lawyer's client does not know what to worry about the most, his opponent's case or his lawyer's fees. Basic professional services do not reach all people who need them. And even the successes of the professions, their very considerable successes (for example, medical technology) have generated moral quandaries which a purely technical education does not address.

Feeling marginal and beleaguered, professionals tend to obscure for themselves their duties as wielders of great power. Their obligations to the public and to the common good seem at best remote, peripheral, and occasional. They tend to focus on minimal rules to keep themselves out of trouble, while the larger issues of the common good and the problems that beset our common life disappear from the agenda.

This weakened sense of commitment to the public weal defects from the classical understanding of a vocation and a profession. Professionals moved a long way from Roscoe Pound's statement in 1953 that a profession refers to a group "pursuing a learned art as a common calling in the spirit of public service—no less a public service because it may be incidentally a means of a livelihood."

The University Setting for Professional Education

Universities played a major role in the development of knowledge-based power but they less consistently accepted responsibility for shaping its moral uses. From the seventeenth century forward, universities increasingly fostered the development of the sciences and their technological spin-offs and benefits. In the course of time, as society embraced the prodigal benefits of technology, the moral formation of its professional graduates seemed less one of its core tasks. Further, professionals flocked to the universities for their credentialing at the beginning of the twentieth century, just as positivists increasingly dominated the universities philosophically and made moral education in the academy seem illegitimate. The positivists established a sharp cleavage between facts and values. Facts are hard and objective; values are soft and spongey and subjective. We read them into things. Thus in the classroom, teachers should stick to the facts, just the facts. As Max Weber, the apologist for the modern positivist university, put it: If you want to be a teacher and a pedagogue, you must leave your values out in the cloakroom, along with your hat and coat before entering the class room.

This brand of objectivism in the university tended to produce an unabashed careerism in its graduates. The university can hand out a stock pile of knowledge that generates power but without questioning its uses. Historically, the word "professional" and the equally ancient term, "calling," had a moral and public ring to them that the word "career" does not. A career is a kind of self-driven vehicle, a car, as it were, that one drives into the public thoroughfares while heading toward one's own private destination. Courses in professional responsibility, when offered at all, tended to deal minimally with the rules of the road that will keep the practitioner out of trouble, not with the question of means and ends, goals and values in the larger setting of the common good.

Why does a student owe something to the common good? No student zigzagging his or her way through a modern university can think of himself or herself as self-made. A huge company of people at a university will have contributed to what students have become and the credentials they have acquired by their graduation. Teachers will have taught them; workers will have cared for campus buildings, mowed the lawns, run the kitchens, and cleaned up the bathrooms. Secretaries and staff members will keep the operation humming; and the vast research traditions of each of the disciplines will have set the table for that sharing. In addition to this investment of labor, institutions such as SMU will need and seek further support beyond the tuition fees generated by their students' education. Students are not self-created; in response to what they have received, they owe some expenditure of themselves on behalf of others and the common good. It would be strange for a university to hand out all that potential power and ordain a ruling class without posing questions about the ends to which those rulers direct their power.

The leadership of SMU believed that the move of the sciences and professions into the university is an incomplete project, to the degree that the university fails to attend to the moral education and public responsibilities of those whom it empowers. In establishing a Center for Ethics and Public Responsibility, SMU aspired to complete that project.

The Field of Ethics in the University

The task of studying ethics in a university center for ethics and public responsibility calls for developing what might be termed corrective vision. The metaphor of vision links ethics with some form of knowledge. It implies that ethics in the classroom should not seek to bend the will or manipulate feelings but to illuminate understanding. Moral insight supplies a type of corrective lens. It differs from the vision available to the senses or through the instruments of science. Moral reflection attempts at its best a knowledgeable re-visioning of the world that human practice presents. It does not merely scan the world as it is or prepare leaders for the professions as they are. It entails a thoughtful re-visioning of foundations and ends. Through this cognitive illumination, ethics serves, in some limited way, the human capacity for resolution and decision. It helps us to serve the worlds in which we work, not perfectly, but well.

While emphasizing the importance of "corrective vision" in teaching ethics, one must recognize that the moral life entails more than that. It also requires the willing heart. The apostle Paul confessed that he knew what he ought to do but also needed the resolution of will to do it. The old Methodist tradition referred to the need for the "heart strangely warmed." The stirring of the moral imagination can occur in courses in history and literature as well as philosophy and theology and also in service/study experiences that open students to a range of human need beyond the confines of their origins.

The Liberal Arts and Ethics

In several ways, the study of ethics helps carry forward the ancient purposes of a liberal education: the honing of critical intelligence, the cultivation of the civic self, and the formation of a good teacher (whether the student goes into the teaching profession or not). Ethics in the liberal arts distinguishes between two forms of intelligence, operational and critical. Operational intelligence tells one how to get from here to there. Critical intelligence asks whether the "there" is worth getting to. It poses what has been recently and incessantly called the questions of ends, goals, and values. It assumes that value questions are not merely a matter of private preference. Critical intelligence prepares us for making responsible appraisal and judgments in our common life together.

We keenly need such critical reflection not only in the humanities as we make disciplined and discriminate judgments as to worth and value in the spheres of art, literature, politics, economics, science religion, and philosophy, but also in the professions. What is the primary goal of medicine? The fight against death or the pursuit of health? The goal of the law? Order or justice? The goal of business? Maximizing profits or economic performance at a profit? What balances must be struck in engineering between increases in productivity and decreases in the destructiveness of industrial processes? What trade-offs, between liberty and equality, the local and the national, the individual and the communal, in our political life? What roles should religious and educational institutions and the media play in the formation of citizens? Responses to these questions about means and ends fatefully affect our understanding of the professions and civilization itself.

Second, the university, if it would serve more than the private aims of its students, must nurture what might be called the civic self. This duty trivializes if it means straining for relevance by ingratiating curricula units in civics or ethics into the latest headlines. Rather, it calls for connecting education throughout to critical inquiry. Ultimately, the nurturing of the civic self and the encouragement of critical inquiry are part of the same enterprise if value questions are not merely matters of private preference. To engage in critical inquiry is itself a social act that teases the mind out of the bottle of private preference and opens it out toward a community of inquirers. It makes a person publicly responsible for his or her judgments and decisions and assumes these judgments to be interpretable in civil discourse.

In a privileged moment, a teacher delights in seeing a sophomore take her first stammering steps out of the closet of private preference and into the public arena, as she begins to do more than express her likes and dislikes and argues for her judgments, and explains why this novel is important, why that play is trash. Or when, in a paper, she no longer invokes the technical language—the Morse code—the professor has taught her, but begins to run with her subject and teaches what she knows through her writing. Strictly speaking, we do not need to leave the classroom in order to go public. The classroom is already a public place; the library, a commonwealth of learning; and disputation within the humanities, a kind of parliament of the human mind.

In effect, the cultivation of the citizen overlaps with the third goal of the liberal arts—becoming a good teacher of what one knows, whether one goes into the teaching profession or not. A society such as ours requires leadership through the word. Professional schools have increasingly come to realize the importance of their graduates knowing how to teach what they know. As needed, doctors, lawyers, accountants, social workers, labor and business leaders, do not simply dispense technical services. The day of "doctor's orders" is over. A good doctor needs to explain those orders. Words are to a prescription what the preamble is to a constitution. They help make sense of the regimen. Without words, medicine is a kind of veterinary practice on men and women. Effective leaders of durable institutions in business, labor, religious, and political positions must lead, at least partly, by persuasion.

This sort of leadership looks to ancient Athens rather than to Sparta for its ideal. Sparta, a military society, depended upon leadership through command and obedience. It was essentially a taciturn society; it relied on the bark of command and the grunt of obedience. But the city of Athens created a political, rather than a military culture. It relied on *logos*, the word or, more precisely, on *rhetor*, the art of persuasion, to function as a society. The truly effective professional, citizen, and leader must learn how to teach, that is, how to persuade colleagues or clients to make good in common cause.

The Notion of *Public Responsibility*

The *public* to which the citizen, the professional or the political leader responds is not simply an amorphous, indeterminate public. The health of the public at large includes and depends upon the health and flourishing of specific publics within the public at large. The society depends upon the vigor and responsibility of such public institutions as hospitals, schools, voluntary communities, synagogues and churches, neighborhood associations, professional guilds, the media, and corporations. At the same time, such publics are more than interest groups within the society. The good of the society at large cannot long flourish if it merely consists of overlapping interest groups. Groups, solely defined by their interests, can underlap, as well as overlap, or exhaust themselves in profitless competition. The public at large depends on some determinate publics within its life that surely attend in part to their interests, but that also keep at least a wall-eye on the question of the common good.

The Idea of the Common Good

Some interest group theorists question the very possibility of invoking the ideal of the *Common Good*. The existence of contrary views of the good from society to society (and the challenge of counter instances to any particular claims within a society like ours) lead them to hope at best for shifting and partly overlapping and underlapping articulations of interest. Other theorists counter that a sense of the common good does in fact incipiently inform our life. It arises in part "from a deep common experience of the bad . . . Wanton cruelty, slavery, poverty, malnutrition, vulnerability and humiliation are bad without having a fully articulated unitary account of the good."[1] It may be difficult to articulate a unitary sense of the common good since the goods constituting the common good are plural in number and often competing. Nevertheless, it is possible to sketch out a working grid of multiple goods on which a society such as ours depends and which its members imperfectly serve.

The first good of a society is *belonging*, not only because belonging supplies the ticket to other goods, but because belonging is a good in itself. Additionally, a society and its members need a range of *fundamental goods crucial to survival*—food, clothing, shelter, safety, basic education, safety, and health care; and they need a set of *higher goods that permit members not merely to survive but to flourish*—art, culture, higher education, work, love, friendship, citizenship, honors, and play. While we can depend partly on the marketplace for generating and distributing many of these goods, some of the high goods (such as love, friendship, and honors) we cannot buy or sell without corrupting them; and other fundamental goods (such as food, clothing, shelter, health care, public safety, and education) are so basic to life that we cannot treat them exclusively as mere commodities. The marketplace may go a long way toward distributing basic goods. But a decent society must find ways, at an adequate level, to provide its members with access to the necessities; and a fully flourishing society encourages and supports the pursuit of the higher goods.

Since no expert or pundit can supply a society with a fixed hierarchical ordering of these goods, a society also needs the *goods of process*—the principles and procedures, appropriate civil rights, and rules—that can help the society reach fair decisions about priorities. It also needs leaders who, working within the constraints of these procedures, can reach wise decisions. Lawful procedures alone do not ensure equitable outcomes.

A sober footnote here. The diversity and vertical range of the competing goods that comprise the common good make politics inherently among the most difficult of professions. Each of the professions serves an important human good difficult to pursue. The politician differs from other professionals in that he or she purportedly serves not a particular good,

---

1. Galston, *Liberal Purposes*, 182.

such as health, education, and abundance, but the common good constituted by a medley of particular competing goods that need regularly to
be rebalanced and prioritized. (That is why from Aristotle forward, many
moralists saw a powerful connection between ethics and politics. Ethics
describes the fitting pursuit of the good; politics, the common good. They
form two sides of the same coin.) Regrettably, the entire world needs good
political decisions coming out of the United States, while Americans tend
to dismiss politics as a despised profession.

Finding Common Ground in the University

The liberal arts college in the nineteenth century, largely Protestant in origin and small town in its setting, found its common ground in a general
consensus on ends and goals that shaped its life. Reflecting this consensus,
the president of the college often taught a course in ethics for all graduating seniors. This arrangement may have produced courses badly taught
but it also offered an important symbol. *Ethics had not yet contracted into
a subspecialty in religious or philosophical studies; it served rather to crown
the student's education.*

Various factors contributed to the affirming of common ground. The
college owed its existence and support to a specific religious tradition.
Scripture supplied the institution with its uncontested canon. (Methodist
institutions, such as SMU, included Tradition and Reason, in addition to
Scripture, as part of their extended teaching authority.) In the course of
time, some of these colleges drifted from their specific religious origins, but
faculty members still sustained a sense of common ground. They had not
burrowed so deep into various areas of specialization as to lose their sense
of themselves as a *collegium.*

Further, although explicitly religious values lost their binding power to
unify all faculty members, the professoriate still informally agreed upon the
"greats," the *auctores,* an acquaintance with whom defined the educated person. These authors constituted a *quasi-religious sacred canopy* under whose
sheltering presence Western civilization would presumably continue to flourish. Education was a matter of traditioning the young; that is, handing on the
past, honored as a valued past on which to build. So went the ideal. (Roman
Catholic colleges and universities at the time maintained in their own way
a theological identity based on Scripture and Tradition and a philosophical
identity usually based on a Thomist account of Reason.)

In the twentieth century, a minority of Protestant colleges differed from the earlier ideal. They reacted against the certainties of science and the loosening of personal behavior—in favor of a biblical fundamentalism, which mimicked science with certainties of its own and extracted selectively from Scripture a code of behavior that would shield students from the impurities of the wider culture. In this case, the university of religious origin tended to define itself increasingly as an *embattled fortress* rather than a sacred canopy. Similarly, some Catholic institutions, turned inward and saw themselves as a sacred shelter in an alien environment.

The Twentieth Century Positivist University, as noted, did not agree substantively on a set of values to supply the institution with its common ground. Instead, teachers (and derivatively their students) needed to shed their values before entering the classroom in the disinterested pursuit of the truth. Further, the great size and scope of the university undercut the very notion of having a common ground. Robert Hutchins, President of the University of Chicago, after surveying the vast array of disciplines in the liberal arts college and the proliferation of financially independent professional schools, with "every tub sitting on its own bottom," wryly observed that the heating plant supplied the modern university with its only unifying ground.

Nevertheless universities, although cut off from a defining tradition in origin, usually found their common ground by offering themselves essentially as a *training ground*. The university prepared students operationally for a rich array of careers that would open the doors to a more promising future than available to parents on family farms or to immigrant parents from Europe. As a training ground, education no longer oriented to a valued past, but equipped students for a better future.

However, enthusiasm about the university as a training ground dampened for students in the 1960s and 1970s who viewed the future with increasing anxiety and distaste. The national goal of victory over Communism stalled in Vietnam and male graduates faced the uneasy prospect of being drafted. The reward of a good job for decent grades famously earned student contempt for dangling before graduates nothing grander than a "plastic" promised land. Students in the counterculture movement of the sixties and seventies oriented neither to past tradition nor future prospects. They pronounced themselves the "Now Generation." Their parents, whether conservative or liberal, worried that their flower children would become the cut flower children.

The moment of the "Now Generation" quickly passed with the end of the draft. Students and the universities in varying ways disaggregated. Some students followed the idealistic path into the Peace Corp or Americorp; others held back from the corporate market place and started small shops and businesses around their universities. The vast majority revisited conventional careers in large scale organizations. Still others invented new ways or areas for professional practice—doctors in preventive medicine, pain management, and palliative care; lawyers in family law and public law; engineers at work on environmental issues; or technicians inventing (and investors devising business models for) the new ways of communicating in the century ahead.

Clearly, the universities could no longer define themselves for the century ahead as shaped by a single religious tradition (in the manner of the old liberal arts college). Their students, their faculty members, service workers, patrons, and funders, intermixed from diverse backgrounds. Indeed, the religious tradition of origin itself contained often competing strands. Adding to this mix, faculty members, no longer under the thrall of positivism, could not claim the commanding heights of a traditionless transmission of knowledge that students might convert as they please into careers. How then, might one credibly conceive of common ground for a university that was neither an isolated shelter/fortress, nor a relatively seamless sacred canopy, nor simply a training ground, few questions asked, for high-flyers in the professions?

The proposal for the Cary M. Maguire Center for Ethics and Public Responsibility at SMU grew out of the conviction that *the old word "campus"* supplied the starting point for describing the common ground today both for the university and the work of the field of ethics. The Latin root for "campus" refers literally to an open field, a flat place, the traditional site where rival armies encamped and fought. The university provides one of those precious open spaces in a civilization where the deep cultural conflicts within a civilization can surface. Just as the legal system permits us to substitute a contest in the courts for a brawl in the streets, in order that justice be done; so the campus allows us to marshal arguments, rather than troupes, in order that our common life in the truth may be pursued and prized.

Engaging one another within and across traditions within a university—attentively, civilly, and thoughtfully—entails that a given tradition in the university, including even the founding tradition, does not simply perpetuate itself umbilically. A tradition needs to grow beyond its umbilical cord.

Contest and dialogue with other traditions opens up a cognitive distance from origins that allows receivers of a tradition to discover itself afresh. The aliveness of a tradition depends upon this re-visiting.

This openness to the presence of alternative traditions (in an institution such as SMU, shaped by the specifics of its Methodist heritage) differs from a grudging accommodation to diversity, as though diversity in a pluralistic world is an unwanted complexity one is simply stuck with. This openness also asks for more than a thin politeness, in which one side in an argument waits out the speech from the other side before launching into a speech of its own. Vital exchanges on a campus sometimes call for what the philosopher Charles Taylor once called a readiness to honor excellences alien to one's own. Indeed, the lively presence of other traditions in its life can help a campus recover features of its own heritage which may lie obscured in the shadows, if left unchallenged.

The French philosopher Paul Ricoeur once recognized this dialectics at work in his book *The Symbolism of Evil*. The book described four contending "Myths" for the understanding evil, but affirmed one myth, the "Adamic Myth," as superior to the other three. But Ricoeur did not close his book with the dismissal of the other three accounts of evil. Indeed, he argued, their continuing presence in the conversation on the subject of evil helped keep alive features of the Adamic sensibility itself which might otherwise be obscured.[2]

A Center Rather than an Institute

The choice of the word *center* rather than *institute* to describe what SMU hoped to achieve was deliberate in this proposal. Universities have usually established institutes to draw financial support to research in particular departments and schools. That goal is certainly worthy. However, institutes often have limited relations either to the rest of the university or to the region of which the university is a part. Institutes often subsist in a university like a benign tumor. They are *in* but not *of* the university (or the region). We did not want an ethics institute that would be only incidentally in SMU and accidentally in Dallas. Instead, we envisaged a center that would serve as a resource and meeting ground across liberal arts and professional schools to explore ethical issues both within the university and in the still broader setting of the Metroplex and a concern for the common good.

2. Ricoeur, *Symbolism of Evil.*

In discharging this broader mission, the Center would invite a variety of conversation partners to the table—professional, disciplinary, and non-academic. Thus the term "public responsibility" would define not only the field of inquiry but also the kind of writing and speaking, which the Center hoped to encourage as it provided a public forum for participants that transcended the traditional academic enclaves.

The Context for Speaking and Writing in an Ethics Center

The trajectory for most writing and speaking in the entire educational system points *upward*. Students secure their ascent by impressing their teachers, who single them out with good grades that send them up into the colleges and eventually into graduate and professional schools where at length a select few students gain approval to write a thesis for a dissertation committee of three. Thereafter, most academics, with job in hand, continue to write *up* for the gatekeepers in their disciplines. Their publishing record provides academics with the leverage of job offers elsewhere, which may be useful in improving their position where they are or, alternatively, in "writing their way out" of their current location to a more prestigious institution. This orientation of academic writing results in very important quality control over research; however, it also often offers limited access to the public.

The conventional alternative to writing *up* is to write *down*, either by turning out the potboiler of a textbook for beginners or by placing some pieces in popular magazines. Such writing may be financially rewarding, but it too often disconnects the task of writing from discovery. One simply packages what one already knows. One learns nothing new through the packaging. We hoped to encourage a third vector for both teaching and writing, as we designed the grants and programs at the Maguire Center for Ethics and Public Responsibility, writing neither *up* nor *down*, but *out* to a larger audience of intelligent inquirers. (Machiavelli, it should be remembered, wrote his essay on *The Prince*, not for the gatekeepers in political science, but for princes.) In recovering this social vector for communication that opens out to a wider audience, our model was the Renaissance tradition of the essay rather than the twentieth century convention of the article.

We hoped to engage academics in the important task of teaching through their writing. Such teaching would also, by virtue of its social matrix, lead the writer to view his or her subject with the eyes of the stranger, that is, the non-specialist. We hoped that the grant activities of the Center would provide faculty members with opportunities to discover their subject anew as they shared their work with a diverse and perceptive reading audience. At their best the social acts of teaching (and teaching though one's writing) are heuristic acts in which one's thought is not merely packaged but discovered.

From Concept to Founding

With some of these thoughts in mind about the animating vision for a Center, Tom Mayo, a professor of law and scholar of legal ethics, and I had meetings with Provost Ruth Morgan and Acting President James Kirby to discuss the basic mission, the staff structure of the Center under the authority of the Provost, and the creation of a faculty advisory committee (including representatives from UT Southwestern Medical School) and the recruitment of a council of scholars and leaders in the region to help the Center serve Dallas and the North Texas area. William S. Babcock, the provost *ad interim,* successor to Provost Ruth Morgan, eventually drafted the specifics on these issues, including a statement of objectives and anticipated activities sponsored by the Center. A copy of this formal Charter, signed by President R. Gerald Turner and William S. Babcock Provost *ad interim,* on 15 June 1995, is included as an appendix to this chapter.[3]

However, the Center would also need a donor if the above musings on the role of ethics in a university and the not-yet written charter for a center at SMU were to move from a series of file folders and come alive. SMU Trustees Robert Dedman and Ray Hunt arranged for me to make a presentation to Trustee Cary M. Maguire for his support. At the meeting, I explained the proposal (mercifully in much less detail than contained in this essay), and recall Mr. Dedman asking me whether such a center, serving the college and the professionals schools, would be unique. I said, No, it was not unique, but it was distinctive. (At the time, Case/Western Reserve and the Cleveland Clinic connected the schools of law and medicine on the subject of ethics. Further, the Hastings Center, though not university based, had begun to expand beyond bioethics to include work groups spanning several professions.) I wondered whether my admission that we could not claim the proposal to be absolutely unique helped or hurt its prospects at SMU.

3. See Appendix A.

Shortly, however, after this meeting with the three trustees, Professor Tom Mayo of the Law School and I received an invitation to meet Mr. Maguire for lunch at the Petroleum Club in Dallas. There we soon realized that Mr. Maguire was going to do something more significant than pay for our vichyssoise. Mr. Maguire asked me whether I would give the time to serve the proposed center as its founding director if he pledged the funds to bring the center into being. Commitments were made.

Programs Developed by the Maguire Ethics Center in Its Founding Years

Course Development Grants

This program would enable faculty members to develop courses (or curricular units in already established courses) to explore ethical issues in their discipline or in their field of professional practice. We instituted the important custom of entrance and exit interviews with winners of these grants on which occasions they would share their maturing projects with colleagues, both within and beyond their disciplines. Such meetings would allow for substantive intellectual exchanges between faculty members. In my experience, such discussions rarely occur at meetings of faculty curriculum committees. They had an important task of monitoring the quality of courses offered, but they tended to function managerially to protect established courses and programs from overlapping and crowding one another. We wanted these grants not simply to be private awards, but to stimulate collegial exchanges about ethics across disciplinary lines. Cecil O'Neal, associate professor and former chair of the theater department, served as the first Maguire Teaching Fellow, 1996 and 1997, to work on a new course on the topic of the "Artist as Citizen." The artist as suspect citizen had vexed thinkers, writers, and artists, most famously from Plato and forward. In the last twenty or so years, the ethics center has provided funding for the creation of nearly sixty courses in ethics.

Grants under a Maguire Scholars Program in Ethics

This program would enable appropriate faculty members, *following* a sabbatical or summer leave, to offer a public lecture or a seminar. On this occasion, they would share their research with colleagues both within and beyond the traditional boundaries of their discipline. Too often faculty members write only for specialists in their own discipline located elsewhere. They are not part of a *collegium* in their own institution. Both the community and the individual faculty member suffer from this privatization of scholarship. The community is deprived of the fruits of a colleague's ideas and research. Meanwhile the grant winner suffers from the lack of what every writer and teacher needs; that is, some deadlines to inspire the completion of their work. Most faculty members fantasize about how great the summer or the sabbatical would be without students around, but during the leave they discover a drop in their metabolic rate without the amphetamine kick of the classroom. They don't get the project accomplished. Meanwhile, back in the class room again in the fall, they are engrossed in the weekly round. The project gets buried into private worry time and delays. The exact format for this event, whether a public lecture, a seminar, or an occasional paper published by the Center would depend on the skills of the researcher. Professor James Hopkins of the history department delivered the first public lecture under the Maguire Scholar Program on the subject of "The Public Intellectual." Professor Hopkins recognized that the academy, perhaps intimidated by disciplinary boundaries, tended to produce few free ranging public intellectuals, such as Reinhold Niebuhr and Daniel Moynihan. The Center named two Maguire Scholars for the following year. Associate Professor of English Michael Holahan, who presented a remarkable paper in a seminar on "A Soft Voice and the Construction of Character in King Lear." It traced the movement from the tempestuous, childish king in the first act to the old man of gentle, childlike voice at the play's end. Associate Professor of English Bonnie Wheeler lectured in Spring 1998 on "Pilgrimage and the Desire for Meaning." Her subject grew out of an interdisciplinary, team-taught course on the medieval practice of pilgrimage.

Summer Grants for Students

These grants would enable students to work for service organizations that might expand their horizons morally beyond the conventional demands of their career track. Middle class students come out of a kind of ghetto—not economically impoverished but of limited experience. Education means literally being "led out" into a broader horizon than the parameters of one's origins. Stirring the moral imagination through such experience can be an important first step in reflection on ethics. In framing this program of grants and commitments for the summer, we instituted entry and exit sessions at which winning students met together and reported on their prospective proposals and reported again at the end of the summer on their experiences to their reassembled colleagues. Their applications included letters from the sponsoring non-profit agencies. Their reports at the end of the summer, in addition to the benefits of the shared experience, helped us vet agencies for future use. A few students received outright research and writing grants; and, indeed, one student's project eventually yielded a chapter in a book published by the Center on the Ethics of Philanthropy. Today, the Center has awarded summer fellowship stipends totaling over $400,000 to 181 SMU students for public service and research in ethics. The fellowship program has supported volunteers in more than 150 agencies across eighteen states, twenty-five countries, and five continents.[4]

Student Participation in the "Ethics Bowl"

Dick Mason, the second director of the Center, recruited and helped prepare students for participation in this national competition sponsored by the Association for Professional and Applied Ethics. As eventual leaders, students would need those analytical and forensic skills bearing on ethics that will help move their moral reflections from private complaint into the public arena.

Sponsoring Public Conferences and Lectures

In discharging its mission to the North Texas Region, as well as the SMU community, the Center established a series of public conferences and lectures, some of them producing occasional papers and books and, in other cases, chapters published in yet other settings. The high quality of these occasions would lead to the creation of a constituency of townspeople who looked forward to the Center's conferences. The Center also joined forces with the recently established annual meeting in Dallas of members of the "three learned professions"—law, medicine, and ministry. The guest speaker for each of these events might come from elsewhere, but the heart of the occasion was the meeting across professional boundaries

4. See "Public Service Fellowships."

of doctors, lawyers and religious leaders from Dallas and vicinity. The Center also collaborated on other projects with UT Southwestern Medical School, Austin College, North Texas State University, Texas Christian University, and the University of Dallas.

In planning public events, we felt it important to avoid a trap into which some universities fall. While we welcomed distinguished guests to speak at our public conferences, we would not spend our limited resources on bringing celebrities to campus. Colleges and universities often set aside occasions such as commencement addresses and distinguished lecture series to feature "names," usually media names, to rescue the institution from the obscurity that shrouds it. Universities are particularly prone thereby to squander their opportunities to identify voices, including local voices, with something to say to the community. They reveal their own marginality when they obeisantly hand over teaching occasions to media-crowned figures.

The J. Erik Jonsson Ethics Award

In carrying through further on the idea that Dallas should honor its own, the Center also established the J. Erik Jonsson Ethics Award given annually. It included a medallion inscribed with the American Revolutionary phrase, "public virtue," a phrase that fairly described Mayor Jonsson's service to the city and his self-expenditure on behalf of Dallas and the region. Ethics is not simply taught, it is taught by example. We undertook responsibility for identifying exemplary figures in the region. While that was the original intention of the Award, it also provided a public occasion for outside board members of the Center to meet many others in the Metroplex who became interested in the Center's work. Curtis W. Meadows Jr. was the first recipient of the now annual J. Erik Jonsson Ethics Award.

Organization Structure of the Ethics Center

This brief round-up of activities at the Maguire Center calls for comments about the structure and personnel at the time of its founding that helped make the lift-off for the Center doable. Both the Provost and Trustee Cary Maguire at the time felt that the Center director ought to report to the provost and not simply to one of the university's liberal arts departments or professional schools. The reasons at that time for this design were twofold, intellectual and strategic. As taught at most universities, ethics usually divided into the disciplines of philosophy and religious studies, and then, if taught further at all, entirely within the separate professional schools theology, medicine, business, law, engineering, and journalism. While such specialization was valuable, the intellectual loss could be considerable. Without a wide-angle lens, university might tend to neglect the family resemblances across the professions and the ways in which the professions variously answer to turbulences and drives deep in the human spirit. Locating the center in the provost's office would also support explorations of moral issues across conventional boundaries in literature, the arts, history, and the social and natural sciences.

Reporting to the provost also seemed important at that time for a further strategic reason. SMU as a university did not predate the twentieth century. It lacked the deep funding for the liberal arts of the kind available to institutions with roots in the liberal arts colleges of the eighteenth and nineteenth centuries. Enthusiastic alumni at a twentieth-century university such as SMU might be inclined to fund largely their professional schools and their respective dean's offices, not the College of Arts and Sciences or the provost's office. At an earlier time, SMU President Willis M. Tate recognized the need for central discretionary funds in realizing the Master Plan for SMU (1963). Later, the provost's office helped support such undertakings as the capstone courses for undergraduates and faculty seminars across disciplinary and professional boundaries that helped maintain SMU as an intellectual universe, even while enrollments and financial support expanded at the periphery.

In the 1990s, I sensed some agreement on this matter of reporting to the provost. It led to the charter's design that called for both a broadly based faculty advisory committee and a regional council of scholars and leaders, both appointed by the Provost. The task of recruiting the faculty advisory committee fell to me; the second, more largely to the center's benefactor, Mr. Maguire. The faculty committee included 18 original members, eight from Dedam College of Humanities and Sciences and the rest from the university's professional schools (business, engineering, arts). The regional council of scholars and leaders grew across the first three years of the Maguire Center's operation. In effect, Mr. Maguire helped fund the center not simply with the pledge of money but also by recruiting leaders from the metropolitan area for the Council.

The original design also called for a director of the center, an associate director, and an administrative assistant, each on part-time assignment to the work of the center. At the Center, Ms. Rivers helped mount all public events and managed the transmission of information concerning applications for student and faculty grants. Professors Charles Curran, Richard Mason, Tom Mayo and, as needed, all other of the eighteen members of the faculty advisory committee gave generously of their thought and time to the undertaking. As the Center grew, so did the demand for resources, and the once part-time positions were expanded to full-time positions including the newly endowed director position and a full-time associate director. Professor Rita Kirk, the current William F. May Endowed Director, *which humbles me*, is not as conventionally trained in the academic study of ethics as her predecessors, but she has striking organizational gifts and a grasp of seismic changes in modern media that have major consequences for the study of ethics as it bears on politics and education. This new direction has provided a necessary "lift" to the focus of ethics at SMU and allowed the Center to expand its message to new audiences.

I have mentioned in the course of this essay my gratitude to Charlie Curran and Tom Mayo who were helpful conversational partners in the course of developing the proposal for the Maguire Center. They are creative people in their own right. Had they been charged with designing the Center, they might have brought other thoughts and themes and priorities to bear on its formation. The shortfall in the foregoing belongs to me, not to them.

Cary M. Maguire supported my work in the Maguire Chair of Ethics from 1985 to 2001 and my service as founding director of the Maguire Center for Ethics and Public Responsibility from 1995 to 1998. Both settings made possible my work on four books and the revision of a fifth. Other of my essays and lectures, delivered elsewhere, grew out of the milieu which the ethics center helped engender.

However, this particular essay grows out of the cultural soil of SMU itself. I went there when I was fifty-eight years old. The university allowed me to study and actually teach in a range of professional schools. Bill Bridge let me sit in on his course on legal ethics. Later I taught collaboratively a course at the law school. Dick Mason and I co-taught a course in business ethics at the Cox School of Business. When the journalist Phil Seib departed from SMU for another institution, his department let me teach in his absence a semester course on ethics and journalism. Periodically, I also revisited my origins by teaching undergraduates in the Department of Religious Studies and the Perkins School of Theology. Regular teaching in "capstone courses" let me think through my convictions on the subject of environmental ethics, eventually published under the title, "The Engineer: From Nature's Adversary to Nature's Advocate?" As all teachers know, the act of teaching and teaching through one's writing permits one to remain a student. This final assignment of writing about the Center grew out of my own continuing education.

9

Higher Education and Public Moral Discourse

Robin Lovin

Introduction

POLITICS TODAY IS IN a state of crisis. Public discussions are sharply polarized between ideologies at the extremes of the political spectrum, even though the margin of victory in elections is measured in a few percentage points. Legislative gridlock and conflict between branches of government prevents the solution of problems, and in any case, there is little practical consideration of what those policy solutions might be. What is most surprising, perhaps, is that this is all happening in the world's oldest and most experienced democracies, beginning with the United States. That is disturbing, but it should suggest that this is not a problem that can be blamed a single leader, on one or both political parties, or on something peculiar to contemporary culture. The origins of the problem lie far back in history, sometimes in the very strengths that have allowed democracy to develop and endure. The deterioration of public discourse is a reminder that political goals almost always have unintended consequences when pursued over a long period of time. Part of the task of maintaining a society is identifying those historical ironies before they become truly tragic and working to correct them in ways that are mindful that these corrections, too, will have their own unintended consequences.[1]

---

1. Niebuhr, *Irony of American History*.

Education has played an important role in this history, not only in modern democracies, but from the beginnings of Western culture. The connection begins before there were institutions of higher education and continues down to contemporary research universities. This history means that higher education has both considerable responsibility for the ironic dysfunctions in our public discourse and important possibilities for contributing to its renewal. We will explore those possibilities in this essay in four steps: First, a very brief history of education and ethics, focusing on the importance of practical reason and moral discernment; second, a discussion of modern public discourse, showing how the distinction between desire and discernment has been obscured; third, an analysis of how this change in public discourse affects the public role of the university; and finally, a reassertion of the university's ethical task that clarifies the mission of higher education and offers resources for the renewal of public moral discourse.

I. Education and Ethics

The connection between education and ethics goes back to the beginning of the Western tradition and affects the shape of higher education everywhere in the world today. Aristotle explained the task of reason, especially what he called "practical reason" as a process of discernment.[2] Among the great many things that we might desire to have, or to do, or to be, we must discern which are truly good, and we must arrange these many different goods in such a way that they work together in a sustained way that gives us the best life.[3] This is difficult enough, given that many things that we desire turn out not to be good for us, and developing the virtues that enable us to pursue the ones that really are good takes a lot of practice. But discerning the good immediately leads a person into what we today would call public questions, because many goods have to be agreed on and kept in being by a whole community of citizens. That is why Aristotle said that the human being is a *zōon pōlitikon*, a "political animal."[4] What he meant is simply that human beings are meant to live in a *polis*, a city; but this implies that practical reasoning has to go on in groups, as well as individually. Ethics leads us into politics, and discernment of what is really good, as distinct from

2. Aristotle, *Politics and the Constitution of Athens*, 114–16.
3. Aristotle, *Politics and the Constitution of Athens*, 3–22.
4. Aristotle, *Politics and the Constitution of Athens*, 13–14.

what is desired, is something on which we have to agree. There are many important goods that we will not be able to create or keep in being without that public discussion.

Of course, what Aristotle had in mind when he thought of politics involved a very limited group of people: men, of course, and free male citizens, at that. Slaves and women were excluded, and so were foreigners who happened to be in the city for whatever reason. (Aristotle himself was in Athens to teach his theories about ethics and politics. Ironically, he was not a citizen.) What distinguished the people who were involved in politics was that they had time to engage in moral discernment. They had leisure (*scholē*), while those who kept the herds, tended the crops, and took care of the household (*oikos*) had their work cut out for them. So, those who had time for discernment also had a need for it. Unlike those who did the work, their choices had not already made. Much of the subsequent history of ethics and education can be glimpsed in the etymological observation that Aristotle's leisure is also the starting point for our words "school," "scholar," and "'scholastic," while the household realm of necessity became "economics."

The social context changed considerably over the centuries after Aristotle, and for some time after the end of the Roman Empire in western Europe, public moral discourse largely disappeared. Scholarship became the work of the church, especially the monasteries, and religious vocation replaced the citizen's leisure. By the late twelfth century, however, a more complex, urban society was emerging, knit together by extended networks of trade and information, and the tasks of education and ethics had become too large for the monastery and the church alone. Universities developed from groups of a few scholars living together in Paris, Bologna, Oxford, and other European cities into organizations with curriculums, faculties, students, libraries, and degrees.[5] It was at this point that European scholars rediscovered Aristotle through Arabic sources, and Thomas Aquinas gave Aristotle's understanding of practical reason in the curriculum.[6] It was also at this point that the university's role in public discourse begins to take a shape that we might still recognize today. But these medieval and early modern scholars were not like leisured citizens of Aristotle's Athens. The increasing complexity of European life demanded discernment that extended into what had been the realm of economic necessity, and law and medicine

5. Janin, *University in Medieval Life.*
6. Rubenstein, *Aristotle's Children.*

joined theology as a systematic body of knowledge taught by university faculties. Vocation was no longer confined to the monastery, and life in the city was no longer identified with leisure. Vocation meant a place in the work of an emerging modern society where human goods—material, political, cultural, and religious—required specialized knowledge in addition to practical reason to recognize, create, and maintain them.

Later, with the rise of democracy in the eighteenth century, the public purposes of higher education became explicit alongside vocational goals. Education was important because it prepared students to make discerning choices among the goods available to them in politics and legislation, as well as in personal and professional life. This was true especially in nineteenth century America, where the capstone of a liberal arts education was often a course in moral philosophy, taught to students in their final year by the president of their college.[7] Moral philosophy was the practical application of what they had learned in all their other classes in history, logic, literature, or science. But "practical" did not primarily mean that it was useful. It drew in this context on the enduring Aristotelian idea of practical reason, which discerns genuine goods among the many possible objects of desire. This liberal education was to be the foundation for a lifetime vocation. Before the middle of the nineteenth century, higher education in America was principally the task of colleges, and professional education was conducted through various forms that were more like apprenticeships. There were few universities with graduate and professional programs of a sort we might recognize today.

Perhaps this aspiration to a liberal education prepared its students for democratic moral discourse was always more an elite ideal than a social reality. American public discourse in the early nineteenth century could take sophisticated philosophical forms in the right publications, but on the stump, in popular newspapers, and even in the halls of Congress, it could be a rough, partisan affair that would startle even used to today's vitriolic tweetstorms.[8] In any case, the moral philosophy courses largely disappeared after the Civil War, and what took their place was a different kind of university and a different political philosophy that largely shapes our public discourse today.

7. Smith, *Professors & Public Ethics*.
8. Wilentz, *Rise of American Democracy*.

II. The Transformation of Public Discourse

The years after the Civil War saw enormous growth in the American economy and major transformations in American society. What Mark Twain called "the Gilded Age" ushered in a new collaboration between the leaders of new industries and the political "bosses" of the new, urban manufacturing centers with their poor and largely uneducated working populations. If the ideal of a liberally educated citizenry making political choices after reasoned public discussion was no more than a distant vision before the Civil War, it had even less connection to political reality by the end of the nineteenth century.[9]

Changes also took place in higher education, where specialized knowledge was increasingly tied to scientific research and technical innovations. The economic connection began already during the Civil War, with provisions for the creation of new land-grant colleges and universities under the Morrill Act of 1862. Then the ideal of the research university took hold at Harvard, Johns Hopkins, and the University of Chicago and spread soon after to other schools, including ambitious colleges that transformed themselves into universities, especially for the benefit of cities and regions that had not had these centers of research and professional education in the past.[10] Specialization transformed the image of higher education from a liberal arts college in a small town in the Midwest to the urban ivory tower, preferably with a laboratory in the tower.

One effect of this was to encourage and reward academic specialists who were cautious about making claims that extended beyond the range of their research. If colleges were no longer producing liberal arts graduates who saw themselves prepared for the tasks of citizenship, the new corps of research scholars was professionally uninterested in moral discernment. Claims about the human good fell uncomfortably beyond the range of scientific demonstration.

One further development was required to set aside the Aristotelian approach to practical reason that had shaped the disciplines of earlier universities and produce the forms of public discourse that are familiar to us today. Economics was transformed from the realm of necessity to the realm of choice. As discernment of the good faded from public consideration, the marketplace provided a forum for the satisfaction of desire. By

9. White, *Republic for Which It Stands.*
10. Menand, *Rise of the Research University.*

154

the end of the nineteenth century, many came to believe that deliberating about what goods politics should pursue was less efficient than asking people to decide what they want by declaring the price they are willing to pay for it. Markets provide a self-regulating social mechanism that reduces the number of political questions to a minimum and virtually eliminates the need for moral discernment. Within broad limits established by law, goods of whatever sort can be exchanged for money, which can be used in turn to procure whatever other sort of goods you prefer. This applies not only to goods for personal use, like food and clothing, but also to the goods produced by social institutions. How society values M.B.A. degrees or symphony concerts can be measured by the combination of tuition payments and tax revenues, of ticket sales and annual fund contributions that are required to maintain the institutional arrangements that produce these goods. The language of the market thus provides general terms in which a wide range of desires can be satisfied without having to adjudicate between them, while other values that are not so easily quantified or exchanged tend to drop out of public discussion.

This was perhaps not quite the intention of Adam Smith, whose economic theories introduced the ideas of free markets and specialized division of labor. Smith linked market mechanisms to a quite specific good that he called "opulence," by which he meant a level of wealth that so far exceeds the requirements of survival that it leaves people with real choices about how to use it.[11] Since Smith was a professor of moral philosophy before he turned his attention to the workings of the market, he perhaps expected that once opulence had been achieved, it would be discussed with the same moral vocabulary that had long been used for such purposes. He might even have expected a new era of moral discernment in politics, since wealthy nations have many more choices to make collectively than poor ones do. It was probably not his intention that efficiency and productivity, which characterize the good functioning of markets, should become the general terms in which political choices would be discussed. But that was the result.

Discernment of the good, which had first been seen as the essence of politics, now appears to be unnecessary. Economic expertise spares us the hard task of comparing goods that are really different and deciding what combination of them is best for our wellbeing as a community. The price of so much education can now be directly compared with the price of so much

---

11. Smith, *Wealth of Nations*, 115.

health care, culture and nature each finds its place within the constraints of a budget, and even future possibilities can be compared to present ones on the basis of appropriately discounted costs. Especially insofar as the market promises a general increase in wealth over time, inability to satisfy all desires simultaneously requires only the postponement of some goods, not a real choice between them. The sequence of satisfactions can easily be decided by comparing the sum total of wealth available under each of the alternatives, future possibilities again appropriately discounted. Given the right information, the economic specialist can point policy in the right direction without contentious public arguments.

It is just at this point, when we can compare the vision of public moral discourse anticipated by market economics and academic specialization with the reality of our contemporary politics, that the irony of history becomes apparent. Politics, which seemed to be on its way to becoming a managerial task, appears now to have become unmanageable. Parties and leaders seem unable to offer clear policies, while the public increasingly believe that politics is irrelevant to their wellbeing and disconnected from the things that really matter to them. People will mobilize quickly to counter immediate threats to their material interests, but the big questions about the future—the environment, the provision of social services, and the needs of future generations—cannot even be framed for political deliberation.[12]

This narrowing of the range of public discussion does not mean that people will stop making choices between goods. It means that they will only discuss those choices in private forums, with people who already agree with them. People begin to think of moral ideas as beliefs that need to be cultivated among like-minded people, rather than criteria for discernment that can be applied in public discourse. People conclude that their values are unimportant, or even incomprehensible, to their neighbors. The result is polarization, and those who aspire to political leadership are driven to define the extremes, not toward the center. Leaders must convince what political analysts now call their "base" that they uphold values and virtues that belong uniquely to them, and that these values and virtues are under threat from anonymous, indifferent, or even hostile forces that do not share them.

So instead of providing a neutral forum for making public choices, politics conducted in the language of the market succumbs to gridlock. Nothing can be done because nothing can really be discussed. There is no moral vocabulary on which the parties might draw, and suspicion of others'

12. Sandel, *What Money Can't Buy*, 13–15.

motives renders compromise impossible. Ultimately, this polarization threatens democracy itself, because it tempts us to think that unresolved political questions result from the stubbornness of our opponents. That fatal deterioration of politics is not the inevitable outcome of the mechanisms of the market. Political dysfunctions are the result of many factors, including some that are strictly local and contingent. But the problems of politics as we now experience them are not a momentary aberration. They reflect an understanding of ethics and politics that has developed for over a century. The duration of the problem, as well as its urgency, requires us to think about other ways of relating discernment and desires.

III. Institutions, Vocations, and Ethics

The public role of the university needs reconsideration in light of these developments. It might seem that a simple solution is to reassert the importance of ethics or moral philosophy at all levels in a university education. Graduates who have some exposure to important ways of thinking about human goods and some practice in addressing the basic questions of ethics that arise in personal, professional, and public life may be less likely to settle for appeals that speak only to immediate needs and wants. They should acquire skills in critical thinking that leave them unsatisfied with conspiracy theories and stereotypes that explain away the moral claims that underlie protests and reform movements. Above all, they should be able to distinguish between narrow concern for self and the larger values represented in the social groups of which they are a part, from the family and local community right up through the nation and global humanity. Loyalties are easily confused, and ideals of civic spirit, patriotism, and environmentalism are always bent in particular directions by self-interest. But a healthy skepticism in these matters must not be confused with moral cynicism. Unless some practice in making and responding to moral arguments is part of a comprehensive education, public moral discourse decays for want of adequate preparation among the public who must participate.

Still, more ethics courses cannot be the whole answer to the problems of public life today. Universities are actually quite well supplied with such courses, not only in philosophy and religion departments, but across a range of fields where research methods, fiduciary responsibilities, and potential conflicts of interest require ethical awareness along with technical expertise. Especially in graduate and professional education, programs in engineering and business have increasingly followed the established models in legal and medical education in requiring ethics education for graduation and professional certification. But it is worth noting that this expansion of ethics courses and programs has taken place concurrently with the decline of public discourse that has been described above. There appears to be little relationship between the focus on ethics within disciplines and degree programs and the discussions that go on among a wider public.

One reason for this disconnect may be that universities have adapted rather easily to the shift from discernment to desires that characterizes most forms of public communication today. As the number of educational options multiplies and competition for students and financial support increases, universities spend less time articulating—to the public or to themselves—the purposes of higher education and more time becoming "market-smart." It becomes urgent to demonstrate that the university offers good value for money, measured primarily in terms of skills and connections that will produce a good job upon graduation and also reassure employers, donors, or legislators that its graduates will solve the problems they have in mind when they support its services.[13] Ethics education thus tends also to be explained and structured in terms of the skills it is supposed to provide. Especially in graduate and professional education, these skills focus largely on the obligation to provide effective, competent services, untainted by conflicts of interest or personal prejudices. That is extremely important. Given the complexity of the transactions in which a lawyer, physician, financial adviser, architect, or engineer becomes involved today, knowing how to meet these obligations from the beginning has to be an important part of professional preparation. But it means that larger questions like the availability of medical care, the regulation of markets, and the environmental impacts of infrastructure and urban development go largely undiscussed in courses on professional ethics. The ethical provider of services navigates largely within the social framework provided for getting those services to those want them, and for the "market-smart" university, that is chiefly what ethics education is about. Larger social questions seem best left to professional associations or activist groups within the professions.

This tendency to narrow moral discourse to specialized questions of professional practice has produced a reaction within in many universities, especially among faculty in the humanities, who fear that basic questions about virtue and human good that have historically been the concern of

13. Zemsky et al., *Remaking the American University*.

their disciplines will disappear from the education of future generations, whose moral lives will focus on important and difficult, but nonetheless highly specialized, questions of professional practice.[14] The dystopian vision emerges of an elite of scrupulously correct service providers, who do their work strictly according to professional code, but who are unable to raise coherent questions about their place in a larger society.

The concern is appropriate, but it must not take the form of a polarizing reaction against "market-smarts" in the university. A university, like a computer chip maker, a symphony orchestra, or a manufacturer of chocolates or plastic trash containers, survives in part by demonstrating that it produces something that other people find immediately to be delightful, or useful, or both. The satisfaction of needs and desires, usually mediated through some sort of market, is basic to what keeps most organizations going, whether they produce a tangible product or provide a service, whether they are non-profit or for profit, and whether the people who work in them are employees or volunteers. However high-minded the aspirations, the goods are not purely for the contemplation of those who create them, and each product or performance must satisfy some needs and meet some expectations among those to whom it is offered. We have tended to forget that in higher education, and we are understandably being called up short and asked to account for ourselves in those terms. The difficult task is to do that in a way that does not sacrifice persuasion to satisfaction, because a university's contribution to public moral discourse depends both on its aspirations and its effectiveness.

These competing forces drive the strategic plans of today's universities and often define the conflicts between faculties and educational philosophies within them. We might summarize it as a tension between aspiration and effectiveness or analogize it to the dialectic between discernment and desires in political argument, but the complex relationships at work require more detailed discussion, which can be developed around an analytical distinction between *organizations* and *institutions*.

An *organization*, in this somewhat artificial terminology, is a concrete collection of persons, facilities, resources, and events organized for purposes that are generally shared among the participants and generally recognized among the public. Smith's Hardware Store is an organization, and so is Middletown Community Hospital. So is General Motors. So, too, are the New York Philharmonic, the Pleasant Valley Community

---

14. Nussbaum, *Not for Profit.*

Chorus, Thomas Jefferson Middle School, and Harvard University. You get the idea: An organization, large or small, belongs to a larger genus of organizations and draws on the particular resources it has available to create and maintain a rather specific list of goods and services by which it sustain itself as an organization, either because people want to consume these things or because the participants themselves value the opportunity to create them. A Ford pickup, a performance of a Beethoven symphony, an MBA degree, and the weekly meetings of a bridge club are all things that organizations produce.

An *institution*, for present purposes, is more abstract. It can be most easily identified with the set of normative ideas that people have in mind, with varying degrees of precision, when they set up an organization. An institution is the more general set of goals and values that gives shape to the life of an organization. It helps people in organizations explain, to themselves and to others, what they are trying to do. It gives them terms in which to evaluate what they have done and stake their claims on the resources they need to continue doing it. If an organization consists of specific persons, places, and things, an institution holds together reference points that transcend generations and geography. If the Ford Motor Company is an organization, the manufacturing industry, encompassing all those organizations that deploy raw materials and workers to produce a finished product, is an institution. The New York Philharmonic is an organization. Classical musicianship is an institution. An institution is not structured by an organizational chart, but by goods and virtues. It is in that sense the expression of a history of moral discernment.

The goods include both the final goods that define the institution's purposes and the instrumental goods that must be created and maintained to reach the more ultimate goals. The virtues summarize the human dispositions, habits, and disciplines that experience has shown essential to achieving the goods. Middletown Community Hospital is an organization that has a CEO and a director of nursing services. The hospital as an institution has goals of healing and care, and it will devote considerable attention to discerning what is best to do when both of those goals cannot be achieved for a particular patient. It cultivates virtues of accuracy and teamwork and seeks dispositions toward patience and compassion in pursuit of its goals.

There is a level of abstraction in this account of institutions that may suggest that they exist primarily in the minds of those who participate in them, or perhaps only in the mind of one who writes about them. But institutions are not simply reducible to a set of ideas. They take form concretely in the organizations where these ideas are remembered, debated, put into practice, and revised in light of experience. In that sense, institutions really exist as part of the social world around us. We can trace their histories, chart their development and differentiation into new forms, and occasionally note their disappearance.

As we saw at the very beginning of this essay, it is these institutions that set the modern world apart from the forms of social organization that preceded it. In contrast to Aristotle, who divided society into a realm of necessity organized by the *oikos* and a *polis* where citizens had leisure to discern what the human good is and organize themselves to pursue it, ours is a world of vocations or callings, in which we discover our good by participation in institutions that create and maintain different human goods and instill in us the virtues that this participation requires. Vocation is a discourse of call and response, different both from the economic necessity that compelled Aristotle's household and the leisured pursuit of happiness that he took to be a good life. We learn what that good is in the context of an institution, rather than simply by individual experimentation. At the same time, we enter into a vocation by discernment, rather than because we must. Some institutions, especially those of the modern state, do have coercive power.[15] But we arrive at a vocation when the institution and the particular organization on which we have settled persuades that its goods are also our own. We may try a number of vocations before we are persuaded that this is the right one.

It is also important not to identify vocation too closely with a role in the market economy. We may find our true vocation in a different institution from the one in which we happen to earn our livelihood. Indeed, many people have multiple vocations simultaneously: the physician on the hospital ethics committee may also be a volunteer at the local food pantry and serve on the board of the art museum. Vocation is not determined by what it requires in time or contributes to income. It rests on a judgment that this institution and its goods are important human goods, so that our way of living makes a case to others that these goods are real and deserve to be supported in ways that will make them endure and keep them available to others.

This is different from being contented or not with the particular organization that mediates a vocation to us. Vocation is not about whether I

15. Weber, "Politics as a Vocation."

like my job. Nor are its satisfactions like the satisfactions provided by the various consumer choices that modern citizens make in the limited leisure that their vocations allow. I may truly enjoy a symphony concert and believe that it is a good thing these performances continue, but this is not the same as the vocation of the conductor, the concertmaster, or the bassoonist in back among the woodwinds. This distinction is important for understanding the role of institutions in public moral discourse. Businesses, local religious organizations, and even individual colleges and universities come and go as they succeed or fail in meeting the needs of those who try their services. The corporation, the universal church, or the university live by claiming social space for the distinctive human goods that they create and maintain. The social world we have in modern times is thus a product both of desire and discernment, of market forces and moral choice.

IV. Public Moral Discourse and the Vocation of the University

The loss of the distinction between discernment and desire in contemporary public discourse confuses the distinction between organization and institution. Institutions attempt, often successfully, to maintain a strong moral discourse around their central purposes and the virtues expected of the people who participate in them. We see this, as noted earlier, in the growth of ethics courses as a part of professional education. Reflection on professional ethics has expanded well beyond law and medicine, where these discussions began, and codes of ethics have been devised for a whole range of businesses, professional services, voluntary organizations, and community groups that need to tell the public what they can expect and, perhaps even more important, need to spell out for organizations working within the institutional framework what they must do to remain there in good standing. The Association for Practical and Professional Ethics now counts more than fifty different subspecialty areas within its field of concern.[16] As public expectations have become more ambiguous and conflicted, more energy is devoted to explicit statements of institutional values.

Because they locate their organizations and the goods they seek within a wider social framework, the ethics of institutions constitute an important resource for public moral discourse. This is not because the institutional purposes automatically adjust to one another like prices is a market. The

16. Association for Practical and Professional Ethics, "Mission, Vision, and Bylaws."

institutions of a society, viewed as a whole, do not constitute a seamless social ethics. In fact, they highlight important issues that need to be addressed. Neighborhood purposes will conflict with business values around land use, housing availability, and public spaces. The integrity of a national political community will be in tension with institutions that in one way or another require a global frame of reference, whether that frame is a global market or a global community of faith. Institutions devoted to tradition and historic preservation may clash with institutions whose organizations seek a more inclusive society, raising questions about which statues belong in the public square. None of these disagreements are easily resolved, but if those involved recognize the real goods at stake on both sides, the possibility for discernment emerges, instead of an escalation of desires.

The present state of public discourse, however, encourages the opposite result. For reasons noted earlier in this essay, even organizations that understand very well the institutional goods they represent feel constrained to enter the public discourse with the message that they are well-positioned to satisfy particular desires. If you want a better home, a cheaper product, a new career, or a cost-effective place to make your tax-deductible charitable contributions, our organization provides it. In this discourse, in fact, the more we can distinguish ourselves in the competition with other organizations that share our institutional purposes, the better.

This tension between organization and institution is especially evident in disputes within contemporary universities over the way they present themselves to the public. The academic achievements of the faculty may be neglected when a message about athletic facilities, placement rates, and extracurricular options is targeted to the desires of prospective students. Seemingly endless lists of rankings allow a school to claim first place in value for money, or eleventh in its region in academics, or a spot among the top one hundred in the nation according to some set of criteria. Discernment about the purposes of higher education is rarely prominent among the messages.

Criticisms of this marketing effort, however, largely miss the point. Universities are particularly aware of their institutional context, because they have a long history in the work of moral discernment, and because they encompass disciplines that study that history and make a vocation of clarifying moral arguments. This does not mean that universities should ignore what their prospective students, graduates, and surrounding communities desire and try to live exclusively on the high plane of institutional purposes. The university can make a case for moral discernment and claim the resources it needs to keep this history and knowledge available. But the individual university must also hope that it can make discernment something to be desired.

The point is that universities have unusual resources for reintroducing discernment into public discourse, as well as a particular interest in doing so. Here, we will consider just three things that the universities bring to this task: 1) a broad understanding of human goods, 2) a detailed knowledge of the moral discourses in actually use at all levels of society, and 3) a similarly detailed analysis of moral discernment itself, across different ways of reasoning in a range of disciplines.

The broad understanding of human goods is evident at once in the long list of disciplines in the departmental directory of a major university. Each field of study, indeed each faculty position, represents a story of contributions to human flourishing, distractions and dead-ends to be avoided, and promising lines of inquiry yet to be explored. Contrast this with a business that offers a particular range of products, even a very large one, or with an arts institution that focuses on excellence in one type of music or drama, and the reasons why new possibilities emerge especially from the university become clear. History is a record of innovations and failures, and over time the institutional infrastructures that give rise to human goods become known, along with the demands these institutions make on the wider society in order that those goods may continue. Anthropology, sociology, and other social sciences provide a comparative understanding of possible social arrangements and the forces that make for conflict or social cohesion. Literature explores the same questions with different methods and a different angle of vision. Psychology and medicine integrate knowledge of human flourishing from the conceptual to the physiological level. Even basic chemistry, biology, and physics contribute to the understanding of life as a planetary phenomenon, with the limits and possibilities of an Anthropocene in which humans remake their evolutionary environment.[17]

The university's contribution to public moral discernment thus begins with a range of resources that should make our vision broad while keeping our hopes realistic, allowing us to measure possibilities on timelines that range from immediate legislative initiatives to institutional transformations that may take decades, and building in allowances for the ironic reversals that always happen, even when we try to anticipate them. In this way, the

17. Grinspoon, *Earth in Human Hands*.

disciplines of the university nudge us from various directions toward an ethics of responsibility,[18] in which we make use of the full range of possibilities available to us without committing ourselves to choices that outrun our ability to see the consequences. Of course, every real university includes a fair number of narrowminded, overconfident, or even reckless individuals. The culture of a university may actually encourage such vices. But the multiplicity of viewpoints has a restraining effect, and the institutional values of open debate and freedom of inquiry should provide the public with sufficient resources for informed and responsible discernment, as well as models for how it is done.

Not all of the models are found within the university, however, nor are they as visible as the discernment that goes on in learned journals, on the op-ed pages of the newspapers of record, or symposia at the Council on Foreign Affairs. Much of the moral discernment that shapes a society goes on at a very local level, measured against goods and virtues that have become important in the life of a particular neighborhood, shape the mission of a congregation, or activate the networks of communication and action that respond to emergencies, defend community interests, and come to the aid of neighbors in distress. These, too, are public discourses. Unlike the polarized networks on social media, they generally understand themselves as open discussions, subject to questions from the margins and accessible to new voices. Their public may be quite small, but they see themselves in relation to other similar groups that occupy adjoining spaces or face similar problems in other places. What we know about the cumulative effect of these groups comes largely through the work of university programs in sociology, social work, religious studies, social psychology, and similar disciplines whose students and faculty become participant observers, interns, and consultants in these communities.[19] Precisely because we usually think of public discourse as amplified through mass media, we suppose that all of it has the uniform appearance and limited moral vocabulary that mass media impose. Engagement with local publics provides the level of detail we need to understand all of the institutions that shape society, even when the units of organization within those institutions are quite small and sometime little noticed beyond their immediate neighborhoods.

These engagements are most informative when they are genuine collaborations, rather than observations from a distance. Obtaining insight

18. Weber, "Politics as a Vocation."
19. Nyden, *Public Sociology.*

into moral discernment at a local level can, of course, raise its own ethical issues. There is a danger that local community partners will be exploited, even inadvertently, to advance a research agenda. Empathy and enthusiasm can stretch the protocols for objective investigation, and in any case most research proposals will need to be cleared by standards for research with human subjects. Placements in unfamiliar neighborhoods or potential conflict situations raise questions about the risks to which students and faculty may be exposed. But the cumulative experience of a university that undertakes these engagements can be focused in ongoing centers for community research and learning that can shape future research and establish trust that may be transferable to future researchers. Without these efforts which the institutional infrastructure of a university supports, our knowledge of public moral discourse would be limited to the discussions that know how to attract public attention or happen to stumble into it.

Finally, of course, there are those scholars in philosophy, law, theology, and other disciplines whose work focuses specifically on the ways that moral reasoning is done. The institutional and vocational differentiation that developed within the modern university did not, at least initially, imply the fragmentation of ethics. The classical figures, especially Plato and the Stoics, joined by Aristotle rediscovered through Arabic sources, continued to provide the patterns of moral reasoning. Over time, this practical reason took on some of the characteristics of the different contexts in which it was deployed, so theologians speak of "moral theology"[20] and lawyers speak of "legal reason."[21] Nevertheless, concepts of good, duty, and virtue and ideas about how these are related to one another still provide recognizable frameworks for moral reasoning in very different personal, professional and social contexts. The formulation of ethical theories that transcend the problems to which they are applied is an important academic contribution to the understanding of public moral discourse, and we will no doubt continue to need at regular intervals summary works like C. D. Broad's *Five Types of Ethical Theory*[22] or William Frankena's typology of deontological and teleological norms.[23] These provide a vocabulary that facilitates comparison of substantive ethical positions across disciplines, traditions, and cultures.

20. Curran, *Development of Moral Theology*.
21. Weinreb, *Legal Reason*.
22. Broad, *Five Types of Ethical Theory*.
23. Frankena, *Ethics*.

Even more important for public moral discourse are analyses that trace the implications of institutional norms for social policy on a wider scale. We have noted the tendency in professional ethics to resolve ethical issues within the framework of existing institutional structures and avoid challenging the political, economic, and social systems within which professions are practiced. Clearly, however, the claim that a vocation should be lived in a way that produces specific human goods leads on to questions about how a society is organized to make use of those goods and distribute them. Medical ethics has given careful attention to decisions at the end of life between therapies that aim at cure and palliative care. How those choices become part of practice has implications for the design of medical facilities, the social expectations placed on families and caregivers, and the benefits required from public and private insurance programs. The growth among educational institutions of post-secondary schools as gateways to a wide range of careers has implications for how these opportunities should be funded, distributed, and evaluated. Raising these questions is part of the vocation of medicine or education, precisely because the goods these institutions provide cannot be maintained without societal attention to the answers. More developed reflection on the links between the ethics of professional practice and social ethics should be part of what the university contributes to public moral discourse.

Conclusion

The connections between ethics and education go back to the beginning of the Western tradition, and the university as an institution has played an important role in shaping public moral discourse through the differentiated vocations and specialized professions that began in the first European universities and have continued to develop right down to the present. The suspicion, misinformation, and polarization that characterize politics today pose a challenge to the university to renew this contribution to public discourse and to rethink its public responsibilities, just where these connections have the longest history and the most complex relationships.

Some aspects of this history have become problematic. The isolation of professional ethics from social ethics and the isolation of professions and disciplines from one another within the university need particularly to be questioned. Nevertheless, the central element in the university's vocation endures. Its task is to carry on critical, knowledgeable, and open discernment of human goods and to identify the virtues that are necessary for these goods to be created and maintained. In the process, universities will provide many useful services and marketable skills for the places where they are located and the students who attend them. But the task of discernment is more basic to the mission of the university than the satisfaction of desires, and the public and its discourse will be best served by universities that build that priority into their own organizations.

Appendix A

Charter

The Cary M. Maguire Center for Ethics and Public Responsibility

Southern Methodist University

I. Mission Statement

THE BOARD OF TRUSTEES and the leaders of Southern Methodist University have declared ethics to be one of its priorities for the 90s. At an earlier defining moment in its history, the Master Plan of 1963, the University affirmed the formation of the citizen as one of its three educational goals. The University believes that it has not fully discharged its responsibility to its students and to the community at large if it imparts knowledge (and the power which that knowledge eventually yields) without posing questions about its responsible uses.

In keeping with this heritage and its stated mission, Southern Methodist University has sought and secured an endowment of two and a half million dollars from a member of the Board of Trustees, Cary M. Maguire, to establish the Cary M. Maguire Center for Ethics and Public Responsibility.

As an integral part of SMU, the Maguire Center will encourage, augment, and focus scholarship and teaching on Ethics at the University, not only in its professional schools, but pervasively throughout the undergraduate and graduate programs alike through curriculum development, interdisciplinary seminars and research support. As a part of Dallas and the North Texas Region, the Maguire Center will sponsor colloquia and publications with the expectation that leaders in the Dallas community and the wider society will find the Maguire Center to be a place to share their views on moral issues and where questions can be posed and answers pursued in partnership with the University community.

II. Positions

At its inception, the Maguire Center will be staffed by a Director, an Associate Director (permanent part-time) and an Administrative Assistant (permanent part-time).

A. The Director. The Provost will appoint the Director of the Center with the benefit of the advice of a Search Committee that includes the holders of the Scurlock and Maguire Chairs and such other faculty members as the Provost designates to insure a broad representation from the University community. The Search Committee will seek to recommend as Director a person who commands the intellectual respect of the faculty, is grounded in the field of ethics within the setting of at least one discipline or profession, and is interested in dialogue across disciplinary and professional lines. The person should possess the requisite leadership and administrative skills and be sufficiently public-spirited to invest the necessary time, energy and imagination on behalf of the Center's support and programming.

The appointment will be made for a period up to, but not exceeding, three years. The Director of the Maguire Center will make an annual report, retrospective and prospective, to the Provost, to the Center's Faculty Advisory Board, and to the donors supporting the Center's work. The Provost will appoint and authorize a Review Committee to conduct a comprehensive review of the Center and the Director's work, well in advance of the appointment/re-appointment of the Director. This Review Committee will be composed of a representative body such as the Search Committee.

The duties of the Director as specified by the Provost *ad interim* in the appointment of the first Director of the Maguire Center, read as follows: "Your duties as Director will include the initiation and oversight of the Center's program of activities as listed in the Statement of Objectives for the Maguire Center, and, as Director, you will work with an Advisory Board of senior SMU faculty members, to be appointed by this office, which will assist you in setting priorities and in carrying out the program of the Center." —William S. Babcock, Provost *ad interim*, May 17, 1995.

B. The Associate Director will be appointed by the Director. Ideally, the credentials of the Associate Director should include a degree in one profession, with some formal background in the field of ethics. In addition to these formal credentials, the Associate Director must have the personal and intellectual stature to be able to deal credibly and successfully with faculty members and community leaders. The Associate Director will make some substantive decisions collaboratively with the Director of the Maguire Center and many implemental decisions on his or her own, assisted in the latter by an Administrative Assistant and such other workers as the Maguire Center may from time to time require and who, along with the Administrative Assistant, will report to the Associate Director.

III. The Faculty Advisory Committee

The Provost of the University will appoint an Advisory Board of senior SMU faculty members (with the initial addition of two faculty members from The University of Texas Southwestern Medical Center) with whom the Director will work and who will assist the Director in setting priorities and in carrying out the program of the Maguire Center. As specific activities of the Center may change in the course of time, membership on the Advisory Committee will be set for limited periods of time and subject to renewal at the Provost's discretion.

IV. The Council of Scholars and Leaders

In its efforts to serve the Dallas community and the North Texas Region and to build enduring alliances with other institutions, academic and non-academic, tbe Director will, over a two-year period, recruit persons to be appointed by the Provost to a Council of Scholars and Leaders. This Council will include not only academicians and other professionals but other leaders whose voices should be heard at the table as the Maguire Center focuses on questions concerning the common good.

V. Statement of Objectives and Activities

Subject to available resources and perceived needs, the Center will undertake projects in the spirit of those envisaged at its inception. They include:

A. Organize continuing seminars, colloquia, workshops in the Dallas area, featuring SMU scholars and visiting lecturers. These programs will address topics of national import in such a way as to attract and interest scholars in related fields, yet speak to the concerns of Dallas and the general populace. It is anticipated that the Center will sponsor in its first year an Inaugural Event featuring an academic speaker of high regard and a speaker widely known to the public. In subsequent years, the Center will sponsor an annual symposium addressing a topic of public interest and importance.

B. Support the editing and publishing of papers and books that grow out of the work of the Center and that meet its standards of interest to the public. It is anticipated that several speakers from the Inaugural event and seminars in the first year and from symposia and seminars in subsequent years will submit papers for publication. Up to three publications per year are planned depending on the publishable quality of the submissions and the availability of funding.

C. Support faculty research and establish faculty seminars that cut across disciplinary, professional, racial/cultural and gender lines. The directors for these seminars will be drawn from the faculty and, in some instances, the seminars will provide faculty members returning from a sabbatical leave with an opportunity to share the results of their research with colleagues. The Center will offer one SMU Faculty Research Seminar in each of the first two years and increase to two per year in the third year.

D. Begin SMU Faculty Teaching Seminars so as to support efforts to: (a) strengthen teaching in values in the semester-long "Capstone" courses which all graduating seniors at SMU are required to take; (b) develop the ethics component in core interdisciplinary courses required of underclass students; (c) encourage faculty members to launch new undergraduate courses bearing on ethics and public responsibility; and (d) strengthen the work in professional responsibility at each of SMU's professional schools. The first Teaching Seminar will begin in the second year of operation.

E. Conduct meetings of Scholars and Leaders of the Council which will always include some substantive discussion of a moral problem or issue.

F. Build and strengthen library holdings in ethics at SMU (available to scholars in the region) including, but not limited to, on-line data services and electronic media.

G. Award grants to SMU graduate and professional students pursuing theoretical and clinical issues in ethics that bear on their chosen fields and provide summer stipends for gifted undergraduates working on topics germane to the Center. These awards will begin after the third year, allowing for a core of faculty sponsors to be developed.

R. Gerald Turner, President   Date
Southern Methodist University

William S. Babcock   Date
Provost *ad interim*

Bibliography

"2018 Edelman Trust Barometer Global Report." https://www.edelman.com/sites/g/files/ aatuss191/files/2018-10/2018_Edelman_Trust_Barometer_Global_Report_FEB. pdf.

Ahern, N. R., et al. "Risky Behaviors and Social Networking Sites: How Is YouTube Influencing Our Youth?" *Journal of Psychosocial Nursing and Mental Health Service* 53.10 (2015) 20–29.

Allen, Joseph L. "Politics as a Calling." Cary M. Maguire Center for Ethics and Public Responsibility, Occasional Paper No. 17, Southern Methodist University, 1998. https://www.smu.edu/-/media/Site/Provost/Ethics/pdfs/99214-AllenTextFA. pdf?la=en.

Allinson, Robert. *Global Disasters: Inquiries into Management Ethics*. New York: Prentice Hall, 1993.

American Bar Association. "The Lawyers of Watergate." *American Bar Association Journal.* http://www.abajournal.com/gallery/Watergate/589.

———. *Model Rules of Professional Conduct*. American Bar Association. June 11, 2019. https://www.americanbar.org/groups/professional_responsibility/publications/ model_rules_of_professional_conduct.

American Medical Association. "Code of Medical Ethics Overview." https://www.ama-assn.org/delivering-care/ethics/code-medical-ethics-overview.

Aristotle. *Nicomachean Ethics*. Edited by Roger Crisp. New York: Cambridge University Press, 2000.

———. *The Politics and the Constitution of Athens*. Edited by Stephen Everson. New York: Cambridge University Press, 1996.

Association for Practical and Professional Ethics. "Mission, Vision, and Bylaws." https:// appe-ethics.org/mission-and-activities/.

The Association of Theological Schools. "The Commission on Accrediting." https://www. ats.edu/uploads/resources/institutional-data/annual-data-tables/2019-2020%20 Annual%20Data%20Tables.pdf.

Auden, W. H. "The Art of Healing (In Memorium David Protech, M.D.)." In *On Doctoring: Stories, Poems, Essays*, edited by Richard Reynolds and John Stone, 126–28. 3rd ed. New York: Simon & Schuster, 2001.

Bankowski, Zenon, and Maksymilian del Mar, eds. *Moral Imagination and the Legal Life: Beyond Text in Legal Education*. Surrey: Ashgate, 2013.

Berg, Paul. "Meetings that Changed the World: Asilomar 1975: DNA Modification Secured." *Nature* 455 (2008) 290–91.

Bidwell, Allie. "More Students Earning STEM Degrees, Report Shows." *U.S. News and World Report*, January 27, 2015. https://www.usnews.com/news/articles/2015/01/27/more-students-earning-degrees-in-stem-fields-report-shows.

Birden, Hudson, et al. "Teaching Professionalism in Medical Education: A Best Evidence Medical Education (BEME) Systematic Review. BEME Guide No. 25." *Medical Teacher* 35.7 (2013) e1252–66. https://www.tandfonline.com/doi/full/10.3109/0142159X.2013.789132.

Bolman, Lee G., and Terrance E. Deal. *Reframing Organizations: Artistry, Choice, and Leadership.* 6th ed. Hoboken, NJ: Jossey-Bass, 2017.

Bostrom, Nick. *Superintelligence: Paths, Dangers, Strategies.* Oxford: Oxford University Press, 2016.

Brauer, David G., and Kristi J. Ferguson. "The Integrated Curriculum in Medical Education: AMEE Guide No. 96." *Medical Teacher* 37.4 (2015) 312–22.

Broad, C. D. *Five Types of Ethical Theory.* New York: Harcourt Brace, 1930.

Brooks, Arthur. "Our Culture of Contempt." *New York Times*, March 2, 2019.

Brooks, Lucy, and Dominic Bell. "Teaching, Learning and Assessment of Medical Ethics at the UK Medical Schools." *Journal of Medical Ethics* 43.9 (2017) 606–12.

Brooks, Peter, and Paul Gewirtz. *Law's Stories: Narrative and Rhetoric in the Law.* New Haven: Yale University Press, 1996.

Brown, Brené. *Dare to Lead: Brave Work, Tough Conversations, Whole Hearts.* New York: Random House, 2018.

Brynjolfsson, Erik, and Andrew McAfee. *The Second Machine Age: Work, Progress, and Prosperity in a Time of Brilliant Technologies.* New York: Norton, 2016.

Buchanan, Allen. *Better than Human: The Promise and Perils of Biomedical Enhancement.* New York: Oxford University Press, 2017.

Callahan, Daniel. *The Roots of Bioethics: Health, Progress, Technology, Death.* New York: Oxford University Press, 2012.

Camp, Mary E., and John Z. Sadler. "Moral Distress in Medical Student Reflective Writing." *AJOB Empirical Bioethics* 10.1 (2019) 70–78.

Campbell, Alastair V., et al. "How Can We Know That Ethics Education Produces Ethical Doctors?" *Medical Teacher* 29.5 (2007) 431–36.

Campbell, Ted A. "'The Wesleyan Quadrilateral': A Modern Methodist Myth." In *Doctrine and Theology in the United Methodist Church*, edited by Thomas G. Langford, 154–61. Nashville: Kingswood, 1991.

Carrese, Joseph A., et al. "The Essential Role of Medical Ethics Education in Achieving Professionalism: The Romanell Report." *Academic Medicine: Journal of the Association of American Medical Colleges* 90.6 (2015) 744–52.

Carver, Raymond. *All of Us: The Collected Poems.* New York: Knopf, 1998.

Cavanaugh, William. *The Myth of Religious Violence.* Oxford: Oxford University Press, 2009.

Chin, Jacqueline J. L., et al. "Evaluating the Effects of an Integrated Medical Ethics Curriculum on First-Year Students." *Annals of the Academy of Medicine, Singapore* 40.1 (2011) 4–18.

Chiu, Priscilla P. L., et al. "Experience of Moral Distress among Pediatric Surgery Trainees." *Journal of Pediatric Surgery* 43.6 (2008) 986–93.

Chopra, Deepak, et al. "Did God Discover the God Particle?" *San Francisco Gate,* July 13, 2012. http://www.sfgate.com/columnists/chopra/article/Did-God-discover-the-God-particle-3705245.php.

Chung, Eun-Kyung, et al. "The Effect of Team-Based Learning in Medical Ethics Education." *Medical Teacher* 31.11 (2009) 1013–17.

Coase, Ronald. "The Nature of the Firm." *Economica* 4.16 (1937) 386–405.

Cohen, Mitchell J. M., et al. "Identity Transformation in Medical Students." *The American Journal of Psychoanalysis* 69.1 (2009) 43–52.

Collins, Billy. "Introduction to Poetry." In *Sailing Alone Around the Room,* 16–17. New York: Random House, 2001.

Colt, Henri, et al., eds. *The Picture of Health: Medical Ethics and the Movies.* New York: Oxford University Press, 2011.

Cone, James H. *Black Theology and Black Power.* New York: Seabury, 1969.

————. *A Black Theology of Liberation.* Philadelphia: Lippincott, 1970.

Covert, Ed, and Angela Orebaugh. "Ethical Challenges of the Internet of Things." *The Cybersecurity Source,* January 29, 2014. https://www.scmagazine.com/home/opinions/ethical-challenges-of-the-internet-of-things/.

Cruess, Richard L. "Teaching Professionalism: Theory, Principles, and Practices." *Clinical Orthopaedics and Related Research* 449 (2006) 177–85.

Curran, Charles. *The Development of Moral Theology: Five Strands.* Washington, DC: Georgetown University Press, 2013.

De George, Richard. *Business Ethics.* 5th ed. Upper Saddle River, NJ: Prentice Hall, 1999.

Department of Health, Education and Welfare. "The Belmont Report." https://www.hhs.gov/ohrp/sites/default/files/the-belmont-report-508c_FINAL.pdf.

Doudna, Jennifer, and Samuel Sternberg. *A Crack in Creation.* Boston: Houghton Mifflin Harcourt, 2017.

Doukas, David J., et al. "Perspective: Medical Education in Medical Ethics and Humanities as the Foundation for Developing Medical Professionalism." *Academic Medicine: Journal of the Association of American Medical Colleges* 87.3 (2012) 334–41.

Doukas, David J., et al. "Transforming Educational Accountability in Medical Ethics and Humanities Education toward Professionalism." *Academic Medicine: Journal of the Association of American Medical Colleges* 90.6 (2015) 738–43.

DuBois, James M., and Jill Burkemper. "Ethics Education in U.S. Medical Schools: A Study of Syllabi." *Academic Medicine: Journal of the Association of American Medical Colleges* 77.5 (2002) 432–37.

Eckles, Rachael E., et al. "Medical Ethics Education: Where Are We? Where Should We Be Going? A Review." *Academic Medicine: Journal of the Association of American Medical Colleges* 80.12 (2005) 1143–52.

"Editorial: 'God Particle' Searchers Still Need a Little Faith." *The Republican,* July 4, 2012. https://www.masslive.com/opinion/2012/07/editorial_god_particle_searche.html.

Edson, Margaret. *Wit.* New York: Faber and Faber, 1999.

Ehmke, Rachel. "How Using Social Media Affects Teenagers." *Child Mind Institute.* https://childmind.org/article/how-using-social-media-affects-teenagers.

Evans, John H. *The History and Future of Bioethics.* New York: Oxford University Press, 2012.

Ferrey, Tom. "NCAA's Once-Rabid Watchdog Loses its Bite." *ESPN Go,* November 28, 2002. http://static.espn.go.com/ncf/s/2001/1126/1284940.html.

Feudtner, C., et al. "Do Clinical Clerks Suffer Ethical Erosion? Students' Perceptions of Their Ethical Environment and Personal Development." *Academic Medicine: Journal of the Association of American Medical Colleges* 69.8 (1994) 670–79.

Foley, Anna. "Penn State History Lessons: We Are Penn State." *Onward State*, September 11, 2015. http://onwardstate.com/2015/09/11/penn-state-history-lessons-we-are-penn-state/.

Ford, John C. "The Morality of Obliteration Bombing." *Theological Studies* 5.3 (1944) 261–309.

Fox, E., et al. "Medical Ethics Education: Past, Present, and Future." *Academic Medicine: Journal of the Association of American Medical Colleges* 70.9 (1995) 761–69.

Frankena, William. *Ethics*. Englewood Cliffs, NJ: Prentice-Hall, 1963.

Freeman, Edward. *Strategic Management: A Stakeholder Approach*. Boston: Pitman, 1984.

Friedman, Thomas L. *Thank You for Being Late: An Optimist's Guide to Thriving in the Age of Accelerations*. New York: Farrar, Straus & Giroux, 2016.

Galston, William A. *Liberal Purposes: Goods, Virtues, and Diversity in the Liberal State*. Cambridge: Cambridge University Press, 1991.

Gaufberg, Elizabeth, et al. "In Pursuit of Educational Integrity: Professional Identity Formation in the Harvard Medical School Cambridge Integrated Clerkship." *Perspectives in Biology and Medicine* 60.2 (2017) 258–74.

Gaufberg, Elizabeth H., et al. "The Hidden Curriculum: What Can We Learn from Third-Year Medical Student Narrative Reflections?" *Academic Medicine: Journal of the Association of American Medical Colleges* 85.11 (2010) 1709–16.

Giberson, Karl. "God and the God Particle." *Huffington Post*, July 9, 2012. https://www.huffingtonpost.com/karl-giberson-phd/god-and-the-god-particle_b_1655942.html.

Goldie, John. "Review of Ethics Curricula in Undergraduate Medical Education." *Medical Education* 34.2 (2000) 108–19.

Goldie, John, et al. "The Impact of Three Years' Ethics Teaching, in an Integrated Medical Curriculum, on Students' Proposed Behavior on Meeting Ethical Dilemmas." *Medical Education* 36.5 (2002) 489–97.

Gordon, Richard, ed. *The Literary Companion to Medicine: An Anthology of Prose and Poetry*. New York: St. Martin's, 1996.

Gottfried, Jeffrey, and Elisa Shearer. "News Use across Social Media Platforms 2017." Pew Research Center, September 7, 2017. http://www.journalism.org/2017/09/07/news-use-across-social-media-platforms-2017/.

Grinspoon, David. *Earth in Human Hands: Shaping Our Planet's Future*. New York: Grand Central, 2016.

Gutiérrez, Gustavo. *A Theology of Liberation: History, Politics, and Salvation*. Maryknoll: Orbis, 1973.

Hafferty, Frederic William. "Beyond Curriculum Reform: Confronting Medicine's Hidden Curriculum." *Academic Medicine: Journal of the Association of American Medical Colleges* 73.4 (1998) 403–7.

———. "Professionalism and the Socialization of Medical Students." In *Teaching Medical Professionalism*, edited by Richard L. Cruess et al., 53–70. Cambridge: Cambridge University Press, 2008.

Harden, R. M. "What Is a Spiral Curriculum?" *Medical Teacher* 21.2 (1999) 141–43.

Hariharan, Janani. "Uncovering the Hidden Curriculum." *Science* 364 (2019) 702.

Hawthorne, Nathaniel. "The Birthmark." http://www.online-literature.com/poe/125/.

Head, Alison J., et al. "How Students Engage with News: Five Takeaways for Educators, Journalists, and Librarians." Project Information Literacy. October 2018.

Heald, Paul J. *Literature and Legal Problem Solving: Law and Literature as Ethical Discourse.* Durham: Carolina Academic Press, 1998.

Held, Virginia. *The Ethics of Care: Personal, Political, and Global.* Oxford: Oxford University Press, 2006.

Herkert, Joseph R. "Microethics, Macroethics, and Professional Engineering Societies." In *Emerging Technologies and Ethical Issues in Engineering: Papers from a Workshop, October 14–15, 2003,* 107–14. Washington, DC: National Academic Press, 2004.

Hilliard, Ri, et al. "Ethical Conflicts and Moral Distress Experienced by Paediatric Residents during Their Training." *Paediatrics & Child Health* 12.1 (2007) 29–35.

Himes, Kenneth, ed. *Modern Catholic Social Teaching: Commentaries and Interpretations.* 2nd ed. Washington, DC: Georgetown University Press, 2017.

Hinduja, Sameer, and Justin W. Patchin. "Cyberbullying: Identification, Prevention, & Response." https://cyberbullying.org/Cyberbullying-Identification-Prevention-Response-2018.pdf.

Holden, Mark, et al. "Professional Identity Formation in Medical Education: The Convergence of Multiple Domains." *HEC Forum: An Interdisciplinary Journal on Hospitals' Ethical and Legal Issues* 24.4 (2012) 245–55.

Holden, Mark D., et al. "Professional Identity Formation: Creating a Longitudinal Framework through TIME (Transformation in Medical Education)." *Academic Medicine: Journal of the Association of American Medical Colleges* 90.6 (2015) 761–67.

Howell, R. J. "Google Morals, Virtue, and the Asymmetry of Deference." *Noûs* 48.3 (2014) 389–415.

Huijer, M., et al. "Medical Students' Cases as an Empirical Basis for Teaching Clinical Ethics." *Academic Medicine: Journal of the Association of American Medical Colleges* 75.8 (2000) 834–39.

Hunt, Daniel, et al. "The Influence of Computer-Mediated Communication Apprehension on Motives for Facebook Use." *Journal of Broadcasting & Electronic Media* 56 (2012) 187–202.

Hunter, James Davison. *Culture Wars: The Struggle to Define America.* New York: Basic Books, 1992.

Jameton, A. "Dilemmas of Moral Distress: Moral Responsibility and Nursing Practice." *AWHONN's Clinical Issues in Perinatal and Women's Health Nursing* 4.4 (1993) 542–51.

Janin, Hunt. *The University in Medieval Life.* Jefferson, NC: McFarland, 2008.

Johnson, Bobbie. "Privacy No Longer a Social Norm, Says Facebook Founder." *The Guardian,* January 10, 2010. https://www.theguardian.com/technology/2010/jan/11/facebook-privacy.

Johnstone, D. Bruce. "Financing Higher Education: Who Should Pay?" In *American Higher Education in the Twenty-First Century: Social, Political and Economic Challenges,* edited by Philip G. Altbach et al., 347–69. 3rd ed. Baltimore: Johns Hopkins University Press, 2011.

Joy, Bill. "Why the Future Doesn't Need Us." *Wired,* April 1, 2000. https://www.wired.com/2000/04/joy-2/.

Kälvemark, Sofia, et al. "Living with Conflicts—Ethical Dilemmas and Moral Distress in the Health Care System." *Social Science & Medicine* 58.6 (2004) 1075–84.

Kant, Immanuel. *Metaphysics of Morals*. Translated by Mary J. Gregor. Cambridge: Cambridge University Press, 1991.

King, Martin Luther, Jr. "Pilgrimage to Nonviolence." *Christian Century*, April 13, 1960.

Klement, Brenda J., et al. "Anatomy as the Backbone of an Integrated First Year Medical Curriculum: Design and Implementation." *Anatomical Sciences Education* 4.3 (2011) 157–69.

Kolhatkar, Sheelah. "In Meredith Whitney We Trust?" *New York Magazine*, March 20, 2009.

Krishnan, Archanan, and David Atkin. "Individual Differences in Social Networking Site Users: The Interplay between Antecedents and Consequential Effect on Level of Activity." *Computers in Human Behavior* 30 (2014) 111–18.

Kuo, Caroline Y., and Donald B. Kohn. "Gene Therapy for the Treatment of Primary Immune Deficiencies." *Current Allergy Asthma Report* 16.5 (2016) 39.

Kurzweil, Ray. *The Singularity Is Near: When Humans Transcend Biology*. New York: Viking, 2005.

Ladd, John. "The Quest for a Code of Professional Ethics: An Intellectual and Moral Confusion." In *AAAS Professional Ethics Project: Professional Ethics Activities in the Scientific and Engineering Societies*, edited by Rosemary Chalk, Mark Frankel, and Sallie Burket Chafer, 154–59. Washington, DC: AAAS, 1980.

Ledwon, Lenora. *Law and Literature: Text and Theory*. New York: Garland, 1996.

Lehmann, Lisa Soleymani, et al. "Hidden Curricula, Ethics, and Professionalism: Optimizing Clinical Learning Environments in Becoming and Being a Physician: A Position Paper of the American College of Physicians." *Annals of Internal Medicine* 168.7 (2018) 506–8.

Lehmann, Lisa Soleymani, et al. "A Survey of Medical Ethics Education at U.S. and Canadian Medical Schools." *Academic Medicine: Journal of the Association of American Medical Colleges* 79.7 (2004) 682–89.

Lempp, Heidi, and Clive Seale. "The Hidden Curriculum in Undergraduate Medical Education: Qualitative Study of Medical Students' Perceptions of Teaching." *British Medical Journal* 329.770 (2004) 770–73.

Li, Jing, et al. "Experiments That Led to the First Gene-Edited Babies: Ethical Failings and the Urgent Need for Better Governance." *Journal of Zhejiang University Science B.* (2019) 32–38.

Lloyd, Vincent W. *Black Natural Law*. Oxford: Oxford University Press, 2016.

Loewy, E. H. "Teaching Medical Ethics to Medical Students." *Journal of Medical Education* 61.8 (1986) 661–65.

Lomis, Kimberly D., et al. "Moral Distress in the Third Year of Medical School; a Descriptive Review of Student Case Reflections." *American Journal of Surgery* 197.1 (2009) 107–12.

"Looking Back: Kim Lawton." *Religion & Ethics Newsweekly*, February 24, 2017. https://www.pbs.org/wnet/religionandethics/2017/02/24/looking-back-kim-lawton/34736/.

MacIntyre, Alasdair. *After Virtue: A Study in Moral Theory*. Notre Dame: University of Notre Dame Press, 1984.

Mackie, J. L. *Ethics: Inventing Right and Wrong*. New York: Penguin, 1977.

Mann, Karen V. "Thinking about Learning: Implications for Principle-Based Professional Education." *The Journal of Continuing Education in the Health Professions* 22.2 (2002) 69–76.

Marginson, Simon. "Higher Education and Public Good." *Higher Education Quarterly* 65.4 (2011) 411–33.

Martimianakis, Maria Athina (Tina), et al. "Humanism, the Hidden Curriculum, and Educational Reform: A Scoping Review and Thematic Analysis." *Academic Medicine: Journal of the Association of American Medical Colleges* 90.11 (2015) 5–13.

Mason, Richard, and Ian Mitroff. *Challenging Strategic Planning Assumptions.* New York: Wiley, 1981.

Mattick, K., and J. Bligh. "Teaching and Assessing Medical Ethics: Where Are We Now?" *Journal of Medical Ethics* 32.3 (2006) 181–85.

May, William F. *Beleaguered Rulers: The Public Obligation of the Professional.* Louisville: Westminster John Knox, 2001.

May, Win, et al. "A Ten-Year Review of the Literature on the Use of Standardized Patients in Teaching and Learning: 1996–2005." *Medical Teacher* 31.6 (2009) 487–92.

Mayo, Thomas Wm. "Twyla Tharp Goes to Law School: On the Use of the Visual and Performing Arts in Professional Education." In *Moral Imagination and the Legal Life: Beyond Text in Legal Education*, edited by Zenon Bankowski and Maksymilian del Mar, 169–87. Surrey: Ashgate, 2013.

McIntyre, Lee. "Making Philosophy Matter—or Else." *Chronicle of Higher Education*, December 11, 2011. http://www.chronicle.com/article/Making-Philosophy-Matter-or/130029/.

Mead, Margaret. *Continuities in Cultural Evolution.* New Brunswick, NJ: Transaction Publishers, 1999.

Menand, Louis, ed. *The Rise of the Research University: A Sourcebook.* Chicago: University of Chicago Press, 2017.

Milewski, John. "We Are Penn State' and What That Means Today." *Huffington Post*, September 15, 2012. https://www.huffingtonpost.com/john-milewski/we-are-penn-state_b_1671744.html.

Mill, John Stuart. *Autobiography.* London: Penguin, 1989.

———. *Utilitarianism.* Indianapolis: Hackett, 2002.

Morawetz, Thomas, ed. *Literature and the Law.* New York: Aspen, 2007.

———. "Self-Knowledge for Lawyers: What It Is and Why It Matters." *Journal of Legal Education* 68 (2018) 136–53.

Morris, Norval. *The Brothel Boy and Other Parables of the Law.* New York: Oxford University Press, 1992.

Mozur, Paul. "Google's AlphaGo Defeats Chinese Go Master in Win for A.I." *The New York Times*, May 23, 2017. https://www.nytimes.com/2017/05/23/business/google-deepmind-alphago-go-champion-defeat.html?_r=0.

Mukherjee, Siddhartha. *The Gene.* New York: Scribner, 2016.

Muller, Jessica H., et al. "Lessons Learned about Integrating a Medical School Curriculum: Perceptions of Students, Faculty and Curriculum Leaders." *Medical Education* 42.8 (2008) 778–85.

Musick, D. W. "Teaching Medical Ethics: A Review of the Literature from North American Medical Schools with Emphasis on Education." *Medicine, Health Care, and Philosophy* 2.3 (1999) 239–54.

Nagel, Thomas. *The Last Word.* New York: Oxford University Press, 2001.

Negroponte, Nicholas. *Being Digital.* New York: Knopf, 1995.

Niebuhr, Reinhold. *The Irony of American History.* New York: Scribner's, 1952.

―――. *Moral Man and Immoral Society: A Study in Ethics and Politics*. New York: Scribner's, 1932.

―――. *The Nature and Destiny of Man: A Christian Interpretation*. 2 vols. New York: Scribner's, 1941, 1943.

Nietzsche, Friedrich. *Beyond Good and Evil*. New York: Modern Library, 1886.

Nussbaum, Martha. *Not for Profit: Why Democracy Needs the Humanities*. Princeton: Princeton University Press, 2010.

Nyden, Philip. *Public Sociology: Research, Action, and Change*. Thousand Oaks, CA: Pine Forge, 2011.

O'Brien, David J., and Thomas A. Shannon, eds. *Catholic Social Thought: The Documentary Heritage*. Maryknoll: Orbis, 2010.

Ogden, Paul E., et al. "Clinical Simulation: Importance to the Internal Medicine Educational Mission." *The American Journal of Medicine* 120.9 (2007) 820–24.

Owen, David. *The Hubris Syndrome: Bush, Blair and the Intoxication of Power*. York: Methuen, 2007.

Parker, Lisa, et al. "Clinical Ethics Ward Rounds: Building on the Core Curriculum." *Journal of Medical Ethics* 38.8 (2012) 501–5.

Parker, M. H., et al. "Teaching of Medical Ethics: Implications for an Integrated Curriculum." *Medical Education* 31.3 (1997) 181–87.

Parnas, D. L. "Software Aspects of Strategic Defense Systems." *Communications of the ACM* 28.12 (1985) 1326–35.

Patil, Lalit, et al. *Educate to Innovate: Factors That Influence Innovation; Based on Input from Innovators and Stakeholders*. Washington, DC: National Academies Press, 2015.

Pettit, Emma. "How Kevin Kruse Became History's Attack Dog." *The Chronicle of Higher Education*, December 16, 2018. https://www.chronicle.com/article/How-Kevin-Kruse-Became/245321.

Pollack, Robert. "Bridging Evolutionary Barriers." https://www.dnalc.org/view/15158-Bridging-evolutionary-barriers-Robert-Pollack.html.

Porter, Jean. *Nature as Reason: A Thomistic Theory of the Natural Law*. Grand Rapids: Eerdmans, 2005.

Posner, Richard. *Law and Literature*. Rev. ed. Cambridge: Harvard University Press, 1998.

Prato, Lou. "Lou Prato: We Are . . . Cheer Was Years in the Making." *Statecollege.com*, December 28, 2011. http://www.statecollege.com/news/columns/lou-prato-we-are-cheer-was-years-in-the-making,970985/?_ga=2.248671623.1461559232.1508 777772-1074829321.1508777772.

The President's Council on Bioethics. "Being Human: Readings from the President's Council on Bioethics." https://bioethicsarchive.georgetown.edu/pcbe/bookshelf/index.html.

Quinn, Philip. *Divine Commands and Moral Requirements*. Oxford: Oxford University Press, 1978.

Rauschenbusch, Walter. *Christianity and the Social Crisis*. New York: Macmillan, 1907.

―――. *A Theology for the Social Gospel*. New York: Macmillan, 1917.

Reynolds, Richard, and John Stone, eds. *On Doctoring: Stories, Poems, Essays*. 3rd ed. New York: Simon & Schuster, 2001.

Rhode, Deborah L. "Ethics by the Pervasive Method." *Journal of Legal Education* 42 (1992) 31–56.

Ricoeur, Paul. *The Symbolism of Evil*. Boston: Beacon, 1992.

Rosenbaum, Thane, ed. *Law Lit: From Atticus Finch to* The Practice; *A Collection of Great Writing about the Law.* New York: New Press, 2007.

Rubenstein, Richard. *Aristotle's Children: How Christians, Muslims, and Jews Rediscovered Ancient Wisdom and Illuminated the Middle Ages.* New York: Harcourt, 2003.

Sandburg, Carl. "The Lawyers Know Too Much." In *Law Lit: From Atticus Finch to* The Practice; *A Collection of Great Writing about the Law,* edited by Thane Rosenbaum, 173–74. New York: New Press, 2007.

Sandel, Michael. *What Money Can't Buy: The Moral Limits of Markets.* New York: Farrar, Straus & Giroux, 2012.

Sarat, Austin, et al., eds. *Law and the Humanities: An Introduction.* New York: Cambridge University Press, 2010.

Shapiro, Fred. R., and Jane Garry, eds. *Trial and Error: An Oxford Anthology of Legal Stories.* New York: Oxford University Press, 1998.

Shapshay, Sandra, ed. *Bioethics at the Movies.* Baltimore: Johns Hopkins University Press, 2009.

Shashkevich, Alex. "Moral Judging Helps People Cooperate Better in Groups, New Stanford Research Says." *Stanford News Service,* April 7, 2017. https://news.stanford.edu/press/view/13552.

Silver, David, and Demis Hassabis. "AlphaGo: Mastering the Ancient Game of Go with Machine Learning." Google AI Blog. https://research.googleblog.com/2016/01/alphago-mastering-ancient-game-of-go.html.

Simpson, Brent, et al. "The Enforcement of Moral Boundaries Promotes Cooperation and Prosocial Behavior in Groups." *Scientific Reports,* February 17, 2017. https://www.nature.com/articles/srep42844.

Singer, Peter, and Renata Singer, eds. *The Moral of the Story: An Anthology of Ethics through Literature.* Malden, MA: Blackwell, 2005.

Smith, Adam. *The Wealth of Nations.* London: Penguin, 1999.

Smith, Holly. "Culpable Ignorance." *The Philosophical Review* 92.4 (1983) 543–71.

Smith, Wilson. *Professors & Public Ethics: Studies of Northern Moral Philosophers before the Civil War.* Ithaca: Cornell University Press, 1956.

Southern Methodist University. "McFarlin Auditorium." https://www.smu.edu/BusinessFinance/CampusServices/McFarlin/About/History.

———. "Public Service Fellowships." https://www.smu.edu/Provost/Ethics/Student Engagement/Fellowship.

Specter, Michael. "How the DNA Revolution Is Changing Us." *National Geographic,* August 2016.

Spiegel, Max. "Origins of We Are Penn State Cheer." *YouTube,* November 2, 2009. https://www.youtube.com/watch?v=Afot8ypldsg.

Stone, John. "The Truck." In *All This Rain,* 16. Baton Rouge: Louisiana State University Press, 1980.

Stout, Jeffrey. *Blessed Are the Organized: Grassroots Democracy in America.* Princeton: Princeton University Press, 2010.

Stravridis, James, and Dave Weinstein. "The Internet of Things Is a Cyberwar Nightmare." *Foreign Policy,* November 3, 2016. http://foreignpolicy.com/2016/11/03/the-internet-of-things-is-a-cyber-war-nightmare/.

Taleb, N. N., et al. "The Precautionary Principle (with Application to the Genetic Modification of Organisms)." Extreme Risk Initiative—NYU School of Engineering Working Paper Series, 2014.

Taylor, Charles. *A Secular Age*. Cambridge: Belknap Press of Harvard University, 2007.

Thompson, Dennis. "Moral Responsibility of Public Officials: The Problem of Many Hands." *The American Political Science Review* 74.4 (1980) 905–16.

Tsai, Janice Y., et al. "Location-Sharing Technologies: Privacy Risks and Controls." *I/S: A Journal of Law and Policy for the Information Society* 6 (2010) 119–51.

Tsukayama, Hayley. "Google's Focus on AI Means It Will Get Even Deeper into Our Lives." *The Washington Post*, May 21, 2017. https://www.washingtonpost.com/news/the-switch/wp/2017/05/17/googles-focus-on-ai-means-it-will-get-even-deeper-into-our-lives/.

Turing, A. M. "Computing Machinery and Intelligence." *Mind* 59 (1950) 433–60.

Urry, Meg. "Will the 'God Particle' Destroy the World?" *CNN*, September 12, 2014. http://www.cnn.com/2014/09/12/opinion/urry-god-particle/index.html.

US National Library of Medicine. "Recombinant DNA Technologies and Researcher's Responsibilities, 1973–1980." https://profiles.nlm.nih.gov/spotlight/cd/feature/dna.

Veatch, R. M., and S. Sollitto."Medical Ethics Teaching: Report of a National Medical School Survey." *Journal of the American Medical Association* 235.10 (1976) 1030–33.

Velasquez, Manuel. *Business Ethics: Concepts and Cases*. 5th ed. Upper Saddle River, NJ: Prentice Hall, 2002.

Vidic, Branislav, and Harry M. Weitlauf. "Horizontal and Vertical Integration of Academic Disciplines in the Medical School Curriculum." *Clinical Anatomy* 15.3 (2002) 233–35.

Walrave, M., et al. "Whether or Not to Engage in Sexting: Explaining Adolescent Sexting Behavior by Applying the Prototype Willingness Model." *Telematics and Informatics* 32.4 (2015) 796–808.

Walters, LeRoy, and Julie Gage Palmer. *The Ethics of Human Gene Therapy*. New York: Oxford University Press, 1997.

Weber, Max. "Politics as a Vocation." In *The Vocation Lectures*, edited by David Owen and Tracy B. Strong, 32–94. Indianapolis: Hackett, 2004.

———. *The Protestant Ethic and the Spirit of Capitalism*. Translated by Talcott Parsons. London: Routledge, 1992.

Weinreb, Lloyd. *Legal Reason: The Use of Analogy in Legal Argument*. Cambridge: Cambridge University Press, 2005.

West, C. P., et al. "Physician Burnout: Contributors, Consequences and Solutions." *Journal of Internal Medicine* 283.6 (2018) 516–29.

Whitaker, Albert Keith. "Neoconservative Nathaniel: Bioethics and 'The Birth-Mark.'" http://www.hawthorneinsalem.org/ScholarsForum/MMD2448.html.

White, James Boyd. *The Legal Imagination: Studies in the Nature of Legal Thought and Expression*. Boston: Little Brown, 1973.

White, Richard. *The Republic for Which It Stands: The United States during Reconstruction and the Gilded Age, 1865–1896*. New York: Oxford University Press, 2017.

Wiggleton, Catherine, et al. "Medical Students' Experiences of Moral Distress: Development of a Web-Based Survey." *Academic Medicine: Journal of the Association of American Medical Colleges* 85.1 (2010) 111–17.

Wilentz, Sean. *The Rise of American Democracy: Jefferson to Lincoln*. New York: Norton, 2005.

Winner, L. "Engineering Ethics and Political Imagination." In *Broad and Narrow Interpretations of Philosophy of Technology*, edited by Paul T. Durbin, 53–64. Boston: Kluwer, 1990.

Zemsky, Robert, et al. *Remaking the American University: Market-Smart and Mission-Centered*. New Brunswick, NJ: Rutgers University Press, 2005.

Zimmermann, F., and M. Sieverding. "Young Adults' Social Drinking as Explained by an Augmented Theory of Planned Behavior: The Roles of Prototypes, Willingness, and Gender." *British Journal of Health Psychology* 15.3 (2010) 561–81.

Zuger, Abigail. "Dissatisfaction with Medical Practice." *The New England Journal of Medicine* 350.1 (2004) 69–75.

CPSIA information can be obtained
at www.ICGtesting.com
Printed in the USA
JSHW011139160920
7926JS00002B/4